THE PROPHETIC MELVILLE

THE PROPHETIC MELVILLE

Experience, Transcendence, and Tragedy

ROWLAND A. SHERRILL

THE UNIVERSITY OF GEORGIA PRESS

ATHENS

Copyright © 1979 by the University of Georgia Press
Athens 30602

Set in 10 on 12 point Sabon type
Printed in the United States of America

Library of Congress Cataloging in Publication Data

Sherrill, Rowland A
  The prophetic Melville.
  Includes bibliographical references and index.
    1. Melville, Herman, 1819–1891—Criticism and inter-
pretation. 2. Melville, Herman, 1819–1891—Religion
and ethics. I. Title.

PS2387.S48   813'.3   78-20436
             ISBN 0-8203-0455-7

*For my mother and father,
Elise Rowland Sherrill and
Raymond Edward Sherrill*

Divine imaginings, like gods, come down to the groves of our Thessalies, and, there, in the embrace of wild, dryad reminiscences, beget the beings that astonish the world.

Redburn

CONTENTS

Acknowledgments

So many people have entered into my thinking about the subject of this book that it is impossible to name them all, but some have contributed in ways which make me think that any success it has is mainly due to them and that any failures must be the consequences of my inability to hear what they were saying to me. Among these direct and indirect mentors, a special few stand out: Donald A. Ringe of the University of Kentucky, who first introduced me to the complexities of Melville's work; Nathan A. Scott, Jr., of the University of Virginia, who presented me with the rich variety of the field of religion and literature; Robert E. Streeter of the University of Chicago, who "gifted" me with his broad and sensitive understanding of early American life; Anthony C. Yu of the University of Chicago, whose acumen in criticism and theory of literature was always a boon. In this regard, however, my deepest debt is to Giles Gunn of the University of North Carolina who, over the years, has given himself continuously to my education by his generous and thoughtful responses to my work, by his own inquiries into "the shaping environment" of American culture, and, not least, by his keen and humane sense of the requirements, responsibilities, and possibilities of scholarship in our time.

Other friends and colleagues have read and commented on portions of the book, and for this I should like to thank James G. Moseley and Peter Vasile as well as, in my own university, Richard Turner, Warren French, Paul Nagy, Jan Shipps, and some attentive students who have listened to my incessant talking about Melville. My chairmen, James F. Smurl and Rufus Reiberg, besides responding carefully out of their own alert senses to my subject, have been most gracious about arranging teaching schedules and freeing time for me as much as possible.

Acknowledgments

For a Summer Faculty Fellowship for 1977, which in part enabled me to carry out a revision of portions of the original manuscript, I want to thank the Office of Research and Sponsored Programs in my home university.

Thanks are due also to Ray L. Hart, editor of the *Journal of the American Academy of Religion,* for permission to use materials from chapter 4 of this study which first appeared in the supplement to the December 1977 issue of that journal under the title of "'Flood-Gates of the Wonder-World': Melville's Religious Drive and the Generic Question of *Moby-Dick.*"

The editorial staff of the University of Georgia Press has been astute and helpful with suggestions for the style and format: Robert Buffington, Malcolm MacDonald, and Karen Orchard have throughout been prompt, gracious, and efficient in their handling of the manuscript, and Carol McDonald Fisher has done an alert and sensitive job of copyediting.

My final and continuing indebtedness is to Joy, my wife, for her work, her encouragement, and her love. Her giving is past counting.

A Note on Texts and Citations

All parenthetical page references to *Typee, Redburn, White-Jacket,* and *Pierre* are to the Northwestern-Newberry edition of *The Writings of Herman Melville,* edited by Harrison Hayford, Hershel Parker, and G. Thomas Tanselle, 6 volumes (Evanston: Northwestern University Press and Newberry Library, 1968–1971). Since this authoritative edition of Melville's works remains incomplete to this date, I have used, in quoting from other primary works, the following editions: *Moby-Dick,* edited by Harrison Hayford and Hershel Parker (New York: W. W. Norton, 1967); *The Confidence-Man,* edited by Hennig Cohen (New York: Holt, Rinehart, and Winston, 1964); and *Billy Budd,* edited by Harrison Hayford and Merton M. Sealts, Jr. (Chicago: University of Chicago Press, 1962). In each case, the citation is according to the following abbreviations:

T	*Typee*
R	*Redburn*
W	*White-Jacket*
M	*Moby-Dick*
C	*The Confidence-Man*
P	*Pierre*
B	*Billy Budd*

One special matter is important: while I have cited *page* numbers following quotations from each of the other works, I have used *chapter* numbers in quoting from *Moby-Dick* for the convenience of readers using the numerous available editions of that work.

I have omitted full discussions of *Omoo, Mardi,* and *Israel Potter,* other major fictions by Herman Melville, both because of considerations of space and because my concern in this study, as the introduction will suggest, has been not so much to provide a complete reading of any of Melville's works as to trace the growth of an idea and of Melville's sense of himself in his vocation as these are adumbrated in the fictions.

THE PROPHETIC MELVILLE

INTRODUCTION

The vague phrase that history is the knowledge of the individual claims for it a field at once too wide and too narrow: too wide, because the individuality of perceived objects and natural facts and immediate experiences falls outside its sphere, and most of all because even the individuality of historical events and personages, if that means their uniqueness, falls equally outside it; too narrow, because it would exclude universality, and it is just the universality of an event or character that makes it a proper and possible object of historical study, if by universality we mean something that oversteps the limits of merely local and temporal existence and possesses a significance valid for all men at all times. These too are no doubt vague phrases; but they are attempts to describe something real: namely the way in which thought, transcending its own immediacy, survives and revives in other contexts; and to express the truth that individual acts and persons appear in history not in virtue of their individuality as such, but because that individuality is the vehicle of a thought which, because it was actually theirs, is potentially everyone's.

R. G. Collingwood, *The Idea of History*

The chapters which follow were written in part in order to address a specific problem in interpreting the fictions of Herman Melville—the problem which has beleaguered critics in their grappling with the notion that Melville could "neither believe, nor be comfortable in his unbelief," as Nathaniel Hawthorne recorded his sense of the matter in his *English Notebooks* for 20 November 1856, after his last meeting with Melville. Although Hawthorne's little account has itself proved enigmatic to the critical generations which have followed, the sheer particularity of the remarks, his retention of what was specifically mem-

I

orable about the meeting, indicates how crucial he at least found Melville's concern to be in persisting after "knowledge of Providence and futurity and all that lies beyond human ken." Hawthorne's observations represent only a preliminary clue, of course, but no one who has read *Moby-Dick* can doubt that Melville's masterwork derives much of its energy and power from the author's commitment to enter into the ambience of "infinite Pacifics."

In the interpretive effort of this study, then, the attempt has been to isolate and define the ways in which three of the early fictions—*Typee, Redburn,* and *White-Jacket*—each contributed to Melville's progress toward an idea of the transcendent, to assess the genesis, emergence, and shape of this idea in its most fully articulated form in *Moby-Dick,* and to discern in *Pierre* and *Billy Budd* how this idea became a controlling factor in Melville's mature vision of life. As the chapters undertake this interpretive task, that is, as they provide a style of commentary on Melville's renditions of the meaning of experience and on his use of the forms of fiction, they seek to recover and to clarify a dimension of Melville's thought and life which decisively oriented his creative intelligence.

If the origins, forms, and trials of this idea of transcendence occurred in these three distinct, or at least discernible, stages in Melville's fiction, the nature and composition of the fictions themselves, along with some of the other writings, reveal the sources and development in deeply associated stages of Melville's sense of the prophetic requirements of his art in relation to his age. A second, more generally critical task of this study has therefore been to approach the texts as disclosive, in their prophetic styles of expression, of Melville's consciousness of himself in his career as writer. In such an inquiry into his work, however, the term *prophetic* is not used to refer to the clairvoyant or futuristic arts so much as it is intended to suggest an attitude of mind about, and modes of address toward, history and the contemporary culture.

In the early works, those which preceded *Moby-Dick,* the prophetic character of Melville's authorial voice emerges in the strenuousness with which he attempted both to issue a radical critique of the cultural alternatives of his time and to penetrate to the fundamental levels of human nature and experience. He sought on behalf of the culture to discover the essential terms and conditions of the culture, but, even with his recognition that his identity belonged to the community, he assumed an adversary stance in relation to it, thus distancing himself, like the prophet, in order to preserve the detachment which would not compromise his critique and to underscore the essential seriousness of his concern.

By the time of Melville's writing of *Moby-Dick,* the sense of detachment displayed in the early works had become an anxious sense of isolation—less assumed now than discovered—and with this newly realized conception of himself as author, Melville's understanding of the prophetic dimensions of his fiction were also altered. The early works had brought him to a perception of the world of human experience which challenged the comforts of common belief in his age, and, in the writing of his masterpiece, he recognized that he worked under the demand on Jonah, as Father Mapple in *Moby-Dick* interprets it, "'To preach the Truth to the face of Falsehood!'" The form of this "preaching" in *Moby-Dick* is visionary, for Melville thought he had "bottomed upon the truth," had located a new or newly discovered reality, and he wanted his fiction to articulate its sources, nature, and implications. As estranged as he might have felt from the community in his composition of *Moby-Dick,* he wanted the book to fulfill the prophetic responsibility by presenting his vision of reality to the eyes of that community. The deeply reformative thrust of the book suggests his convictions that fiction needed to bear accountability to its auditors as well as to its own central vision, that his prophetic speaking in fictive forms could be effectual, and, therefore, that changes of cultural perception were possible.

The treatments of Captain Ahab in *Moby-Dick,* the title character in *Pierre,* and Captain Vere in *Billy Budd* begin to reveal a third and final, and again altered, sense of prophetic authorship on Melville's part, for with these characters he explores and tests the kinds of perceptions which obstruct the birth of his fictive vision into history. But it is the structure, style, and tone of *Billy Budd* which finally betray the tragic denouement of the writer-prophet's sense of himself. In the final stage of his career, Melville comes closer than at any other moment to the oracle, the specialist in the predictive arts. But, during the writing of his last fiction, the new role of seer stems, ironically, less from confidence about the efficacy of his vision than from a Teiresias-like understanding of himself as "mere" seer and of the incapacities of his art to create changes in historical perception and action.

If Melville felt at the last, however, that his age spurned the possibilities he wanted to add to it, there is nonetheless a sense in which his work provides our own time with a special entrance into his time. Although his prophetic efforts served in many respects to place him at a great remove from the main currents of his period, his fictions continuously restore to us a record of a distinctive mind at work in his period in the formal struggle that narrative art singularly entails. This more personal history of a mind is the preoccupation of the study which follows: it seeks to recover the thought of that Melville most urgently committed "to wrestle with the angel—Art"—which was, essentially for him, to grapple with the complex, "pulsed" life he felt in history; it is animated by the possibility, derived from Collingwood, that there is unspent significance in this "thought [which], transcending its own immediacy, survives and revives in other contexts."

PART ONE

The Necessity of Experience

CHAPTER ONE

THE HAPPY VALLEY
Typee *and the Impossibility of Paradise*

When Herman Melville undertook to write *Typee,* his first book, he was, as is well known, completely untutored in the craft of fiction. Imperfect as the book may be, however, Melville's little "Peep at Polynesian Life" (the subtitle), which draws on his own South Sea adventures, gives evidence even in this first effort of the kind of "deep-diving" mind he was later to admire so much in Nathaniel Hawthorne, for, if by many tests Melville lived at a great remove from his age, *Typee* perhaps instinctively addresses one of the most compelling metaphors of the regnant cultural mentality in America. After a few weeks' sojourn in the valley of the Typee, Tommo, the narrator of the book, discloses that, "when I looked around the verdant recesses in which I was buried, and gazed up to the summits of the lofty eminence that hemmed me in, I was well disposed to think that I was in the 'Happy Valley,' and that beyond those heights there was nought but a world of care and anxiety" (*T,* 124). In this frame of mind, Tommo seems to have discovered the locus of a prelapsarian situation and seems willing himself to become the new resident of that paradise garden. He seems, in short, to be the embodiment at last of the image of "the American Adam" which inspirited many of Melville's contemporaries.[1] In the Marquesan Valley, "embosomed for a season in nature," as Ralph Waldo Emerson had put it in *Nature* (1836), Tommo apparently shakes free from the habits and corruptions of civilized life and seeks out all the fresh possibilities of innocence, born with the American, in a new and undefiled

7

world. But it is important also to notice, along with F. O. Matthiessen, that *Typee* was only scarcely noticed by Ralph Waldo Emerson, Henry D. Thoreau, and a man then known as "Walter" Whitman.[2] Despite Tommo's nostalgia for Eden, these notable exemplars of the Adamic impulse, like the general reading public, failed to regard *Typee* as much more than an adventure story. Whitman recommended the book in the Brooklyn *Eagle* (5 May 1847) as "thorough entertainment."[3]

Even in view of Professor Lovejoy's admonitions several decades ago that students of culture should be wary of mentioning *romanticism* except in the plural form and that one should always be prepared to carry on "discriminations of romanticisms,"[4] it seems safe enough to remark that the period of Melville's coming of age in America was brimming with the *romantic*—especially if one means that term to be charged specifically with premises about the necessity of avoiding the corruptions of civilization, the virtues of communion with the natural world, and, thus, the implicit logic of the idea of the *noble savage*. With respect to these premises at least, a main current of the mid-nineteenth-century American mentality was emphatically and inveterately romantic. In the sense that Melville understood the general pressures of this romanticism to be some determining forces of the milieu and in the sense that he was infatuated with these specific persuasions of the romantic imagination, often in their transcendental guises, he bears out the adage that a writer, in expressing himself, dramatizes the energies of his age. As Perry Miller has pointed out, Melville's romances were in many ways "defiantly, unrepentantly, transcendental."[5]

As Miller also suggests in a different context, however, Melville frequently "utilized the conventions of this romance to destroy the romantic thesis."[6] To regard *Typee* as a sign of Melville's being seduced by the historical alternative posed by Adamism would be a mistake. However attracted Melville might have been to the Edenic metaphors which animated his contemporaries, however hungry he might have been to define a genuine innocence as a possibility for the American self-conception, *Typee* tests the idea of paradise and finds it wanting. Even in the moment before Tommo considers himself in "the Happy

8

Valley," he has mentioned with relief that a long-lingering despair "now seldom obtruded" (*T,* 124) on his thoughts, but,
in the course of his career in the valley, Tommo's melancholy
returns frequently and poignantly, even in the midst of this
ostensible paradise. Indeed, the fundamental tension of *Typee*
consists in Tommo's oscillation between his yearning after paradisal innocence and his concomitant realization of the necessity
for full experience. In tracing out the significance of this narrative tension, then, the reader must follow the course of Tommo's
mental alternations as a clue to Melville's dramatic testing of
a major option for the contemporary culture.

These alternations are revealed in Tommo's beginning romantic self-definition, in his locating and singing encomia for what
remains of paradise, in his reflecting critically on his own situation in the valley, and in his finally being unable to accept the
confinements of the primal vale. Each stage is accompanied by a
mental state that is distinct in the narrative and can be isolated
to suggest a progress of mind, on Tommo's part, displayed by
the narration itself. In the retrospective rehearsal of his escape
to and, later, his escape *from* the valley of the Typee, Tommo
constructs, tacitly at least, what has become for him a required
anthropology. His tendency to interpret himself, his need to reflect on the activities and events he recounts, indeed, his ability
to remember at all, are necessary features of a view of modern
man which, he discovers, the easy indolence of the valley cannot
help him sustain.

I

In the first three chapters of *Typee,* the narrator does not appear
in propria persona to the reader. Yet in these early chapters
the overriding narrative voice of the man later to be known as
"Tommo" begins both to reveal the special romantic character
he possesses which will qualify him for the quest after paradise
and to establish the romantic context which will provide the
occasion for this quest. There can be little doubt that the disclosures of this voice are conscious and studied, for in the preface to the book Melville suggests that the story will "excite

the warmest sympathies" even of those sailors who, accustomed to "stirring adventure," find things "strange and romantic . . . as commonplace as a jacket out at elbows" (*T*, xiii). With this, the author reasons, the romantic narrative about to unfold can "scarcely fail to interest those [fireside people] who are less familiar than the sailor with a life of adventure" (*T*, xiii).

Tommo himself emerges, through his voice, as a protagonist whose inclinations are commensurate with a life of adventure and romance.[7] He is quickly aroused, after six months aboard the *Dolly*, by the name of the *Marquesas* and the "strange visions of outlandish things" conjured up for him by that name: "Naked houiris—cannibal banquets—groves of cocoa-nut—coral reefs—tatooed chiefs—and bamboo temples" (*T*, 5). Feeling "an irresistible curiosity to see those islands which the olden voyagers had so glowingly described," the narrator is allured by the antiquity of this place, still "tenanted by beings as strange and barbarous as ever" (*T*, 5). As "the light trade-winds" sweep the *Dolly* toward the islands, even the proximity of this tropical paradise exerts "the influence of some narcotic" (*T*, 9) on the crew, and the narrator says he "could not avoid yielding . . . to the general languor" (*T*, 10). The first close view of Nukuheva, the principal island of the Marquesan chain, inspires his romantic wonderment: "We had perceived the loom of the mountains about sunset; so that after running all night with a very light breeze, we found ourselves close in with the island the next morning; but as the bay we sought lay on its farther side, we were obliged to sail some distance along the shore, catching, as we proceeded, short glimpses of blooming valleys, deep glens, waterfalls, and waving groves, hidden here and there by projecting and rocky headlands, every moment opening to the view some new and startling scene of beauty" (*T*, 12). In this benign natural setting, the narrator surmises, the inhabitants, although now "somewhat corrupted, owing to their recent commerce with Europeans," live in innocence, retaining "their original primitive character, [and] remaining very nearly in the same state of nature in which they were first beheld by white men" (*T*, 11).

This romantic bias for the primitive over the civilized which emerges in the narrator is enforced quickly when he notes that those "hostile clans, residing in the more remote sections of the island, and very seldom holding any communication with foreigners, are in every respect unchanged from their earliest known condition" (*T,* 11). If the hostility of *noble* savages, innocently clothed in purifying nature, should appear incongruous to him, he passes over that possibility with utterly romantic disdain. Rather, "nothing could be more out of keeping than" the six French vessels, "whose black hulls and bristling broadsides proclaimed their warlike character [as they floated] . . . in that lovely bay, the green eminences of the shore looking down so tranquilly upon them, as if rebuking the sternness of their aspect" (*T,* 12). Although as yet not named, Tommo's sense of the debauches of civilization on "the poor savages when exposed to the influence of these polluting examples" (*T,* 15) begins his own self-characterization. Even as his own shipmates indulge in "the grossest licentiousness" with the Marquesan girls, he is forced to conclude, with romantic regret for defiled innocence, that "thrice happy are they who, inhabiting some yet undiscovered island in the midst of the ocean, have never been brought into contaminating contact with the white man" (*T,* 15).

Without such indictments issued against civilization, Tommo could embark on his Marquesan interlude only as a renegade adventurer; armed with his awareness of the debasements civilization has wrought, he qualifies as a romantic quester. He is compelled by more than an itch for visions of "outlandish things," by more than the opportunity to riot in "unholy passions" (*T,* 15) with native girls. His passion, rather, is more sublime; having caught a glimpse of paradise, he wants to regain the innocence it promises: "A high degree of refinement [he concludes] . . . does not seem to subdue our wicked propensities so much after all; and were civilization itself to be estimated by some of its results, it would seem perhaps better for what we call the barbarous part of the world to remain unchanged" (*T,* 17). Implicit in this decision against civilization is the nostalgia for what the narrator romantically supposes to be the pure, artless condition of primordial man, basking in the benevolent light of nature.

On the basis of this decision, the narrator steps forward in person to become more than the voice of the first three chapters.[8] Contaminating white man that he is, his predilection for paradise and innocence over the option of a riotous excursion allows him to distinguish himself from his former anonymous position among the crew members of the *Dolly*. He can look at the bay of Nukuheva with "a pang of regret that a scene so enchanting should be hidden from the world in these remote seas, and seldom meet the eyes of devoted lovers of nature" (*T*, 24), but Tommo himself, brimming with romantic conviction, has not missed the significance portended in the scene. Paradise is before him, and the fact that it is hidden from the world only makes it the more alluring: the glen of Tior—"the loveliest vale eye ever beheld"—attracts him just because, "hemmed in by [the]... stupendous barriers [of rocky vine-clad cliffs], the valley would be altogether shut out from the rest of the world, were it not that it is accessible from the sea at one end, and by a narrow defile at the other" (*T*, 28). No matter that the French have taken possession here, Tommo implies; he has heard of even more remote valleys, even more insulated from the encroachments of modern life, and he will not, cannot, "endure another voyage on board the Dolly" (*T*, 20), that floating envoy of civilization.

Self-conscious about his own special inclinations, indeed able to relish "picturing myself seated beneath a cocoa-nut tree on the brow of the mountain, with a cluster of plantains within easy reach" (*T*, 31), Tommo further severs his romantic character from the "dastardly and mean-spirited wretches" (*T*, 21) of the *Dolly*'s crew when he chooses from among their number a single worthy companion, one Toby, who can frequently be found "leaning over the bulwarks, apparently plunged in a profound reverie" (*T*, 31). Toby, at least in Tommo's initial account of him, is very nearly Byronic in aspect; he has a "strange, wayward being, [which is] moody, fitful, and melancholy" and his physical appearance is "remarkably prepossessing" because, among other things, "a mass of jetty locks clustered about his temples and threw a darker shade into his large black eyes" (*T*, 32). Here is one, Tommo romantically supposes, who, "like myself, had evidently moved in a different sphere of life" (*T,* 32) and whose "gazing wistfully upon the shore" (*T,* 32) signals "that the subject of his meditations might be the same as my own" (*T,* 33). Having already developed with this worthy romantic companion "a certain congeniality of sentiment" in their responses to "the hard destiny it seemed our common fortune to encounter" (*T,* 32) aboard the *Dolly,* Tommo decides to flee this microcosm of civilization, the constituency of which was "as coarse in person as in mind" (*T,* 32), the captain of "which was arbitrary and violent in the extreme" (*T,* 21), and the future of which, therefore, "was little to encourage one in looking forward" (*T,* 23).

If Tommo and Toby fly *from* the "ill usage" (*T,* 21) of civilization, however, they escape *to* another, antique world whose primitive purity, Tommo is convinced, will shelter their yearning for paradise and nourish their hunger for innocence. The depth and extent of their romantic conception of themselves and their situation comes to the fore in the course of their flight to the interior of the island. "Limbs torn and lacerated" (*T,* 38) in working their way through a thicket of canes, "incapacitated for any further exertion" (*T,* 38), Tommo and Toby might well have begun to doubt their idea of a benevolent and nurturing natural world. In their romantic state of mind, however, the hazards are appropriately associated with civilization and the difficulties of freeing themselves from it: Tommo's conception of the reeds as "so many rods of steel" (*T,* 37) suggests that the obstacle of the thicket belongs not to nature but to industrial culture, and against this obstacle, he informs the reader, "I hacked and hewed away without mercy" (*T,* 38). After the experience of the reeds threatens to daunt their romantic aspirations, they regain their "high spirits"—"invigorated," Tommo says, "by the refreshing atmosphere we now inhaled" and, thus sustained by the natural surroundings, they are able to rise to the "lofty elevations" (*T,* 39) *above* civilization:

We must have been more than three thousand feet above the level of the sea, and the scenery viewed from this height was magnificent.
The lonely bay of Nukuheva, dotted here and there with the black hulls of the vessels composing the French squadron, lay reposing at

the base of a circular range of elevations, whose verdant sides, perforated with deep glens or diversified with smiling valleys, formed altogether the loveliest view I ever beheld, and were I to live a hundred years, I should never forget the feeling of admiration which I then experienced. (T, 40)

This elevated position, in short, affords them a view commensurate with their romantic expectations. Later in their escape, when they encounter an apparently impassable ravine, Toby again associates the obstacle with civilization as he suggests that "'it looks blacker than our ship's hold'" (T, 44). As before, however, the hazard of a descent into the ravine—which Toby says "'would batter one's brains to pieces'" (T, 44)—fails to shatter their idea of benign nature; indeed, Tommo thinks that "'this ravine will exactly answer our purpose, for it is roomy, secluded, well watered, and may shelter us from the weather'" (T, 45). In the face of a jagged, cruel natural world, then, Tommo comes closest to a realistic assessment of the situation only in his jocular recommendation "to all adventurous youths who abandon vessels in romantic islands during the rainy season to provide themselves with umbrellas" (T, 48).

Even in the midst of dangerous and difficult situations, Tommo and Toby will not surrender their inveterate romanticism, for, in shaking off the fetters of civilization, they have managed a glimpse of an undefiled world: "As far as our vision extended, not a sign of life, nor anything that denoted even the transient residence of man, could be seen. The whole landscape seemed one unbroken solitude, the interior of the island having apparently been untenanted since the morning of the creation; and as we advanced through this wilderness, our voices sounded strangely in our ears, as though human accents had never before disturbed the fearful silence of the place, interrupted only by the low murmurings of distant waterfalls" (T, 44). Tommo claims that the wearying and dangerous circumstances he now faces "only augmented my anxiety to reach a place which promised us plenty and repose" (T, 52). Propelled forward by the idea of such a place, and armed with their "love of adventure" and of "braving untried difficulties," Tommo and Toby seal their romantic communion in the ceremony of opening "the sacred package" (*T*, 54) and breaking bread together. Even the last mental barrier—the "special stigma" (*T*, 25) of cannibalism which Tommo has from the first associated with the dread Typees—is surmounted when Toby evokes the idea of the noble savage: in view of the valley they had seen at a distance, Toby suggests, the residents must be the better-reputed Happars, for "'it is impossible that the inhabitants of such a lovely place . . . can be anything but good fellows'" (*T*, 56). Tommo's willingness to accede to Toby's opinion, his acceptance of Toby's advice to "'throw away all those stupid ideas about the Typees'" (*T*, 56), finally confirms him as the romantic quester after paradise and prepares him, along with Toby, to make what are literally several leaps of romantic faith into the deep gorges which separate them from the garden spot they have seen from afar. This test culminates their rite of passage, and, having endured it, they qualify to enter the valley.

The choice of words here is studied because critical opinion has frequently and generally agreed that the obstacles and chasms Tommo and Toby surmount figure as *trials* in a quest motif. Richard Chase, for instance, finds at the heart of the American literary tradition a concentration on "the theme of the strenuous journey and the quest that gives it meaning." In the case of *Typee,* the objective which animates the quest is, according to Chase, one of the "two leading imaginative ideas of Melville"—namely, "the golden age with its simple life of innocence and genial emotions, which he [Melville] generically calls 'Typee'." [9] The valley itself, Tommo points out repeatedly, is a cultural island within a larger, geographically insular context; if civilization has already debased the Sandwich Islands and is beginning to defile Nukuheva, the valley of the Typee has not yet experienced the "fatal embrace" (*T*, 26) of the European. Tommo says that he has "no doubt that we were the first white men who ever penetrated thus far into their territories, or at least the first who had ever descended from the head of the vale" (*T*, 74). Here, then, Melville supplies Tommo and Toby with what remains of paradise—a romantic locale which will allow the free play of their apparently incorrigible convictions about the beneficence of the natural world, about the nobility of primal man, and, in contrast, about the ill civilization they have departed.

II

Nature, in the valley of the Typee, seems to confirm all of Tommo's expectations of paradise. In describing the topography of the vale, he presents a picture of the perfect harmony of natural and human life in the "paradisaical abode" (*T,* 195) of the Typees:

I should imagine that there were about two thousand inhabitants in Typee; and no number could have been better adapted to the extent of the valley. The valley is some nine miles in length, and may average one in breadth; the houses being distributed at wide intervals throughout its whole extent, principally, however, towards the head of the vale. There are no villages: the houses stand here and there in the shadow of the groves, or are scattered along the banks of the winding stream; their golden-hued bamboo sides and gleaming white thatch forming a beautiful contrast to the perpetual verdure in which they are embowered. There are no roads of any kind in the valley—nothing but a labyrinth of foot-paths twisting and turning among the thickets without end. (*T,* 194)

Here, the celebrated breadfruit "grows to an enormous magnitude, and flourishes in the utmost abundance" (*T,* 117), and, residing amidst this plenitude, "the idle savage stretches forth his hand, and satisfies his appetite" (*T,* 195). Nor is there any lack of cocoanuts in "this genial climate which causes them . . . to flourish" and to be "brought to perfection by the rich soil of the Marquesas" (*T,* 213). The weather itself is "one unvarying round of summer and sunshine, and the whole year is one long tropical month of June just melting into July" (*T,* 213). Many of the small animals, in this harmonious place, "show their confidence in the kindliness of man" (*T,* 212): the golden lizards are "insensible to fear," and the birds, equally unafraid of humans, take to the "wing slowly, less alarmed at your presence . . . than desirous of removing . . . from your path" (*T,* 211). In the midst of this kind and bountiful setting, there is no contention over property; here, Tommo thinks, the "inhabitants hold their broad valleys in fee simple from Nature herself; to have and to hold, so long as grass grows and water runs" (*T,* 202). In communion with their congenial environment, the Typees enjoy a "continual happiness," Tommo observes, "which . . . sprung principally from that all-pervading sensation which Rousseau has told us he at one time experienced, the mere buoyant sense of a healthful physical existence" (*T,* 127).

Embowered in this paradise, individual members of the Typee clan present themselves to Tommo's romantic sensibilities as fully worthy of the designation *noble savages.* The "splendid islander," Mehevi, ostensible chieftain of the Typees, "might certainly have been regarded as one of Nature's noblemen," Tommo suggests, because of "the excellence of his physical proportions" (*T,* 78) and his striking savage dignity. But for Tommo no matter how honorifically he might describe the others, no one can compare with Fayaway, whose "free pliant figure was the perfection of female grace and beauty" (*T,* 85):

Her complexion was a rich and mantling olive, and when watching the glow upon her cheeks I could almost swear that beneath the transparent medium there lurked the blushes of a faint vermilion. The face of this girl was a rounded oval, and each feature as perfectly formed as the heart or imagination of man could desire. Her full lips, when parted with a smile, disclosed teeth of a dazzling whiteness; and when her rosy mouth opened with a burst of merriment, they looked like the milk-white seeds of the "arta," a fruit of the valley, which, when cleft in twain, shows them reposing in rows on either side, imbedded in the red and juicy pulp. Her hair of the deepest brown, parted irregularly in the middle, flowed in natural ringlets over her shoulders, and whenever she chanced to stoop, fell over and hid from view her lovely bosom. Gazing into the depths of her strange blue eyes, when she was in a contemplative mood, they seemed most placid yet unfathomable; but when illuminated by some lively emotion, they beamed upon the beholder like stars. (*T,* 85–86)

If Tommo's description of Fayaway here seems contrived in tone and artificial or affected in its analogy of her beauty and the natural surroundings, the histrionics serve to reveal both how persistently romantic his own impulses are and how desperately he wants to ratify the possibilities of paradisal innocence. Fayaway, attired in "the primitive and summer garb of Eden" represents the supreme beauty of the valley, but, Tommo says, "the description I have given of her will in some measure apply" (*T*, 87) to all the young native girls. With this in view, Tommo implores, "Judge ye then, reader, what beautiful creatures they must have been" (*T*, 87).

Although Mehevi and Fayaway are the paradigmatically *noble* savages, then, the rest of the Typees share their artless vivacity and generosity. Tommo repeatedly remarks their unstudied gracefulness, their inveterate honesty with each other, and their continued warmth and friendliness toward him, and he observes that their insulation from Nukuheva, the nearest outpost of civilization, protects the Typees from the corruptions which characterize civilized man. No greed exists in the valley because the inhabitants live in an environment bountiful enough for them all, and there is "no Money! That 'root of all evil' was not to be found in the valley" (*T*, 126). Nor do any of the natives demonstrate any will to power. Tommo resides in the valley several weeks before he can conclude that Mehevi is indeed the king, and, even then, Tommo himself must "bestow" (*T*, 188) the title. "No one appeared to assume any arrogant pretentions," and Mehevi, who presides "wholly unattended by the ceremonious pomp which usually surrounds the purple" seems a genuinely democratic leader among a people marked by their "equality of condition" (*T*, 185). Further, nothing obtrudes on the harmony of personal relationships here; sexual jealousy and marital contention are unheard of, Tommo asserts, because the Typees practice a happily polyandrous marital system in which a young wife and her two husbands can "live together as harmoniously as so many turtles" (*T*, 191).

The thing that above all else inspires Tommo's admiration of these savage people, however, is "the unanimity of feeling they displayed on every occasion" (*T*, 203). "The love of kindred I did not so much perceive," Tommo points out, because "it seemed blended in the general love" (*T*, 204). On the basis of these and similar observations, he is convinced that these primitive people, away from civilization, are ruled "by an inherent principle of honesty and charity towards each other":

They seemed to be governed by that sort of tacit common-sense law which, say what they will of the inborn lawlessness of the human race, has its precepts graven on every breast. The grand principles of virtue and honor, however they may be distorted by arbitrary codes, are the same all the world over: and where these principles are concerned, the right or wrong of any action appears the same to the uncultivated as to the enlightened mind. It is to this indwelling, this universally diffused perception of what is *just* and *noble*, that the integrity of the Marquesans in their intercourse with each other is to be attributed. (*T,* 201)

This high estimate of the Typees' character, of course, depends on their insulation from civilization and on Tommo's strong sense of the perversions wrought by civilization on the "universally diffused perception" which he thinks "graven on every breast." The life is reminiscent of Eden before the Fall. "There are no venomous reptiles," Tommo emphasizes several times, and "no snakes of any description to be found in any of the valleys" (*T,* 212). The tenacity of this view stands up to the indisputable fact of Typee cannibalism because Tommo, enslaved by his romanticism, can regard the cannibal trait as an idiosyncratic custom with which foreigners ought not to meddle: "immeasurably as it is to be abhorred and condemned," he claims, "still I assert that those who indulge in it are in other respects humane and virtuous" (*T,* 205). Further, even if the islanders' honesty toward each other "is in striking contrast with the thieving propensities some of them evince in their intercourse with foreigners," Tommo does not waver on the idea of the noble savages. Considering the "wholesale forays made upon them" by Europeans, the native "code of morals" makes the foreigners' property "a fair object of reprisal" (*T,* 201). Tommo is certain that those simple people, left undisturbed by the encroachments of civilization, enact the indwelling principles of virtue and honor. These sentiments, of course, are worthy of Rousseau, and Evert Duyckinck's hasty reading of descriptions like this one accounts, no doubt, for his remarking to Hawthorne, to whom he was sending an advanced copy of the book, that *Typee* was "a Frenchy coloured picture of the Marquesan islanders." [10]

On the basis of these observations which seem to bear out romantic expectations about the natural world and the noble savage, Tommo is inevitably forced to trace out contrasts with the life of civilization:

There seemed to be no cares, griefs, troubles, or vexations, in all Typee. The hours tripped along as gaily as the laughing couples down a country dance.

There were none of those thousand sources of irritation that the ingenuity of civilized man has created to mar his own felicity. There were no foreclosures of mortgages, no protested notes, no bills payable, no debts of honor in Typee; no unreasonable tailors and shoemakers, perversely bent on being paid; no duns of any description; no assault and battery attorneys, to foment discord, backing their clients up to a quarrel, and then knocking their heads together; no poor relations, everlastingly occupying the spare bed-chamber, and diminishing the elbow room at the family table; no destitute widows with their children starving on the cold charities of the world; no beggars; no debtors' prisons; no proud and hard-hearted nabobs in Typee. . . .

In this secluded abode of happiness there were no cross old women, no cruel step-dames, no withered spinsters, no love-sick maidens, no sour old bachelors, no inattentive husbands, no melancholy young men, no blubbering youngsters, and no squalling brats. All was mirth, fun, and high good humor. Blue devils, hypochondria, and doleful dumps, went and hid themselves among the nooks and crannies of the rocks. (*T*, 126)

Indeed, in this "abode of happiness," the largest struggle is in the "outlay of strength and good temper" (*T*, 112) required to start a fire. For Tommo, the comparison is irresistible:

What a striking evidence does this operation furnish of the wide difference between the extreme of savage and civilized life. A gentleman of Typee can bring up a numerous family of children and give them all a highly respectable cannibal education, with infinitely less toil and anxiety than he expends in the simple process of striking a light; whilst a poor European artisan, who through the instrumentality of a lucifer performs the same operation in one second, is put to his wits' end to provide for his starving offspring that food which the children of a Polynesian father, without troubling their parent, pluck from the branches of every tree around them. (*T*, 112)

Typee *and the Impossibility of Paradise*

In this frame of mind, in which everything in the valley appears to be superior to anything in civilization, Tommo can suggest that those things in Typee which are ugly and irritating have either their sources or their equivalents in civilized society. A species of ugly dogs, Tommo informs the reader, are here an alien element, whose source is elsewhere: "Whence, in the name of Count Buffon and Baron Cuvier, came those dogs that I saw in Typee? Dogs!—Big hairless rats rather; all with smooth, shining, speckled hides—fat sides, and very disagreeable faces. Whence could they have come? That they were not the indigenous production of the region, I am firmly convinced. Indeed they seemed aware of their being interlopers, looking fairly ashamed, and always trying to hide themselves well out of it, and back to the ugly country from which they must have come" (*T,* 210). And the mosquito—"that enemy of all repose" (*T,* 212)—which plagues the Sandwich Islands was also, Tommo claims, due to the accidental introduction by foreigners. These are "among some of the numerous afflictions which the Europeans have entailed upon some of the natives of the South Seas" (*T,* 212). Other facts of life which strike Tommo as brutal or offensive are vitiated, in a sense, by his habit of suggesting that civilization contains facts equally, if not more, appalling. The hideousness of the "triply hooped" tatooing on Kory-Kory's face reminds Tommo "of those unhappy wretches . . . gazing out sentimentally from behind the grated bars of a prison window" (*T,* 83). Or again, when hostilities break out between the Typees and their Happar enemies, in a battle with much noise but no Typee fatality, Tommo describes the events in terms of European martial activity—Mehevi, he says, "rather inclined to the Fabian than to the Bonapartean tactics" (*T,* 130)—as if to assure the reader that civilization far outstrips the Typees in the enormities of waging war. With respect to the Typees' reputation for cannibalism, Tommo wonders "whether the mere eating of human flesh so very far exceeds in barbarity" public punishment in "enlightened England" or the "fiend-like skill we display in the invention of all manner of death-dealing engines" of war, or "the horrors we inflict upon those wretches, whom we mason up in the cells

21

of our prisons, and condemn to perpetual solitude in the very heart of our population" (*T*, 125). In view of these examples of "civilized barbarity," he concludes that "the term 'Savage' is . . . often misapplied" and that "four or five Marquesan Islanders sent to the United States as Missionaries might be quite as useful as an equal number of Americans despatched to the Islands in a similar capacity" (*T*, 125). Thus Tommo can pass over the Typees' cannibalism as "mere"—merely, he thinks, "a rather bad trait in their character" (*T*, 125) which they do not frequently indulge and then only with the bodies of slain enemies.

Withal, the islanders have a "free, inartificially happy, and unconstrained" (*T*, 127) life, and, Tommo must ask, "what has he to desire at the hands of Civilization?" (*T*, 124)—the answer to which rhetorical question, of course, is that "the Polynesian savage, surrounded by all the luxurious provisions of nature, enjoyed an infinitely happier, though certainly a less intellectual existence, than the self-complacent European" (*T*, 124). This is the point at which Tommo finds himself "well disposed to think that I was in the 'Happy Valley'," to think, in short, that he has regained a paradise insulated from the "world of care and anxiety" (*T*, 124) which lies beyond it. Flinging himself into the indolent pleasures such a garden spot affords, disporting himself with the "river-nymphs" (*T*, 131), imbibing the abundance of the valley, and, above all, submitting to the tender graces of Fayaway, he determines to make "a point of doing as the Typees did" (*T*, 209), and, with this resolution, he seems to have ratified the possibility of innocence which was the fondest dream of many of Melville's contemporaries.

III

Typee could not end at this point, with this apparent certification of paradise, however, because the understanding of the romantic Tommo who embarks on the quest after Eden has not yet caught up, so to speak, with the knowledge of the retrospective Tommo who, having undergone the entire experience and having reflected on its meaning, recounts the tale. The retrospective narrator cannot forget elements of the adventure that his earlier, romantic self, in his persistent innocence, was all too willing to ignore or to disdain. If the romanticist Tommo can, as he thinks, assume the life of the valley by eating "poee-poee as they did," by walking "about in a garb striking for its simplicity," and by reposing "on a community of couches" (*T,* 209), the reflective Tommo knows full well that in these things he had reified the life of innocence only in the most superficial way. While the early Tommo fancies that he has located a spot reminiscent of Eden, the latter Tommo realizes that this is a paradise impossible for modern man. In the closing distance between the romanticist Tommo and the retrospective Tommo, then, Melville negates the idea of paradisal innocence as a refuge from the world of experience by undercutting Tommo's romantic assumptions and by establishing an anthropology which includes the fact of the Fall.

Even if Tommo is convinced for a time about the virtue of communion with a benevolent natural world, he develops, in the course of the narrative, some sense of his own incapacity to enter into full participation in this life. Although it seems true that the Typees, encamped in a plentiful natural world, enjoy a sheer healthful existence, unmarked by disease and early fatality, Tommo himself is not sustained by any such relationship with therapeutic nature. Mysterious pains in his leg and an accompanying ague and fever plague him intermittently throughout his stay in the valley. The Typee leech applies a natural "species of medical treatment" which includes moistened herbs and "leafy bandages" (*T,* 80)—remedies which apparently work well enough on the Typees—but he only succeeds in creating new pain for Tommo. Later, when Tommo visits the medicinal springs in the valley, he still finds that his leg pains him. Resident in healing nature as he is, he is not healed.

His romantic assumptions are further called into question by his wavering on the idea of the noble savage. If in the daylight hours Tommo can admire their unstudied grace and physical beauty, his "night thoughts" include moments during which the Typees seem diabolical and fiendish. If he can observe the inherent principle of honesty and charity which governs them, he must also own that, out of sheer habit, they wage senseless wars, the sources of which they cannot even remember. As such moments recur more frequently, Tommo's imagination riots with apprehension about his situation. The Typees' strong desire to tatoo him makes Tommo "half wild with terror and indignation" (*T,* 219); and his discovery that they are cannibals, as he had expected, was "a last horrid revelation . . . [with which] the full sense of my condition rushed upon my mind with a force I had never before experienced" (*T,* 238). He begins to learn that the natives excel in cunning and duplicity, and their "glaring falsehood" about their cannibalism, Tommo says, "added to my alarm" (*T,* 233). With his growing recognition of the dark qualities of the Typees, and his awareness of "the craft peculiar to savages," Tommo's romanticism about his entrance into the ostensible paradise begins to diminish.

Now, Tommo's failure to find nurture in healing nature and his inability to take on the full life of the savage do not invalidate the idea of paradise so much as these things indicate that he is incapable of belonging in such a place because of his ties to the life of civilization. Although he can delight in watching "the Marquesan girls, [who] dance all over, as it were," he must add at once that, as "they so sway their floating forms, arch their necks, toss aloft their naked arms, and glide, and swim, and whirl, . . . it was almost too much for a quiet, soberminded, modest young man like myself" (*T,* 152). If Tommo has tongue in cheek here, he does not fail, in retrospect, to remark other reservations he had about entering completely into Typee life. He can eat "poee-poee as they did," but he cannot imitate the natives' habit of eating raw fish, he informs the reader, without first subjecting each fish "to a slight operation with my knife" (*T,* 209). The wild dances of the widows of the valley, which give "public evidence" of their grief strike Tommo as "so indecorous a custom . . . that it did not satisfy me as to its propriety" (*T,* 167). And his deep dread of being tatooed results from his fear that he "should be disfigured in such a manner as never more to have the *face* to return to my countrymen" (*T,* 219). In these and other ways, then, Tommo discloses bonds with civilization so strong that he cannot free himself from them. Paradise remains, with all its opportunities for innocence, but it remains possible only for the man who does not bring with him the legacies of civilized life.

The early Tommo's attempts to enter the society of the Typee valley only mark increasingly how severely the later Tommo knows he was precluded from that entrance. His contributions to life in the valley are either ineffectual or dangerous. Because of his singing ability, Tommo becomes a "court-minstrel" (*T,* 228) who is called upon by Mehevi, "fairly transported" by the chorus of the song, to repeat "the sounds fifty times over" (*T,* 227). In this attitude, Tommo is a kind of court fool who, suggesting that "singing was not the only means I possessed of diverting the royal Mehevi," also practices shadowboxing, "much to the enjoyment" (*T,* 228) of the onlookers. Other efforts to make a contribution are equally useless or trivial. The shoes he had worn into the valley become decorative pendants, hanging from around the neck of Marheyo. Tommo's ability to sew astonishes the natives: "they regarded this wonderful application of science with intense admiration" (*T,* 121). But they have no use for sewing since the making of *tappa*, the native cloth, is only a light task. Tommo's razor induces one of the natives to have Tommo shave his head, an operation during which the fellow "endured the pain," according to the narrator, "like a martyr" (*T,* 122). At another point, Tommo finds himself "engaged in manufacturing popguns" for the children and the adults of the valley; but the situation gets out of control as the natives playfully enter "duels, skirmishes, pitched battles, and general engagements," and Tommo fears falling "victim to my own ingenuity" (*T,* 145). In this, whatever Tommo can give to the valley consists of something useless, like the shoes which decorate Marheyo, or potentially dangerous, like the trivial violence he ushers in with his "attitudes of a pugilistic encounter" (*T,* 228) or his "nursery muskets" (*T,* 145). In short, Tommo offers the natives only the accoutrements of civilization which are negligible for their lives or which would go to undermine the continuing life of this paradise. He himself can only be a guest or visitor here, at best, never a citizen.

Although Tommo's contributions during the experience in the valley seem only minimally threatening, the retrospective narrator understands how thoroughly he belongs to civilization which, from the outset, he has associated with the snake, the Fall, and its potential destruction of paradise: "When the inhabitants of some sequestered island first descry the 'big canoe' of the European rolling through the blue waters towards their shores, they rush down to the beach in crowds, and with open arms stand ready to embrace the strangers. Fatal embrace! They fold to their bosoms the vipers whose sting is destined to poison all their joys; and the instinctive feeling of love within their breasts is soon converted into the bitterest hate" (*T*, 26). Although Tommo has assured the reader that there are "no snakes of any description to be found in any of the valleys" (*T*, 212), the fact is that civilized man, with his capacity to introduce paradise to the Fall, provides the hint of the snake. Tommo and Toby, no matter how extensive their rejection of civilization, cannot escape their connection with this symbol of the Fall: as they escape the *Dolly*, the narrator describes their "crawling on our hands and knees, and screened from observation by the grass through which we glided, much in the fashion of a couple of serpents" (*T*, 39). Later, in trying to account for the pain he suffers in his leg, Tommo "half suspected that I had been bitten by some venomous reptile" (*T*, 48). Finally, as he and Toby hesitate before entering the Typee valley, Tommo sees Toby "recoil as if stung by an adder" (*T*, 68) when he is startled by two young natives.

Because he bears the taint of the Fall, civilized man represents that which could be the end of the innocent life of the Typee valley. Even the missionaries are not immune to the fact of the Fall, Tommo argues, although their work, in the abstract, is "in truth a just and holy cause": "But if the great end proposed by it be spiritual, the agency employed to accomplish that end is purely earthly; and, although the object in view be the achievement of much good, that agency may nevertheless be productive of evil. In short, missionary undertaking, however it may be blessed of Heaven, is in itself but human; and subject like everything else, to errors and abuses" (*T*, 197). As if to prove this case, Tommo has cited the episode in which a missionary's wife enslaves two native men and uses them as draught horses to pull her carriage.

Although he is appalled by this instance, the retrospective narrator cannot forget, and does not fail to mention on several occasions, that he had himself similarly enslaved Kory-Kory as a beast of burden. Civilized man is the interloper in paradise, then, and, despite all his yearning for innocence and his good intentions, Tommo becomes the alien element which threatens the harmony of paradise. In the final scenes of the narrative, as the Typees fight over him, Tommo himself is the factor which disrupts what he had earlier admired most about the natives, "the unanimity of feeling they displayed on every occasion" (*T,* 203). If he can in retrospection conclude that "the penalty of the Fall presses very lightly on the valley of the Typee" (*T,* 195), he must also conclude that any anthropology adequate for modern, civilized man, including missionaries, must contain an admission of his fallen nature, a nature which not only prevents his recovery of innocence but which also destroys the Eden of his yearning.

As might have been expected, given the casual reading usually brought to *Typee,* Melville's observations about the missionaries caused a furor.[11] The fact is, however, that Melville does not deprecate the missionaries' Christianity—which is "blessed of Heaven"—but, rather, that he notes their civilization—"in itself but human" and thus unavoidably tainted by the Fall. Tommo does not exclude himself from these considerations, for he recognizes that he too, despite his romantic yearning, bears the mark of civilization. Such a view helps also to explain, in a large measure, the function of the apparently ill-fitting historical appendix to *Typee.* There, attempting to correct "the distorted accounts and fabrications which had produced in the United States so violent an outbreak of indignation against the English" intercession in the Sandwich Islands, Melville describes "the events which occurred upon the arrival of Lord George Paulet at Oahu" (*T,* 254). This corrective account of Lord Paulet's character and actions is honorific in tone, but the point again seems to be that however noble and well intentioned Paulet might have been, his civilized presence could create nothing but mayhem among the innocent islanders. In this way, the appendix works to enforce the empirical, historical validity of the anthropology Tommo will finally conceive in the narrative proper—it works, that is, to confirm historically the literary idea issued up by the shifts and tensions of Tommo's narration.

This recognition of the threat of civilization to the life of innocence forms a part of the retrospective narration from the first, as for instance when the narrator describes the outcome of his and Toby's initial entrance into the valley: "As soon as they [the Typees] perceived us they fled with wild screams into the adjoining thickets, *like so many startled fawns*" (*T,* 70; my italics). If, after his experience in the valley with the innocent savages, Tommo "will frankly declare . . . [that] I formed a higher estimate of human nature than I had ever before entertained," he adds immediately that he is fully aware of "the pent-up wickedness of five hundred men" aboard a man-of-war (*T,* 203), and he demonstrates how completely his own nature belongs in the fallen context of a man-of-war world when, at the end of the narrative, he admits his sinking a boathook into a Typee neck in order to make his escape.

If Tommo fails to locate a place for himself in the primitive society of the valley, however, and if his suggestion of the snake represents a threat to the innocence of the Typees, there is a deeper reason still why he must enact this extreme measure in order to escape. The consequence of the Fall which banishes him from the life of innocence also exiles him into an encompassing world of experience. Robbed of his Adamic mentality, he must bring to his experience a continuous consciousness, a penalty of the Fall, in order to construct and maintain his self-definition. As the narrative runs its course, Tommo discovers, or at least begins to sense, that, if his fallen nature cannot contribute to the life of the vale, the paradise itself cannot supply either the full diversity of experience or the habit of reflection, both of which are crucial to his self-understanding.

The insular character of the valley, the fact that it is severed from the rest of the world, the very fact which first attracted Tommo to its innocent confines, becomes a danger to his integral selfhood. The breadth of experience in this paradise is as narrow as its topography, and the variety of experience here is as homogeneous as the "unvarying round of summer and sunshine" which marks the climate. Tommo suggests the narrow extent of possible experience in the valley when he rehearses the Typees' mode of living: "nothing can be more uniform and undiversified than the life of the Typees; one tranquil day of ease and happiness follows another in quiet succession; and with these unsophisticated savages the history of a day is the history of a life" (*T,* 149). After describing a typical day, he concludes that the entire day is simply a preparation for the evening:

Unless some particular festivity was going forward, the inmates of Marheyo's house retired to their mats rather early in the evening; but not for the night, since, after slumbering lightly for a while, they rose again, relit their tapers, partook of the third and last meal of the day, at which poee-poee alone was eaten, and then, after inhaling a narcotic whiff from a pipe of tobacco, disposed themselves for the great business of night, sleep. With the Marquesans it might also be styled the great business of life, for they pass a large portion of their time in the arms of Somnus. The native strength of their constitutions is no way shown more emphatically than in the quantity of sleep they can endure. To many of them, indeed, life is little else than an often interrupted and luxurious nap. (*T,* 152)

In the face of this routine, Tommo says he "sought to diversify my time by as many enjoyments as lay within reach" (*T,* 131), but even the pleasures of indolence have a kind of sameness about them. Attempting to convince Tommo to remain, Marnoo enumerates the assets of the valley: "'Why you no like to stay? Plenty moee-moee (sleep)—plenty ki-ki (eat)—plenty whihenee (young girls)—Oh, very good place Typee!'" (*T,* 241). The retrospective Tommo realizes, however, that this constricted range of activity cannot satisfy the demands for full experience that his selfhood requires. After three months in the valley, he had "grown familiar with the narrow limits to which my wanderings had been confined" (*T,* 231) and had come to despair about having "to pass away my days in this narrow valley" (*T,* 239).

Apart from the hint of the snake which it provides, Tommo's leg injury also figures in his physical and mental bondage. The pain in his leg subsides proportionately to his willful submersion into the narcosis of life in the valley and increases in just the measure that he wants to leave the valley. With the growing awareness of his captive state, he reports that "the painful mal-

THE HAPPY VALLEY

ady" in his leg "began again to show itself, and with symptoms
as violent as ever" (*T*, 232). The pain increases whenever his
chances for freedom seem to decrease. It is, in short, a poetic
pain which has to be surmounted even as he hobbles to the beach
to make his escape. The native doctor had not been able to cure
him, and his attachment to civilization is again enforced when he
"reflected that just beyond the elevations which bound me in,
was the medical relief I needed" (*T*, 232).

If the insular character of life in the valley prevents Tommo's
finding the full span of experience necessary for him, the lotus-
eating indolence of the Typees, their drowsy, unreflective mentality, stifles the operation of consciousness which is Tommo's
legacy of the Fall. His inquiries about the Typee monuments and
gods go unanswered; the natives have no memory of and no account for these things. His curiosity about the system of taboos
is never satisfied; although the taboos "guide and control every
action of his [a Typee's] being" (*T*, 221), the natives offer no explanation of the sources or the significance of these dictates.
Even Tommo's constantly comparing the life of the valley to life
outside the valley is an alien habit here; the Typees know nothing and care nothing for things beyond their narrow abode. The
war with the Happars, which briefly interrupts the homogeneity
of experience in the valley, is talked about as "an event of prodigious importance" and "for two or three days . . . was the theme
of general comment" (*T*, 130), but, as quickly as it had erupted,
"the excitement gradually wore away, and the valley resumed its
accustomed tranquillity" (*T*, 130). The Typees take a kind of
infantile delight in the war and then forget it utterly. With no
need to bring any consciousness to their historical activity, they
return immediately to an unvarying round of sleep and tropical
pleasure. Tommo singles out Marheyo in this respect: He "was
so eccentric a character, that he seemed to be governed by no
fixed principles whatever; but acting just according to the
humour of the moment, slept, ate, or tinkered away at his little
hut, without regard to the proprieties of time or place. Frequently he might have been seen taking a nap in the sun at noon-day,
or a bath in the stream at midnight. Once I beheld him perched
eighty feet from the ground, in the tuft of a cocoa-nut tree,

30

smoking" (*T*, 151). In "acting just according to the humour of
the moment," Marheyo is only the extreme example of the lazy,
purposeless life of the valley in general. Although the romantic
Tommo can for a time immerse himself in the narcotic pleasures
of this life, the retrospective narrator remembers that he thought
"a thousand times . . . how much more endurable would have
been my lot had Toby still been with me" (*T*, 231), and he recalls as well that he relished the visits of Marnoo, the native
who speaks a bit of broken English, because "again I should be
able to converse with him in my own language" (*T*, 240). He
cannot surrender the possibility of even the most meager forms
of intellection.

By the end of the narrative, Tommo's expressed need for mental stimulation and intellectual companionship, his most crucial
requirement, has deepened into an awareness that to succumb to
the mindless life of the valley is to annihilate his conscious selfhood. Earlier, in trying to assume the life of innocence by sub-
merging himself in the unconscious life of Typee, he had thrown
off his despondence by sinking "insensibly into that kind of
apathy" in which he "lost all knowledge of the regular recur-
rence of the days of the week" (*T*, 123). However, he had to
develop an "elasticity of mind" (*T*, 123) in order to divorce himself thus from historical consciousness, and later, with this mental flexibility, he "flung . . . [myself] anew into all the social
pleasures of the valley, and sought to bury all regrets, and all
remembrances of my previous existence, in the wild enjoyments
it afforded" (*T*, 144). As it gradually occurs to him that life in
the valley will require this elasticity of mind, this forgetfulness
about the only world which will nourish his self-definition, he
not only regrets but begins "bitterly to feel the state of captivity
in which I was held" (*T*, 231). His description of this state indicates that his intellectual imprisonment is more distressing
than the fact of his physical bondage: "There was no one with
whom I could freely converse; no one to whom I could com-
municate my thoughts; no one who could sympathise with my
sufferings. . . . I was left alone, and the thought was terrible to
me" (*T*, 231). Alone with his "solitary musings" (*T*, 244), Tommo begins to look at life in the valley with a "melancholy eye"

(*T*, 243) because he knows he cannot "pass away my days in this narrow valley, deprived of all intercourse with civilized beings" (*T*, 239). With this knowledge, and with the threat to consciousness posed by the valley, he must make his escape regardless of the cost. The need to escape does not mean that Tommo has rejected the idea of paradise in favor of the grosser barbarities of civilization. Rather, Tommo has learned, under the pressure of Melville's authorship, that the paradise remains; but he has learned as well, as the retrospective narration evinces, that paradise, for all its virtues, cannot supply him with an Adamic identity and that he must cleave to a world—the only possible world for him, with all its fallen quality—in which experience and consciousness nurture his sense of himself.[12]

CHAPTER TWO

DEAR DELUSION
Redburn *and the Test of Tradition*

After *Typee*, and before the appearance of *Redburn* in 1849, Melville published *Omoo* (1847) and *Mardi* (1849). *Omoo* stands, in intention and effect, as a sequel to the autobiographical aspects of *Typee*, and it had its appeal as a narrative of South Sea adventures. If, as with *Typee*, many of the responses to *Omoo* raised the question of the strict veracity of the book, it was favorably regarded.[1] On the basis of the preliminary success of these first two books, Melville determined to earn his living as a writer, but he was soon bitterly disappointed by readers' responses to *Mardi*. With this complex work, he was convinced that he had attempted something much more important than those books which had previously come off his pen, but *Mardi*, an extended and occasionally satirical allegory, usually had a discomposing effect on attempts at interpretation. Charles Gordon Greene, for example, in reviewing *Mardi* for the Boston *Post* (18 April 1849), wrote that "the whole book is not only tedious but unreadable." In the face of flagging sales and a critical financial situation at home, Melville felt himself forced to push aside the abstractions of *Mardi* and to return to the formation of a narrative based on his own experience.[2] Thus *Redburn*, written very quickly in 1849, was founded roughly at least on his own trip to Liverpool in 1839 and was "a thing," according to Melville, "which I, the author, know to be trash, & wrote . . . to buy some tobacco with."[3]

Despite Melville's low opinion of *Redburn*, the book represented a crucial addition to his developing vision, for it enabled

Melville to complicate and extend the understanding which had issued from his very first effort. The careers of Tommo of *Typee* and Wellingborough Redburn, the title character and narrator of Melville's fourth book, are coterminous—at least in the sense that Tommo's test of "the Happy Valley" and his final rudimentary anthropology commit Melville to having the young Redburn live in a fallen world which does not contain, for civilized man, the possibility of Adamic innocence. Redburn claims from the outset that even as a young man he "had learned to think much and bitterly before my time" and that "all my young mounting dreams of glory had left me" (*R*, 10). If he, like the early Tommo, has been disillusioned by the terms of his life, if "upon his young soul the mildew has fallen" (*R*, 11), Redburn, "with the warm soul of me flogged out by adversity" (*R*, 10), cannot imagine, like the romanticist Tommo, a condition of primordial simplicity and purity:

Talk not [he implores the reader] of the bitterness of middle-age and after life; a boy can feel all that, and much more, when . . . the fruit, which with others is only blasted after ripeness, with him is nipped in the first blossom and bud. *And never again can such blights be made good; they strike in too deep, and leave such a scar that the air of Paradise might not erase it.* And it is a hard and cruel thing thus in early youth to taste beforehand the pangs which should be reserved for the stout time of manhood, when the gristle has become bone, and we stand up and fight out our lives, as a thing tried before and foreseen; for then we are veterans used to sieges and battles, and not green recruits, recoiling at the first shock of encounter. (*R*, 11; my italics)

In short, the possibility of taking refuge from experience in a state of Edenic innocence, the possibility which the whole of *Typee* works ultimately to invalidate, is from the first an expressed impossibility for the narrator of *Redburn*. This does not mean, however, that the young Redburn immediately commits himself, after his first shock of encounter, to the world of experience. Nor does it mean that he surrenders his yearning for a certain kind of innocence.

Like the early Tommo, Redburn attempts in his recoil to create a context, apart from the world of experience, which will salve his rough treatment at the hands of that world, and, as in

Typee, the form of this recoil derived from an important strain of conviction in Melville's era. For Redburn, disabused of the possibility of paradise, the refuge is a satisfying past which can be remembered and which, he believes, can be sustained, or rein-augurated to sustain him, in the present. As Redburn retreats from immediate experience, however, he does not demonstrate some merely antiquarian concern. He seeks, rather, to evoke a tradition for himself, the authority of which, he is convinced, will nurture his own self-definition by insuring his continuity with a viable and effective past.[4] His journey to Liverpool is a fictional enactment of an intellectual and emotional pilgrimage and homage, characteristic of many thoughtful people of the day who felt that no adequate American self-definition could be con-ceived apart from what Hawthorne, a few years later, would call *Our Old Home* (1863).[5] While Redburn's early pretensions to aristocracy echo, in some senses, the reservations about the "Dis-advantages of Democracy" James Fenimore Cooper had voiced in *The American Democrat* (1838), the tone of his admiration for the British architectural past and for other evidences of a powerfully substantive tradition belongs squarely to the frame of mind of Washington Irving's Geoffrey Crayon, as that "Gent" rambles about nostalgically in "Westminster Abbey." In short, Redburn's deep needs for a tradition—and his early loyalty to the forms and ideas of the old world—align him directly with the "party of memory" Emerson would identify as one side in the great debate about the American identity.[6]

Melville, like some other serious American writers of his day, probably sensed a need for a long-standing cultural tradition as a resource for his individual talent because, as Henry James per-haps pointed out best, the relatively brief history of the United States could provide writers with nothing of the complex social matrix on which the English drew, could provide no Ascot and no Eton.[7] Regardless of how deeply Melville felt the tug of tra-dition, however, he was no more content in *Redburn* merely to mirror a strain of thought in his age than he had been in *Typee* to succumb to a facile appropriation of the Adamic metaphor. *Red-burn* stands, rather, as a test of the "party of memory" as a pos-sible resource for the American self-understanding—the efficacy of which resource, in the fictive adjudication, depends on the adequacy of its motives, aspirations, and characteristics as they are figured by Wellingborough Redburn. In "His First Voyage" (the subtitle of the book), Redburn's representative convictions are tried in a world imaginatively conceived by Melville to test the vision of the "party of memory" in the full measure. The meaning and significance of *Redburn* must be comprehended in the title character's progress: his initial disjunction from a satis-fying past and the attempt to reestablish his continuity by loyalty to a personally constructed tradition, through his discovery that the authorities he has evoked are given the lie by the direct en-counter with experience, and, finally, to his retrospective assess-ment of the possibilities of tradition and the necessities for his selfhood. If like his predecessor, Tommo, Redburn learns that his innocent expectancies will not suffice, he learns this lesson much earlier in the course of his recoil, and thus Melville has the occasion to develop the kind of reflexive and reflective capability in the growing Redburn's character which was a still-nascent requirement of Tommo's laboriously constructed anthropology. Redburn can at last begin to imagine the sustaining possibilities of a world of experience which Tommo reentered reluctantly because, cast out of Eden, he knew he must.

I

As the retrospective Redburn opens his account of "His First Voyage," he recalls that his taste for the sea and the immediate impetus for his signing on to serve before the mast on a journey to Liverpool had not developed only because of "a naturally rov-ing disposition" but because of some "sad disappointments in several plans which I had sketched for my future life" (*R*, 3). The disappointments had occurred, he informs the reader, be-cause of the poverty of his family after their having been severed by circumstances from a happier, well-to-do time. In his present condition, he is expressly disabused of any felt continuity with a satisfying past, and the sources of this discontinuity lie in his sense of himself as orphaned, at least in part, by the death of his father, for that literal orphanhood represents to him forcefully and poignantly his disjunction from a sustaining personal or familial tradition. Feeling that "desperation and recklessness of poverty which only a pauper knows" (*R*, 12), Redburn retreats from his severe buffeting at the hands of experience into memory, for images from the past seem to him more concordant than his present life with the terms of his self-image. For the briefest time, his recoil begins to resemble Tommo's early flight from the world of experience in *Typee:*

As I grew older my thoughts took a larger flight, and I frequently fell into long reveries about distant voyages and travels, and thought how fine it would be, to be able to talk about remote and barbarous countries; with what reverence and wonder people would regard me, if I had just returned from the coast of Africa or New Zealand; how dark and romantic my sunburnt cheeks would look; how I would bring home with me foreign clothes of a rich fabric and princely make, and wear them up and down the streets, and how grocers' boys would turn back their heads to look at me, as I went by. (*R*, 5)

But even in this moment, the "remote and barbarous countries" —the imaginations of a primitive Eden which allured the early Tommo—are less important to Redburn than the "foreign clothes of a rich fabric and princely make." He does not fly from civilization but wants, rather, to establish his personal continuity with the rich fabric of tradition in such a way that "grocers' boys"—paupers like him in his present condition—will accord him the proper importance he assumes he has.

Without any direct experience of that tradition which inspires him, which indeed represents for him the authoritative element in his projected self-conception, Redburn constructs a beginning personal tradition out of the materials of "certain shadowy reminiscences ... [which] early childhood had supplied me" (*R*, 4). This self-generated tradition springs from Redburn's adolescent dreaming about distant, antique civilizations—the catalysts for which are glimpses of a "wonderful Arabian traveler," examination of "furniture ... brought from Europe," the presence of "several oil-paintings and rare old engravings ... bought in Paris" by his father, the possession of "two large green French portfolios of colored prints" (*R*, 6), and the "long rows of old books ... printed in Paris, and London, and Leipsic" (*R*, 7).

These artifacts, from old and substantive civilizations, constitute for Redburn both a tangible, if secondhand, connection with a past which his youthful sense of himself requires and the foreign associations which will work to inspire his "subsequent rovings" (R, 7). The figurative embodiment of these yearnings is in the glass ship: "That which, perhaps more than anything else, converted my vague dreamings and longings into a definite purpose of seeking my fortune on the sea, was an old-fashioned glass ship, about eighteen inches long, and of French manufacture, which my father, some thirty years before, had brought home from Hamburgh as a present to a great-uncle of mine; Senator Wellingborough Redburn, who had died a member of Congress in the days of the old Constitution, and after whom I had the honor of being named. Upon the decease of the Senator, the ship was returned to the donor" (R, 7). This glass ship, with its intricacy of construction, allows Redburn "to rove in imagination" (R, 8), and to it he brings all his young expectancies about the ways tradition can nurture his own life. The origin and the history of ownership of the glass model represent for him a slender thread of continuity which reaches from a rich European tradition, to his own family's formerly distinguished stature, to the similarly aristocratic definition of himself he wants so desperately to secure.

In the context of these surviving remnants of the past, Redburn's image of his father assumes a large measure of importance just because the late elder Redburn's travels, conversations, and style of life conjoin him vitally in the young Redburn's memory with an abundant and long-standing cultural tradition:

Added to these reminiscences my father, now dead, had several times crossed the Atlantic on business affairs, for he had been an importer in Broad-street. And of winter evenings in New York, by the well-remembered sea-coal fire in old Greenwich-street, he used to tell my brother and me of the monstrous waves at sea, mountain high; of the masts bending like twigs; and all about Havre, and Liverpool, and about going up into the ball of St. Paul's in London. Indeed, during my early life, most of my thoughts of the sea were connected with the land; but with fine old lands, full of mossy cathedrals and churches, and long, narrow, crooked streets without side-walks, and lined with strange houses. And especially I tried hard to think how such places must look of rainy days and Saturday afternoons; and whether indeed they did have rainy days and Saturdays there, just as we did here; and whether the boys went to school there, and studied geography, and wore their shirt collars turned over, and tied with a black ribbon; and whether their papas allowed them to wear boots, instead of shoes, which I so much disliked, for boots looked so manly. (R, 5)

These images of the father, along with the great-uncle senator, sustain Redburn, allowing him to assure himself, even in the midst of his present poor circumstances, that he belongs squarely to a distinguished line of descent which itself belongs to the ages. If he owes his very name to the senator, these recollections serve as well to indicate both how fully the early Redburn's sense of his own impending manhood is tied to the image of his father and how completely, in turn, that image is related to "fine old lands, full of mossy cathedrals and churches." With the death of his father, Redburn feels the entire continuity threatening to break, depending as it does only on shadowy reminiscences and a few transplanted artifacts. His self-definition, his belonging fully aligned with his distinguished ancestry, must remain tentative, he is convinced, until he can himself possess his father's tradition, and he knows this can never be achieved by looking at colored prints of Versailles and by gazing wistfully at "a copy of D'Alembert in French" (R, 6). He will not rest until he can pull on his father's boots or at least walk where those boots have walked, and this, above all else, inspires Redburn to embark on his first voyage. By gaining his proper standing in relation to tradition, by revivifying the past, he will surmount the "blights" of his present condition, he thinks, and will make the authority of the past the definitive factor in a selfhood molded by yet another image from the past: "just as my father used to entertain strange gentlemen over their wine after dinner, I would hereafter be telling my own adventures to an eager auditory" (R, 7). As Redburn sallies forth on his quest to reify his sense of himself as his father's son, his loyalties are all to the past, and he determines that his future actions and attitudes will be mediated by the authority of that past.

The past Redburn conjures to supply himself with a beginning foundation in tradition is one, however, to which he brings no powers of critical intelligence. The rhythms of the prose and the undifferentiated uses of vocabulary in the early chapters betray the fact that the young Redburn cannot yet conceive elements of the past which do not deserve his allegiance. He celebrates "grim-looking warehouses, with rusty iron doors and shutters" (R, 4), equally with "the ball of St. Paul's in London," for the simple reason that each of these images comes to him out of the past—either through dim memories or through his father's accounts of his travels. The images are not themselves important; what inspires Redburn's admiration, rather, is their antiquity—a "mossiness," ascribed to them by his fervor, which blurs any distinctions between them. Linked with this failure of discrimination is a correlative failure on the early Redburn's part to imagine the possibility that even the brightest of these images could contain a darker center. The wharves his adolescent memory recalls so fondly are not scavenged by rats, and the mossy old churches are not dark and damp. He fails to consider that behind the facades of the strange houses fronting the long, narrow, crooked streets of the Old World might exist dimensions of human suffering or that in the London of his projections might lurk crime and disease. He neglects to recall or to mention the voting record of his great-uncle senator or, indeed, to suppose that his dead father's luxurious manner of living might be related to his survivors' present, poor circumstances. In short, despite the fact that his own life has, he says, wounded him painfully, the young Redburn cannot imagine that the past he reveres might have had a similar capacity to scar and blight human life. Because the images he sustains from the past are distant, both in his memory and from his actual experience, he can evoke them and swear his loyalty to them without any sense of the contradictions they might contain.

There is a very real sense in which the Redburn of the first half of the book, as distinguished from the narrator Redburn, seems to be a straw man—that is, a preposterously exaggerated voice for tradition which fails even as it speaks. But the point of view of the book is retrospective, and the later Redburn's presentation of himself as slightly ridiculous, if desperately so, during his adolescence begins to testify to his emerging self-knowledge. Redburn's retrospective disclosures of himself in these early vulnerable moments suggest that he is beginning at least to consider his life honestly.[8] Although Redburn presents himself, in his recollections of his adolescence, as little more than a juvenile exponent of the "party of memory," Melville does not use him, with all his naiveté, to denigrate the frequently voiced need in his America for a defining tradition. In fact, the opposite seems to have been the case, for Melville's journals contain frequent entries which reveal his admiration for long and powerful tradition. In his journal account for 2 May 1857, for instance, Melville recorded his visit to Oxford University as follows:

Most interesting spot I have seen in England. Made tour of all colleges. It was here I first confessed with gratitude my mother land, & hailed her with pride . . . Pulpit in corner of quadrangle. Deer. Garden girdled by river.—Meadows beyond. Oxen & sheep. Pastoral & collegiate life blended.—Christ Church Meadow. Avenue of trees.—Old reef washed by waves & showing detached parts—so Oxford. . . . Learning lodged like a faun. . . . I know nothing more fitted by mild & beautiful rebuke to chastise the presumptuous ranting of Yankees.—In such a retreat old Burton sedately smiled at men.[9]

Indeed, Melville no doubt felt—as he had with the Adamic impulses of Tommo in *Typee*—real sympathy for Redburn's drive to achieve some continuity with the past, for there are enough autobiographical elements in the narrative to indicate Melville's working through his sense of his own personal and cultural orphanhood. But the real point here, however, is that Melville used *Redburn*—again, as he had in *Typee*—for crystallizing the forms with which human beings perceive their experience, for allowing those perceptions and the attitudes they evoke full play in circumstances designed to tax them to the fullest extent, and finally, for presenting, in the fictive world, occasions for those perceptions to shift or to confirm themselves in this world of their living. Quite apart from any body block dealt the "party of memory," the young Redburn's flight from the shock of encounter with direct experience, his retreat into the refuge of tradition, must be understood as stemming from his deeply felt, if apparently fanciful, conviction that this is the most meaningful way to answer the fundamental questions of his life. If, in his perceptions, Redburn rehearses in an elemental fashion the modes and motives of those Americans who would cling to the manners of the Old World, he begins his career not as a caricature of the traditionalist but as Melville's test of tradition as a resource for the contemporary American culture.

II

Immediately upon setting forth on his journey, the young Redburn begins to marshal his defenses—to rely on relics from the past—in order to make his way in a world which his senses of his present experience tell him is hostile: he dons the shooting jacket, carries an old fowling gun, and depends, from the very outset, on a family connection to get him a comfortable berth on a voyage abroad. In one sense or another, each of these defenses belongs to another time, but, as yet, Redburn has no conception that they might fail to obtain in his altered situation. Even if the incongruity of the jacket and the gun, in this new context, might have been brought home to him by the stares of the people around him on board the steamer which takes him down the Hudson to New York, Redburn believes instead that the stares are because "the scent and savor of poverty was [sic] upon me" (R, 12). This incident confirms, at the time, the young man's view that the world was a cold and cruel place, for with it he remembers that "my whole soul was soured within me" (R, 12). The relics he bears, which to this point had been only figurative resources, now become literal defenses as he uses "the ample skirts of my shooting-jacket" to cover "a mighty patch upon one leg of my trowsers" (R, 12) and as he clenches the gun to frighten the people "into respect" (R, 12). Somewhat later still, driven by the "recklessness of poverty" and certain "demoniac feelings" (R, 13), the boy uses the gun to menace the other passengers. In recounting this episode, the retrospective Redburn feels "heartily ashamed" (R, 13), but the fact remains that at the time he was acting in character—in the sense at least that he then attempted to command a position for himself by flourishing weaponry bequeathed him by the past.

Redburn relies on his tradition again when he reaches the city, for here he needs a family acquaintance to help him make his way. His friend abets Redburn's claim to tradition as a life guide; he is fully prepared to utilize Redburn's distinguished ancestry as a way to usher Redburn through his experience. As together they search for a spot for Redburn, they are careful to find a ship's captain who satisfies Redburn's notion of the gentility which should belong to such a maritime figure. They discover Captain Riga, "a fine looking man, about forty, splendidly dressed, with very black whiskers, and very white teeth, and . . . a free, frank look out of a large hazel eye," whom, Redburn informs the reader, "I liked . . . amazingly" (R, 15). Appealing to Riga's aristocratic cut, the well-meaning friend mentions Redburn's line of descent and attempts to persuade Riga that Redburn will ship as an ordinary seaman only because he wants to and not because he must. In retrospect, Redburn recalls this as "a huge fib, which out the kindness of his heart, . . . [my] friend told in my behalf, for the purpose of creating a profound respect for me in the eyes of my future lord." But Captain Riga cares nothing for the friend's recitation of Redburn's "highly respectable family" and offers the young man only a meager berth for the voyage. However, even when confronted with Riga's "levity concerning my great-uncle" (R, 16), his "slanting glance at my shooting-jacket" (R, 18), and his obvious attempt to dupe him and his friend, Redburn's tenacious loyalty to his venerated image of a ship's captain remains intact, for he is certain that, once at sea, this splendid figure of a captain must out of noblesse oblige come to regard him as the "son of a gentleman" (R, 16) he knows himself to be.

In this and other ways, Melville forces Redburn to enter a world even more constricted than the earlier world mediated by his adolescent dreaming. In his reveries, Redburn could at least sustain himself with the shadowy reminiscences and leftover artifacts of the past; now, he must work out his sense of himself in a context within which his family connections and "the respectability of my paternity" (*R*, 17) are, whether real or devised, as anachronistic as the fowling piece and the shooting jacket. These relics he bears not only fail to aid his journey but actually serve to interfere with his success. The fact that he is descended "of one of the first families in America" (*R*, 16), as his friend tells Captain Riga, only allows the captain to offer Redburn less money, since, says Riga, Redburn can depend on these "wealthy relations" (*R*, 17) to finance him. Soon, Redburn will learn also both that the fowling piece will not bring him the money he expected and that the shooting jacket will not serve him well in the ship's rigging.

The challenges to Redburn's attempts to define and guide his life by filtering it through the spectrum of tradition are increased aboard ship, for here he learns that rank and stature are accorded men at sea on the basis of their ability and experience. As a novice, he finds himself unable to comprehend the language of the ship, clumsy in the performance of duties, and often sick at sea. He is no "able seaman," no "artist in the rigging" (*R*, 121), but, instead, a "boy" who is, according to the mate, "'Green as grass! a regular cabbage-head'" (*R*, 30). Therefore, Redburn is "set to cleaning out a pigpen" (*R*, 28), "picking up some shavings" (*R*, 29), and slushing down the top-mast—mean duties which are not, he thinks, commensurate with his standing. His first attempt to create some respect for himself by utilizing the past comes when he displays "an old tortoise-shell snuff-box of my father's, in which I had put a piece of Cavendish tobacco, to look sailor-like" (*R*, 27). When he offers the tobacco to the second mate, however, he is scorned by that worthy who "never carried any such nonsense about him as a tobacco-box" (*R*, 27). Another element of Redburn's naiveté also stems from his dealing exclusively in such images of gentility: "At eight o'clock the bell was struck, and we went to breakfast. And now some of the worst of my troubles began. For not having had any friend to tell me what I would want at sea, I had not provided myself, as I should have done, with a good many things that a sailor needs; and for my own part, it had never entered my mind, that sailors had no table to sit down to, no cloth, or napkins, or tumblers, and had to provide everything themselves" (*R*, 54). He has ar-

rived aboard ship so ill equipped, indeed, that he has no silver-
ware to dip into the common pot at the seamen's mess. The other
sailors' resentment of Redburn's aristocratic pretensions is given
vent here with their question about why "that wealthy gentleman my father [could not] afford to buy his gentlemanly son a
spoon" (*R,* 55).

Although it is not necessary to enumerate all the other ways in
which the efficacy of Redburn's tradition is called into question,
two crucial instances—with the seaman named Jackson and
with Captain Riga—emphasize Redburn's feelings that he is
orphaned, that his life is adrift, and that he must establish some
continuity with his paternity.

In the figure of Jackson, Redburn, in search of a father, encounters a man whose actions and demeanor preclude any solace
the inexperienced young man might have located among the
members of the crew, for "nothing was left of this Jackson but
the foul lees and dregs of a man": his talk is "full of piracies,
plagues, and poisonings" (*R,* 58), and it is "with a diabolical
relish [that he] used to tell of the *middle-passage,* where the
slaves were stowed, heel and point, like logs, and the suffocated
and dead were unmanacled, and weeded out from the living
every morning, before washing down the decks" (*R,* 57). While
it might have occurred to Redburn, listening to this conversation, that here is an example of a tradition of racial superiority
with horrifying results, he is more interested in Jackson's attitude
toward him, for, although "I was young and handsome, [or] at
least my mother so thought me," Jackson continues to "eye me
with . . . malevolence" (*R,* 58). The unaccountable hatred that
Jackson has for him persuades the other members of the crew to
abuse or to avoid Redburn:

[Jackson] had such an over-awing way with him; such a deal of brass
and impudence, such an unflinching face, and withal was such a hideous
looking mortal, that Satan himself would have run from him. And besides all this, it was quite plain, that he was by nature a marvelously
clever, cunning man, though without education; and understood human
nature to a kink, and well knew whom he had to deal with; and then,
one glance of his squinting eye, was as good as a knockdown, for it was
the most deep, subtle, infernal looking eye, that I ever saw lodged in a

human head. I believe, that by good rights it must have belonged to a wolf, or starved tiger; at any rate, I would defy any oculist, to turn out a glass eye, half so cold, and snaky, and deadly. (R, 57)

In moments during which Redburn longs for some paternalism from the older sailors, he discovers that, strangely, something has "made a whole ship's company submit . . . to the whims of one poor miserable man like Jackson" (R, 59) and that "I found myself a sort of Ishmael in the ship, without a single friend or companion" (R, 62). This encounter and its results serve both to rob Redburn of the home he hoped to find aboard ship and to cast into doubt the traditional image he has maintained of the conviviality and nobility of seafaring men.

He brings the same sort of expectations to his confrontation with Captain Riga, and he meets with a similar failure, although the captain is one, Redburn has convinced himself, "who could not fail to appreciate the difference between me and the rude sailors among whom I was thrown" (R, 67). Yearning still for parentage, Redburn suggests: "Indeed, I had made no doubt that he would in some special manner take me under his protection, and prove a kind friend and benefactor to me; as I had heard that some sea-captains are fathers to their crew; and so they are; but such fathers as Solomon's precepts tend to make— severe and chastising fathers, fathers whose sense of duty overcomes the sense of love, and who every day, in some sort, play the part of Brutus, who ordered his son away to execution, as I have read in our old family Plutarch" (R, 67). Of course, the speculations about the "severe and chastising" fathers that sea captains represent belong to Redburn's retrospective thinking, but, even had these thoughts obtruded at the time, the young Redburn would no doubt have decided that a father made by "Solomon's precepts" is better than no father at all. Feeling that he must take his chances, he proceeds, thinking "that Captain Riga . . . would be attentive and considerate to me, and strive to cheer me up, and comfort me in my lonesomeness" (R, 67). He concludes that he will make a social call on the captain, and, for this breach of sailor etiquette, Redburn earns the rage of the captain and an oath from the mate to the effect that, "if I ever repeated what I had done that evening, or ever again presumed so much as to lift my hat to the captain, he would tie me into the rigging, and keep me there until I learned better manners" (*R*, 70). This incident, like his rough treatment by the sailors, challenges Redburn's fondest assurances about the dignity of sea captains and, at the same time, puts him at an even further remove from the possibility of discovering a father.

Observing that Redburn's confidence in tradition meets challenges which could erode it, however, is not at all the same thing as concluding that he surrenders his hold on the past. Rather, the tenacity of his convictions remains intact, and, because these convictions are all he has to sustain himself, his responses to the encounters with Jackson and Riga and to similar events aboard ship are largely predictable. About Jackson and his shipmates, Redburn surmises that they are a rude bunch of fellows, not deserving of his company, and, from his episode with Riga and the captain's later unruly appearance on deck, the young aristocrat begins, he says, to see the man in a new light:

I noticed that while we were at sea, he wore nothing but old shabby clothes, very different from the glossy suit I had seen him in at our first interview, and after that on the steps of the City Hotel, where he always boarded when in New York. Now, he wore nothing but old-fashioned snuff-colored coats, with high collars and short waists; and faded, short-legged pantaloons, very tight about the knees; and vests, that did not conceal his waistbands, owing to their being so short, just like a little boy's. And his hats were all caved in, and battered, as if they had been knocked about in a cellar; and his boots were sadly patched. Indeed, I began to think that he was but a shabby fellow after all. (*R*, 71)

Redburn's decision about Riga's character is largely based upon the evidence of the captain's clothes—which are no match for his own elegantly cut shooting jacket and his "pantaloons, . . . a very genteel pair, made in the height of the sporting fashion, and copied from my cousin's, who was a young man of fortune and drove a tilbury" (*R*, 73). As yet, he has no conception that the captain's tight-kneed trousers, and his garb generally, are more suited for life at sea than his own blossoming pantaloons which give him fits in the rigging. Instead of giving up his traditionalist notions about the gentility of sea captains, however, Redburn maintains them and simply regards Riga as an imposter, and, even if the youth thinks he has a "miserable dog's life" on "this abominable voyage" (R, 66), he remains sufficiently captivated by his secondhand authorities to interpose them between him and his direct experience at sea. Although "vulgar and brutal men [were] lording it over me" (R, 66) and although he is often set to the task of "picking oakum, like a convict" (R, 122), he frequently can be found, he says, "gazing through a port-hole . . . and repeating Lord Byron's Address to the Ocean" (R, 122). In short, the actual experience aboard the *Highlander* represents, to Redburn, less a contradiction of his views about the efficacy of the authority of the past than a confirmation of his initial understanding that the world is fallen. The way to surmount that condition, he is certain, lies still before him in his father's Liverpool—that is, in that past he hopes to bring back to life once he is ashore in the city.

Upon nearing shore, however, Redburn has an experience which foreshadows the complications his loyalty to tradition will encounter throughout the remainder of the narrative: "As I stood leaning over the side, and trying to summon up some image of Liverpool, to see how the reality would answer to my conceit; and while the fog, and mist, and gray dawn were investing every thing with a mysterious interest, I was startled by the doleful, dismal sound of a great bell, whose slow intermitting tolling seemed in unison with the solemn roll of the billows. I thought I had never heard so boding a sound; a sound that seemed to speak of judgment and resurrection, like belfry-mouthed Paul of Tarsus" (R, 126–27). This "boding" moment, which occurs in "answer to my conceit," is borne out in actuality by Redburn's first sight of Liverpool, an image which shatters his expectations:

Looking shoreward, I beheld lofty ranges of dingy warehouses, which seemed very deficient in the elements of the marvelous; and bore a most unexpected resemblance to the warehouses along South-street in New York. There was nothing strange; nothing extraordinary about them. There they stood; a row of calm and collected ware-houses; very good and substantial edifices, doubtless, and admirably adapted to the ends had in view by the builders; but plain, matter-of-fact ware-houses, nonetheless, and that was all that could be said of them.

To be sure, I did not expect that every house in Liverpool must be a Leaning Tower of Pisa, or a Strasbourg Cathedral; but yet, these edifices I must confess, were a sad and bitter disappointment to me. (*R*, 127)

After this first picture of the city, and Redburn's bitter disappointment in the face of it, the narrative successively elaborates the ways in which the entire sojourn in England destroys the young man's notion of tradition as a resource to sustain him. As he records "the general tenor of the life" (*R*, 136) he leads, he does not fail to observe that, far from his previous projections, Liverpool "abounds in all the variety of land-sharks, land-rats, and other vermin . . . [in] the shape of landlords, bar-keepers, clothiers, crimps, and boarding-house loungers" and that it contains "denizens of notorious Corinthian haunts . . . which in depravity are not to be matched by any thing this side of the pit that is bottomless" (*R*, 138). Even as he attempts to avoid these places which prey on sailors by growing, he says in retrospect, "intolerably flat and stupid over some outlandish old guide-books" (*R*, 144), it occurs to him that he is again being robbed of his tradition, for he can see that "this piece of antiquity [the guide-book] enlarges . . . upon previous antiquities" (*R*, 148) of Liverpool, neither of which images from the past bear much resemblance to the Liverpool he now visits.

As Redburn continues rambling about the city, he grows more convinced that the guidebooks which had heretofore guided his life have lied, at least by omission, and are seriously out of date. This conviction culminates when he attempts to retrace the travels marked in his own father's guidebook:

Dear delusion!

It never occurred to my boyish thoughts, that though a guide-book, fifty years old, might have done good service in its day, yet it would prove but a miserable cicerone to a modern. I little imagined that the Liverpool my father saw, was another Liverpool from that to which I, his son Wellingborough was sailing. No; these things never obtruded; so accustomed had I been to associate my old morocco guide-book with the town it described, that the bare thought of there being any discrepancy, never entered my mind. (*R*, 152)

Thus, as he attempts to perform "a filial pilgrimage to spots which would be hallowed in my eyes" (*R*, 154), he reaches a point at which the guidebook tells him to find an old fort and discovers there, instead, a tavern: "this," he reports, "was a staggerer; for how could a tavern be mistaken for a castle?" (*R*, 152). These incursions on his faith in tradition continue to confront him as he finds, in searching for the hotel where his father had stayed, that "this world, my boy, is a moving world; its Riddough's Hotels are forever being pulled down" (*R*, 157) —new knowledge that forces him to think that, "as your father's guide-book is no guide for you, neither would yours (could you afford to buy a modern one to-day) be a true guide to those who come after you" (*R*, 157). He recognizes the impossibility of following in his father's footsteps and determines "here-after [to] follow your own nose throughout Liverpool" (*R*, 159) in order to capture the city for his own conversations over dinner once he returns home.

At this moment in the book, then, Melville commits his young protagonist to face experience directly, and, without the mediating authority of a projected personal tradition, Redburn initiates a process of "making observations upon things immediately around me" (*R*, 161). This represents a dramatic shift from his presentation of himself in earlier parts of the book, for now, during his excursions, he seeks to discover his self-definition by responding reflexively to the life around him instead of trying, as he had before this, to make his sense of himself purely a matter of projecting his own interiority.

Relying now on the empirical evidence, Redburn begins to fashion a critical assessment of his once-dearly-held tradition because "each Liverpool dock . . . [is] an epitome of the world" (*R*, 165), and in these worlds he discovers things beyond his earlier imaginings. He has encountered the most "wretched of starvelings," the corpse hunters, who "are constantly prying about the docks, searching after bodies" in order to collect "standing rewards" from undertakers and in order "to keep from going to the church-yard themselves" (*R*, 179). He has heard, too, the "soul-sickening wail" (*R*, 180) from the gutter under the street called Launcelott's-Hey, where he finds a starving woman and her dying children and where his attempts to help are scorned both by the people of the street and by the authorities of the dock. He has seen the miserably poor—"the scores of tattered wretches, armed with old rakes, and picking-irons, turning over the dirt, and making as much of a rope-yarn as if it were a skein of silk" (R, 185). He has visited the "pestilent lanes and alleys which, in their vocabulary, go by the names of Rotten-row, Gibraltar-place, and Booble-alley, [and which] are putrid with vice and crime" (R, 191). And he has been beseeched by the beggars of the dock wall:

Old women, rather mummies, drying up with slow starving and age; young girls, incurably sick, who ought to have been in the hospital; sturdy men, with the gallows in their eyes, and a whining lie in their mouths; young boys, hollow-eyed and decrepit; and puny mothers, holding up puny babes in the glare of the sun, formed the main features of the scene.

But these were diversified by instances of peculiar suffering, vice, or art in attracting charity, which, to me at least, who had never seen such things before, seemed to the last degree uncommon and monstrous. (R, 186)

These are not the sights "hallowed" in his eyes to which he had intended to make his filial pilgrimage. These examples of human misery, rather, initiate profoundly in him the realization that this is the underside of heralded traditions, for every aristocratic life must have its counterpart in the life of poverty and every Kenilworth must have, at the other extreme, the "Booble-alleys" of the town. Here on the docks Redburn encounters, in short, "all that is dishonorable to civilization and humanity" (R, 186), and, if the wretchedness he descries confirms for him that human life is fallen, the willful corruption and evil manifest themselves in "corroborating Calvin's creed."[10]

With this new empirical reality in tow, one of Redburn's earlier intimations must now return to him forcefully. After having seen, in a sense for the first time, the world which he must inhabit, his noble conception of himself begins to shrink:

Alas! Wellingborough, thought I, I fear you stand but a poor chance to see the sights. You are nothing but a poor sailor boy; and the Queen is not going to send a deputation of noblemen to invite you to St. James's.

It was then, I began to see, that my prospects of seeing the world as a sailor were, after all, but very doubtful; for sailors only go *round* the world, without going *into* it; and their reminiscences of travel are only a dim recollection of a chain of taprooms surrounding the globe, parallel with the Equator. They but touch the perimeter of the circle; hover about the edges of terra-firma; and only land upon wharves and pier-heads. (*R*, 133–34)

If his temperance society views will not allow him to frequent the taprooms, Redburn is, he now recognizes, largely committed nonetheless to the world of wharves and pierheads. Having lately realized that he needs to follow his own nose throughout, he now begins to realize as well that this guide can lead him, at best, only into the "confused uproar of ballad-singers, bawling women, babies, and drunken sailors" and not to "the old abbeys, and the York Minsters, and the lord mayors, and coronations, . . . which, from all my reading, I had been in the habit of associating with England" (*R*, 133). "You are but a sailor-boy," he tells himself again, "and you cannot expect to be a great tourist, and visit the antiquities, in that preposterous shooting-jacket of yours" (*R*, 159). After the unsettling experience of the docks, however, he knows full well that, even were he able to visit the antiquities, something grim or ugly or evil must be hidden behind them. His recognition of his situation is complete, and with it he forfeits his place in the "party of memory," for he now knows, from the evidence of his own senses, how little he can depend on tradition to supply him with his authentic selfhood. He has seen in Launcelott's-Hey that which forces him to ask "What right had anybody in the world to smile and be glad, when sights like this were to be seen?" (*R*, 181).

III

Redburn does not consist simply of the record of the title character's "dear delusions" and the exposition of his subsequent disillusionment, however, because, as he undertakes to respond directly to the world around him, Redburn concomitantly learns that, as blighted as the world might ordinarily be in its confused uproar, that world has moments which contain pattern and meaning. Thus, his attempts to deal with life reflexively, to respond immediately to the stimuli of the things around him after his guides have failed, require him to develop the capacity for reflection which will make that reflexive mode accurate and meaningful. Certain moments and objects and activities and persons seem to him to be at once self-contained, in the sense that they embody some insight, and allusive, in the sense that they seem to refer to some larger pattern and rhythm of life. As he progressively encounters these moments, objects, and persons, and as he attempts to discern their significance, Redburn begins to realize that the meanings he locates are meanings to be possessed for life, that here in the scarred and fallen world is the substantive matter which will go into the construction of his selfhood; he begins, that is, to conceive the sustaining possibility, on Melville's behalf, of a reconciliation with the world of experience, and thus, to overcome the necessity of the resignation of life, "in the spirit of Seneca and the stoics" (*R,* 122), to which he had earlier relented aboard the *Highlander.*

One such poignant and charged moment occurs for Redburn almost immediately after he has become aware of how dearly deluded he has been in his efforts to build his self-definition according to the materials of secondhand guides. Prowling the docks, he suggests that "there was hardly anything I witnessed . . . that interested me more than the German emigrants" (*R,* 168) to the United States, for he sees "something in the contemplation of the mode in which America has been settled" (*R,* 169) which illumines his own orphanhood:

[America is] not a nation, so much as a world; for unless we may claim all the world for our sire, like Melchisidec, we are without father or mother.

For who was our father and our mother? Or can we point to any Romulus and Remus for our founders? Our ancestry is lost in the universal paternity; and Caesar and Alfred, St. Paul and Luther, and Homer and Shakespeare are as much ours as Washington, who is as much the world's as our own. We are the heirs of all time, and with all nations are forming into one federated whole; and there is a future which shall see the estranged children of Adam restored as to the old hearth-stone in Eden.

The other world beyond this, which was longed for by the devout before Columbus' time, was found in the New; and the deep-sea-lead, that first struck these soundings, brought up the soil of Earth's Paradise. Not a Paradise then, or now; but to be made so, at God's good pleasure, and in the fullness and mellowness of time. (R, 169)

With his developing capacity for contemplation then, Redburn begins to sense something of his own connection with what he senses are larger patterns of human life; his orphanhood becomes, with reflection, a condition shared by all his immigrant countrymen, a condition, he muses, portending a future in which the legacy of the Fall will be eradicated. While this passage manifests some of Redburn's deepest spiritual aspirations, its major significance consists certainly in the fact that his double commitment—to experience and to the reflection on it—enables him to discern and to interpret this allusive moment and to decipher what it withholds for his own burgeoning self-definition.

Another scene indicates how dramatically Redburn has reconceived the terms of his dealing with the world. Aboard the *Irrawaddy,* he falls in with a Lascar whose discourse is so instructive to Redburn that, "when we parted, I had considerably added to my stock of knowledge" (R, 172). More important than the information he receives from the Lascar, however, is the man himself and the experience of locating him: "Indeed, it is a God-send to fall in with a fellow like this. He knows things you never dreamed of; his experiences are like a man from the moon—wholly strange, a new revelation. If you want to learn romance, or gain an insight into things quaint, curious, and marvelous, drop your books of travel, and take a stroll along the docks of a great commercial port. Ten to one, you will encounter Crusoe himself among the crowds of mariners from all parts of the globe" (R, 172). At an earlier moment in his journey, Redburn's interposition of tradition between him and his experience would surely have precluded his even conversing with this common Lascar sailor, for the young man's aristocratic sense of himself would have perfunctorily gainsaid any notion that, with this sailor, new insight might be gained. Now, however, Redburn even places odds that one can discover on the docks those wholly strange figures who contain stories and from whom one can gain insight. Further, in the distinction between travel books and experience, he evinces his growing awareness of the possibilities for his life that come with attentiveness to the world and with reflection on the patterns and meanings it discloses to him through the medium of common experience.

As the narrative progresses from this point, Redburn increasingly develops what might be called a democratic attitude toward experience itself, for he is now prepared to acknowledge that the self-contained and yet allusive moments he encounters can spring from the usual and mundane as well as from the beautiful and grand, as he had earlier expected. About the *Irrawaddy,* whose officers are English and whose crew is composed of "Malays, Mahrattas, Burmese, Siamese, and Cingalese" (R, 171), Redburn thinks that, "thus, with Christianity on the quarterdeck, and paganism on the forecastle, the Irrawaddy ploughed the sea" and discovers that, "as if to symbolize this state of things, the *'fancy piece'* astern comprised . . . a cross and mitre; while forward, on the bows, was a sort of devil for a figurehead" (R, 171). Later in his poking about, Redburn enters "the hull of an old sloop-of-war" which is known as the Floating Chapel. Here "on week-days, I used to see an old pensioner of a tar, sitting on a camp stool, reading his Bible," and now Redburn finds that "this old worthy was the sexton" (R, 175). In the Floating Chapel, there occurs another of those moments with its own unicity and force, for "the chaplain was discoursing of future punishments and making allusions to the Tartarean Lake; which, coupled with the pitchy smell of the old hull, summoned up the most forcible image of the thing which I ever experienced" (R, 175). This unique church among the sailors causes Redburn to observe that "even so should Protestant pulpits be founded in the market-places, and at street corners, where the man of God might be heard by all His children" (R, 176). At still another point, Redburn discovers the allusive quality of a piece of old nailrod because, with "this species of rope, I have ever taken, I know not what kind of strange, nutty delight in un-

twisting it slowly, and gradually coming upon its deftly hidden
and aromatic '*heart*'" (*R,* 272). In his process of active seeking,
Redburn can find even this old piece of rope resonant with
"many interesting, mournful, and tragic suggestions": "Who can
say in what gales it may have been; in what remote seas it may
have sailed? How many stout masts of seventy-fours and frigates
it may have staid in the tempest? How deep it may have lain, as
a hawser, at the bottom of strange harbors? What outlandish
fish may have nibbled at it in the water, and what uncatalogued
sea-fowl may have pecked at it, when forming part of a lofty stay
or a shroud?" (*R,* 273). These unified and referential moments
each have their sources, or their catalysts, in the intractable materialities of life—in the fancy-piece of an Indian ship, in the
combination of scene and sense in the Floating Chapel, in the
intricacy and suggestiveness of a piece of rope. They may occur
quickly and pointedly, or they may invite more extended contemplation and interpretation, but these instances can achieve
their significance for Redburn only because, now, committed to
experience, he allows them to give rise to reflection.[11]

Even as he has learned to locate coherence and resonance in
the objects and events he encounters, Redburn realizes that certain human lives also disclose their own patterns and significance
—realizes, that is, that human beings present stories whose
meanings emerge, upon contemplation, as resources for his own
continuing self-understanding. Through the door of the "Dead
House" of the dock, for instance, Redburn catches a glimpse of
"a sailor stretched out, stark and stiff, with the sleeve of his frock
rolled up, and showing his name and date of birth tattooed upon
his arm." With eyes now open for such moments, Redburn recognizes "a sight full of suggestions . . . [because this dead sailor]
seemed his own head-stone" (*R,* 178). This moment, in its
allusiveness, bears a resemblance to an incident similarly fraught
with significance for Redburn when the sailor Miguel dies of
"animal combustion" (*R,* 245): "the whole face, now wound in
curls of soft blue flame, wore an aspect of grim defiance, and
eternal death. Prometheus, blasted by fire on the rock" (*R,* 244).
For Redburn, this moment contains something of a "premoni-
tion of the hell of the Calvinists, and that Miguel's earthly end

was a foretaste of his eternal condemnation" (*R*, 245). The aspect of Promethean defiance disclosed in Miguel's appearance makes him emblematic for Redburn of sailors generally.[12] In another instance, as he returns home aboard the *Highlander*, Redburn encounters the "Horatii and the Curiatii"—the two sets of triplets born, on the same day, of women who are sisters. These six boys "were as like as the mutually reflected figures in a kaleidoscope," Redburn suggests, and "together, as well as separately, they seemed to form a complete figure" (*R*, 267). For him, "all twins are prodigies" (*R*, 269), but this striking incidence of the twinning process, when taken up in a reflective moment, leads Redburn to observe that "all of us in our own persons furnish numerous examples of the same phenomenon. Are not our thumbs twins? A regular Castor and Pollux? And all of our fingers . . . [and] our arms, hands, legs, feet, eyes, ears, all twins; born at one birth, and as much alike as they possibly can be?" (*R*, 269).

How completely such singular moments can be figured in a person and how captivating such a person can become is evident to Redburn when he meets Carlo—"a poor and friendless son of earth, who had no sire; and on life's ocean was swept along, as spoon-drift in a gale" (*R*, 248). Even so, with his eye which "shone with a soft and spiritual radiance" (*R*, 247) and with his organ music which has "subtle power . . . [although] residing in but a bit of steel" (*R*, 249), Carlo becomes for Redburn "such a boy, as only Andalusian beggars are, full of poetry, gushing from every rent" (*R*, 247). This Carlo, Redburn knows, can "make, unmake me; build me up; to pieces take me; and join me limb to limb," for to "list to the organs twain—one yours, one mine— [and to] . . . gaze fathoms down into thy fathomless eye . . . [is as] good as gazing down into the great South Sea, and seeing the dazzling rays of the dolphins there" (*R*, 250). Thus, as with the objects and activities which invite Redburn's reflection, these self-inhering and charged moments which take their figurement in the human can appear in different degrees and in a variety of forms. They may offer him only a brief glimpse into a pattern of life, or they may insist on Redburn's fullest efforts to puzzle them out; they may emerge spontaneously, or they may require him to plumb their depths; but, however variously and deeply they present themselves to him, the significance of these moments, he realizes, must be seized for his life.

If Redburn recognizes the necessity to grasp the significance of these incrassate moments, however, it cannot be claimed that he always exercises his reflective capacity with sufficient sensitivity and depth. As he attempts to decipher these moments, he does not always possess sufficient critical intelligence to grasp their meanings fully for his selfhood. Frequently, the meanings which issue from his observations of the life around him are marked by naive piety and by shrill and histrionic patriotism and by adolescent and inflated rhetoric which cannot do justice to the complications these moments finally involve. All too often, Redburn ignores or at least fails to recognize that certain of these moments are not only subjects for his contemplation but demands for his moral responses, and, in the measure that he misses the real significance of the moment or that he replaces that significance with platitude or nationalistic fervor or, indeed, incommensurate vocabulary, he fails to discern the ways that these informing moments could work to shape the values on which his nascent selfhood will depend. He is, in short, too often possessed *by* his experience and not in possession *of* it. In this condition, Redburn, despite his commitment to experience and to reflection, simply proves himself unable to decode the complex terms of human living without severely reducing those terms.

Certainly the signal instance of Redburn's failure to deal adequately with his experience occurs in his association with Master Harry Bolton, another of those presaging persons whose life seems to contain pattern and meaning. In Harry, Redburn finds one whose "beauty, dress, and manner" make Redburn attempt to "divine what had transplanted this delicate exotic from the conservatories of some Regent-street to the untidy potato-patches of Liverpool." This "courtly youth" charms Redburn with "his appearance" (R, 216) and with "a scorn of fine coats, which exactly harmonized with his reckless contempt, at the time, for all past conventionalities" (R, 218). In the eyes of Redburn, fresh from his own break with "historic mosses" (R, 217), Harry's squandering his patrimony makes him an intriguing figure, although Redburn still cannot understand Harry's resolve "to precipitate himself upon the New World, and there [to] carve out a fresh fortune" (*R*, 218). In conversation, in dress, and in manner, Harry captivates Redburn, and Redburn, for his part, "ever cherished toward Harry a heart loving and true," even when he suspects that Harry frequently lies and even if "at times it made me feel ill at ease in his company" (*R*, 223). In the early stages of the association, then, Redburn clearly cannot marshal the necessary critical distance to imagine that Harry *might* represent a counterfeit of one of those resonant experiences he seeks, and later, when the reader realizes that Harry is as seriously adrift and helpless in the world as Redburn himself had been earlier, Redburn's own knowledge has not yet mastered the fact that Harry's life and his own life have followed a similar pattern. After the experience of "the Horatii and the Curiatii," had he plumbed it completely, Redburn could have discerned the ways in which he and Harry are twinned—at least in situation—and could have recognized that the twinning pattern, far from being a matter of mere symmetry, suggests the necessity of moral responses concordant to this pattern of human sharing and likeness. But Redburn has handled the implications of twinning superficially and has concluded, from his earlier experience, that he cannot help Harry: "after all, every one in this world has his own fate intrusted to himself; and though we may warn, and forewarn, and give sage advice, and indulge in many apprehensions touching our friends; yet our friends, for the most part, will '*gang their ain gate;*' and the most we can do is, to hope for the best" (*R*, 220). Although he suspects that Harry is doomed, Redburn cannot, even at the end of the association, see that Harry's scorn for all past conventionalities is simply the obverse of the pattern of his own earlier reverence toward his historic mosses and that Harry's strategy is equally inadequate. Nor can Redburn see that Harry's resolution to make a future in the New World is equivalent to his own earlier desire to possess for himself the resources of the Old World. Perhaps most destructively, Redburn does not realize, from the evidence of his own change, that the possibility to change exists for Harry as well. With this failure of his critical perception, Redburn does not attempt to help Harry reconstruct the terms of his living, does not act with "a heart loving and true." Rather, in the end, Redburn succumbs to his trivial notion of fate, acts on the banal assurance that Harry must go his own way, and hopes for the best: "I was forced," he says, "to give him up" (R, 312). Only later does Redburn learn that the delicate exotic, so ill equipped to live in the world, has not survived.

Even with such failures of full reflection in view, however, Redburn should not come in for too harsh a critique, for the narrative itself reveals his awareness that he has missed some of the significance of this "his first voyage." [13] At the time of the events he now recounts for the reader's inspection and judgment, he was a very young man, and, during the early stages of the narrative, the scars and blights recently dealt him by his life have, he reveals with candor, impaired his vision and judgment. When he does finally commit himself to confront his experience directly and reflectively, he is, at the very best, a novice in the life of the mind, from whom complete depth and mastery cannot fairly be expected. Moreover, the older and somewhat wiser Redburn who rehearses those earlier events apparently recognizes that, in the midst of those events, he had somehow failed to bring his most meaningful selfhood to birth. As the narrative opens, he deliberately constructs the analogy of his life with the fallen figurine on the glass ship, the little glass sailor who "fell from his perch the very day I left home." This glass figure, he says, "I will not have . . . put on his legs again, till I get on my own" (R, 9). Even after the experiences of the voyage, then, Redburn is struggling to stand up, and the retrospective narration he now begins, one must suspect, has as its motive the attempt to take full possession of the experiences his younger reflections could not completely grasp. If even in retrospection he cannot penetrate to the final significance of his experience, the narrative attempt itself— the effort to understand and articulate the experience as composing a patterned and coherent design—bespeaks the depth and seriousness of his commitment to try.

With respect to the context of Melville's developing vision, then, the judgments about Redburn's young failures should be even less severe, for to observe that his reflections are sometimes attenuated or are occasionally misdirected is, in effect, only to remark that he is not, as yet, the Ishmael of *Moby-Dick* or, indeed, the White-Jacket of the book which will immediately follow. In fact, in the cumulative careers of Melville's early protagonists, Redburn's failures seem, in a sense, to be necessary ones—stemming, as they must, from the first, tentative probings into the experiential and reflective lives. Even with their failures in view, Wellingborough Redburn and *Redburn* represent general advances for Melville on the understanding achieved by Tommo and *Typee*. Redburn, after his early recoil, picks up under Melville's direction the awareness of Tommo at virtually the point at which Tommo's retrospective narration leaves off. After recognizing his "dear delusion," that is, Redburn accepts one of the indispensable elements of Tommo's final anthropology—the need to deal with experience without the interposition of a stratagem of recoil—and, further, attempts to bring to his life the conscious reflection which Tommo's exposure to the narcosis of Typee begins to convince him is a prerequisite for any genuine modern selfhood. Although the depth and sensitivity of Redburn's reflections might be problematical, he has nonetheless taken the crucial step into reflection—a step which will enable Melville to have his successor, White-Jacket, enter the world of experience immediately and to make this entrance in a more fully self-conscious way. Finally, Redburn's drive to seize the significance of the experience he encounters will serve Melville, in the construction of his next protagonist, in still another manner, for, in his effort to possess his experience, Redburn has located moments in that experience which disclose pattern and meaning which inform his life. With these moments of sudden coherence, Redburn realizes that the encounter with the world does not always have to be an armed and dangerous one which forces him to resign himself bitterly and sadly to inhabit a fallen world; he begins to understand that, in these moments, occasions are presented which allow him to reconcile himself meaningfully with a world that, if fallen, contains such possibilities of order and meaning.

CHAPTER THREE

TO NATIONALIZE WITH THE UNIVERSE
Democracy and Identity *in* White-Jacket

The subtitle of *White-Jacket,* Melville's fifth book, is "The World in a Man-of-War," and with that more or less doctrinaire indication of the scope and concern of the fiction he will present, Melville returned to the image for the world of experience which Tommo's retrospective account in *Typee,* conditioned by the sense of the necessity of modern man to acknowledge his fallen state, had given him—"the pent-up wickedness of five hundred men aboard a man-of-war." Although White-Jacket, the protagonist-narrator of the book, finds himself cast into the kind of world which Tommo had come at last to recognize as the only conceivable world for civilized man, the only world remaining after the impossibility of paradise, he enters such a world on different terms than the narrator of Melville's first fiction had been able to discern. White-Jacket walks retrospectively on the decks of the line-of-battle ship armed with much more distinctive self-consciousness; by virtue of Redburn's advances on Tommo's habits of vision, Melville has White-Jacket in immediate and full possession of the requirement of reflection, the notions that his selfhood is inextricably entangled with his experience and that, if he will respond to it reflexively and reflectively, his life will gain pattern and meaning. From the outset, then, Herman Melville did not permit this new narrator to take refuge in geographies of innocence, as in *Typee,* or of tradition, as in *Redburn,* but, rather, committed White-Jacket to encounter his experience straightforwardly. In the career of this new narrator, the author can extend the organicist conception which he began with the young Redburn's struggling to get back on his feet. While *White-Jacket* was written in part as a chronological sequel to the South Sea actions of *Typee* and *Omoo*—in the sense that it picks up Melville's "biography" at the point *Omoo* leaves off—it is sequential in attitude and view to *Redburn,* for White-Jacket's narration reveals his growing awareness of the terms and possibilities of experience in a way which makes it consecutive with what had been the dawning awareness of his immediate predecessor. As sequel to *Redburn,* the narrative both shakes free of the interpositions made between themselves and their experience by the earlier protagonists and allows Melville to build on their cumulative gains toward full experiencing.

To observe that *White-Jacket* immediately surpasses the views of experience which characterize the earlier works, however, is not at all to suggest that the narrator of the book has not had to work his way through a hazardous mode of response of his own which stood in the way of the movement toward meaningful selfhood. Nor is it to suggest that with White-Jacket Melville finally located the most appropriate and integral stance for man to assume in relation to the complex and trying circumstances of his life. The fact is, rather, that *White-Jacket* and its narrator-protagonist take another step forward, on Melville's behalf, in the direction of an answer to the question of the ultimate terms of human identity and possibility. *White-Jacket* itself does not provide that answer; indeed, the book fails even to raise the question in anything like the manner in which Melville's plunging, metaphysical imagination will want to pose it in *Moby-Dick.* As White-Jacket's retrospective narration closes, he might well have discovered, in the couplet which represents the closure of the book, that "'Life is a voyage, homeward bound'" (*W,* 400), but he is not yet home himself, although like Tommo and Redburn before him he bends all his energies in that direction. Unlike his narrator-forbears, however, White-Jacket recognizes that *home* requires radical redefinition on the basis of experiences which have taught him that it is not a place or an institution but a context wherein one finds his fullest and deepest sense of himself. When he boards the *Neversink* at the opening of the narrative, White-Jacket has assured himself that aboard a flagship of the United States he already touches the shores of his democratic homeland, for "a ship," he thinks, "is a bit of terra-firma cut off from the main" (*W,* 23). With this metaphor, White-Jacket accepts the idea that the ship figures as a microcosm of American democracy and notes the "vague, republican scruples about creating great officers of the Navy" which account for the fact that "America has thus far had no admirals" (*W,* 20). The notion of the ship as a microcosm of American society will remain unchanged throughout the narrative, but White-Jacket will learn that, if for a time he had established his own self-definition in terms derived from this conception of home, everything aboard the *Neversink* distorts "republican scruples" and casts into doubt the efficacy of democratic institutions; he must broaden the elements which will go into the making of his selfhood to include that which cannot be gained through social and institutional identities.

In its testing of nationalistic democracy as a form of meaning which might disclose the coherence of contemporary life, *White-Jacket* moves beyond *Redburn* and advances toward *Moby-Dick* with respect to the conception of experience cumulatively working itself out in Melville's fictions. White-Jacket, as narrator, recounts his career aboard ship in a way which indicates that he has freed himself from the problem of indirect experiencing much more quickly than either Tommo or Redburn. Because he is loosed, as it were, to scrutinize the terms of life which crowd in on him, a gain bequeathed him by *Redburn,* he has the advantage over his predecessors of discovering the necessities and possibilities of those terms of living. After the premise that he can achieve his self-definition by way of institutional forms has failed for him, White-Jacket turns to a scrutiny of the nature and course of his encounter with experience, and he learns in this personal engagement that his experience, properly viewed, contains that which endows his life with pattern and substance, the stuff out of which a new idea of himself can emerge.

Democracy and Identity in White-Jacket

White-Jacket begins his retrospective narration having been changed by that voyage of experience which it is now his task to rehearse, and his intention is to describe his career aboard the *Neversink* with an eye toward articulating the nature, reasons, and substance of the changes in his perception. His subtle expositions of the failure of his original premises about institutional democracy and of his altered perceptions of experience finally emerge in the significance of the narrative structures which, designed to render his new conception of experience, indicate something of the substance of that conception. As he records and interprets his experiences aboard ship, White-Jacket portrays the dichotomies which, he now sees, exist between institutional life and personal life and which demarcate in a distinct way the public and the private realms which make claims on the individual man.[1] In his decision in favor of the possibilities of personal and private life, he is not merely repudiating the claims of society, however, for he knows that he cannot elude those claims. His emphatic concern for personal experience and interpretation is nonetheless decisive for him because he gains with it that which he needs most, that which it is beyond the capacity of institutional life to give him: he gains, in short, a sense of his life in relation to a transcendent dimension which at once overreaches his experience and signals its mysterious presence within his experience. Casting his narrative in an episodic form which reveals far more than a documentary mode, he acknowledges his awareness of "another" world intermittently converging on his own in moments which withhold for him the promise of meaning for his life. And it is the necessity of continuing reflection on such moments which requires the retrospective account, for with that reflection White-Jacket transfigures the idea of the home which he and his predecessors had been seeking.

I

In a fundamental way, *White-Jacket* documents the narrator's voyage as a journey on which he embarked in order to locate a context within which to discern the fullest meaning of his life, and the narrative itself stands as a record of the several contexts for self-identification alternately inhabited by the character who becomes the narrator—a record assessed by the narrator's retrospection.[2] As these first alternatives are remembered and exposed as inadequate, they lead, almost by virtue of their failures to suffice, to the narrator's recognition of the necessity to plumb his experience in deeper ways—a recognition which molds and shapes the course of the retrospective narration itself by controlling its direction, mode, and goal. The direction is homeward—toward that context which will suffice; the mode is personal and experiential—beginning where the experience of the voyage has left the narrator; the goal is to discern the pattern and meaning of the experience—locating, that is, the ways it contributes to his sense of himself. Although the beginning of the narrative starts chronologically, with the beginning of the experience of the voyage, the narration, in tone and perception, is oriented from the first by a sensibility constructed out of the stuff of the full voyage, a sensibility which, having undergone all, is radically altered from that of the White-Jacket who "builds" his jacket and whose career aboard ship will be remembered.[3]

White-Jacket's impulse at the outset, as it is recalled by the narrator, is to calculate his identity in terms of the context of American democracy, and, for him, the *Neversink* is nothing if not a floating microcosm of his homeland—"a bit of terra-firma cut off from the main." His premises, tacit at least, are that by inhabiting such a space he is returned home and that by becoming a constitutive part in the institution, by giving his loyalty to it, his own life partakes of, and is thus in part defined by, the meaning of the institution itself. For however brief a time, this meaning issues in a satisfying sense of himself, as he locates in the idea of democracy the elements of reciprocity between community and individual, notions of freedom and responsibility, and idealism and high purposefulness, which increase his own self-esteem. In recollection, however, these elements are demolished by White-Jacket the narrator almost simultaneously with the celebration of them by White-Jacket the actor. If the early White-Jacket insists on the fact that the *Neversink* stands as a microcosm of American life, the narrator, having completed the

entire voyage, has to add that, as an institutional form of democratic society, the ship sadly lacks any of the spirit of democracy:
his experience has forced him to the recognition that the theory
and the practice of democracy are all too divisible. In his observations on the hierarchies of rank aboard ship, the narrator
must own that his initial premises are undercut even if the idea
of the microcosm remains:

For a ship is a bit of terra-firma cut off from the main; it is a state in itself; and the captain is its king.

It is no limited monarchy, where the sturdy Commons have a right to
petition, and snarl if they please; but almost a despotism, like the Grand
Turk's. The captain's word is law; he never speaks but in the imperative
mood. When he stands on his Quarter-deck at sea, he absolutely com-
mands as far as eye can reach. Only the moon and stars are beyond his
jurisdiction. He is lord and master of the sun. (*W,* 23)

Almost immediately, then, the validity of democracy in this particular institutional form is called into question by the narrator.
By virtue of the construction of the institution itself, the captain
assumes the role of king, at the least, and tyrant, at the worst:
"perhaps no mortal man," the narrator reflects, "has more reason to feel such an intense sense of his personal consequence, as
the captain of a man-of-war at sea" (*W,* 23). The rights of the
"sturdy Commons" are dashed against the side of the institutional form which proposes to embody and to maintain those
rights. With these reflections, the narrator establishes from the
first the incapacity of the institution to reify for him, even in the
early moments of his career aboard the *Neversink,* those fond
conceptions of home with which he had supposed to construct a
sense of himself and his place.

From the point of this early recognition of the insufficiency
of the institutional context, the narrative carries on a continuing
critique of democratic culture as it is figured in the rules and
forms of life aboard a line-of-battle ship. The population of the
ship's crew points to it as an image of America as melting pot
and as land of opportunity. As the narrator describes it in the
chapter entitled "A Man-of-War Full as a Nut":

Indeed, from a frigate's crew might be culled out men of all callings and vocations, from a backslidden person to a broken-down comedian. The Navy is the asylum for the perverse, the home of the unfortunate. Here the sons of adversity meet the children of calamity, and here the children of calamity meet the offspring of sin. Bankrupt brokers, boot-blacks, blacklegs, and blacksmiths here assemble together; and castaway tinkers, watchmakers, quill-drivers, cobblers, doctors, farmers, and lawyers compare past experiences and talk of old times. Wrecked on a desert shore, a man-of-war's crew could quickly found an Alexandria by themselves, and fill it with all the things which go to make up a capital. (W, 74)

The catalogue suggests that, just as America promises to accept all, to forgive all, and to give new opportunity to all, the man-of-war crew, in composite, metaphorically embodies the democratic population. Although there may exist an apparent democratic equality among the heterogeneous and sturdy Commons, the social structure within which this egalitarian condition exists nonetheless permits the will of a tyrant to dominate the lot. If the structure of the masses is democratic, the structure of the institution is hierarchical and feudal. A case in point for the narrator is the pomp and circumstance which accrues to the officers and which demeans the common seaman:

While hardly anyone will question that a naval officer should be surrounded by circumstances calculated to impart a requisite dignity to his position, it is not the less certain that, by the excessive pomp he at present maintains, there is naturally and unavoidably generated a feeling of servility and debasement in the hearts of most of the seamen who continually behold a fellow-mortal flourishing over their heads like the archangel Michael with a thousand wings. And as, in degree, this same pomp is observed toward their inferiors by all the grades of commissioned officers, even down to a midshipman, the evil is proportionately multiplied. (W, 166)

The very institution which is the agent and envoy of American society lords it over the smaller, qualitatively equal men who serve within it. But the abuses of democracy by this institutional form of it far exceed these indications of debased feelings among the members of the crew, for the hierarchical and authoritarian construction of navy life allows an intolerable species of arbi-

trary and punitive behavior on the part of the officers with respect to those men over whom they rule and to whom they refer,
in emphatic assertion of "official superiority," as "the people."
The critique continues with the narrator's rehearsals of the undemocratic "constitution" of the ship. There is the evil of flogging which is exaggerated "into a great enormity" by the fact
that it is exercised in a completely arbitrary way. Captains in the
navy can inflict corporal punishment "for nearly all degrees of
transgression" (*W,* 139), and thus, "for things not essentially
criminal," one can "see a human being, stripped like a slave;
scourged worse than a hound" (*W,* 138). The punishment comes
for offences which range in degree to the extent, the narrator
muses analogically, that "the servant-maid who but pilfered a
watch was hung beside the murderer of a family" (*W,* 139). Or,
again, the narrator assesses the failure of the envoy of democracy when he describes "A Knave in Office in a Man-of-War"—
namely the master-at-arms who, in his ex officio function on
behalf of the officers' rule of order, legislates the arbitrary conduct of the quarterdeck on "the people." The narrator concludes
that "such another ineffable villain could not by any possibility"
(*W,* 190) be found, but he does not fail to notice that the master-
at-arms "was a favorite of the Captain's" (*W,* 183). In another
instance, in the satirical sally by the narrator on the surgeon of
the fleet, the undemocratic nature of the ship is again demonstrated in the figure of Cadwallader Cuticle, M.D., who is
"seemingly impervious to the ordinary emotions of humanity"
(*W,* 251) and who yet finds himself perfectly at home in the man-
of-war. If the narrator's jocose tone with respect to the surgeon
seems bluff to all outward appearances, he reports that Cuticle's
low regard for "the people" permits him to cut and maim them
without flinching and that the surgeon's position in the hierarchy
allows him to do so with impunity. In this cruel attitude, the
inhumane figure of the surgeon makes him fully concordant, the
narrator thinks, with the other officers: "Why mince the matter?
The death of most of these man-of-war's men lies at the door of
the souls of those officers, who, while safely standing on deck
themselves, scruple not to sacrifice an immortal man or two, in
order to show off the excelling discipline of the ship. And thus do

the people of the gun-deck suffer, that the Commodore on the poop may be glorified" (*W*, 197). At last, even the "Fun in a Man-of-War" exposes the misuse of the men by the institution itself in what is a dramatic example of the violation of democratic spirit. For the delight of the officers, two Negro members of the crew are ordered into "playful" combat against each other. But the play finally turns to anger, and "retort followed retort; in a word, at last they came together in mortal combat" (*W*, 275). The captain's judgment is, in his own words, that, "'though now and then I permit you to *play*, I will have no fighting.'" In short, he condemns the results of which he has himself been the cause, and "he flogged both culprits in the most impartial manner" (*W*, 276). Such a critique of this institutional form of American democracy continues throughout the book as the narrator surveys outrage on top of enormity.

Now, although the retrospective narrator is concerned in the telling of his tale to expose the inhumane underside of the perverted shipboard democracy, he reveals as well that, at the time, he had himself maintained a personal form of the same undemocratic sense of hierarchy which pervades the institution. Even as a member of the crew, a fact which to all intents makes him simply another member of the sturdy Commons, he had assured himself, he remembers, of his own superiority over some others of "the people." This aristocratic sense of himself comes fully to the fore as he recalls his feelings while beholding the scene of the flogging of the two black men: "Poor mulatto! thought I, one of an oppressed race, they degrade you like a hound. Thank God! I am white. Yet I had seen whites also scourged; for a black or white, all my shipmates were liable to that. Still, there is something in us, somehow, that, in the most degraded condition, we snatch at a chance to deceive ourselves into a fancied superiority to others, whom we suppose lower in the scale than ourselves" (*W*, 277). White-Jacket's own earlier, nondemocratic attitude is drained in this scene as it occurs to him that it is self-deception, fancied superiority underpinning deluded self-conception. He recognizes that he shares the degraded condition and that that which degrades him is the very institutional hierarchy in which he had supposed he had a place. In view of his shared condition, under the sway of what he slowly has learned to see as a perverse context which will not grant him meaningful identity, White-Jacket the actor shifts his loyalties to a new context—"the people"—wherein, among the heterogeneity and broadly shared equality of condition, he hopes to find the spirit of democracy, the sense of community, the place for himself he had not located in the institution.

The shifted loyalties on White-Jacket's part depend on a distinction made throughout the narrative between the institution and the people—or between the public *forms* of democracy and the more vital and less well ordered "people" who compose the constituency. It is a distinction maintained by the officers aboard the *Neversink* in their references to the crew as "the people"— a term tantamount, in their view, to "the rabble." But this distinction is also picked up by "the people," as is evident in the conversation between Lemsford, the poet, and Jack Chase, the Handsome Sailor:

"Blast them, Jack, what they call the public is a monster, like the idol we saw in Owhyhee, with the head of a jackass, the body of a baboon, and the tail of a scorpion!"

"I don't like that," said Jack; "when I'm ashore, I myself am part of the public."

"Your pardon, Jack; you are not. You are then a part of the people, just as you are aboard the frigate here. The public is one thing, Jack, and the people another."

"You are right," said Jack; "right as this leg. Virgil, you are a trump; you are a jewel, my boy. The public and the people! Ay, ay, my lads, let us hate the one and cleave to the other." (*W,* 192)

Now, of course, the distinction is different in the view of it held by the officers and in the version of it celebrated by the crew. For the former, "the people," the conglomerate rabble, is the monster, against which the hierarchy seeks to maintain order. For the latter, the "public" which gives its loyalty to the institutional rigidities is the monster, against which "the people," the true "democrats," define themselves. Once the former has failed for White-Jacket, he seeks out the latter in order to find in that new community the sources of his self-definition.

II

Just as he has learned to discern the failures of the institution, however, the White-Jacket aboard ship discovers no meaningful refuge among "the people." He had counted on the heterogeneity and pluralism of the crew, and the sense of a mutuality of condition shared by its members, in order to gain admission to a diverse and yet closely bonded community. Within such a social structure, he thought it possible both to achieve and to maintain a unique sense of himself and his identity, but if he had found a tyrannous aspect rearing its ugly head in institutional forms, he finds among "the people" the tyranny of the masses. Although it is a fact that the constituency of the crew is pluralistic, "the people" do not celebrate that fact as a virtue; their impulses, rather, are to establish hierarchies of value of their own —according to experience, rank, and shipboard function—the results of which are species of infighting, rivalry groups, and snobbism. Although it is also a fact that there is a shared sense of condition, "the people" are not so much bonded by that fact as they are made exclusive by their sense of it. White-Jacket learns quickly that admittance is difficult without complete conformity; his only uniqueness, the jacket he wears, is the very factor which stands as an obstacle to his joining the sturdy Commons, for they view it, at first, as a sign of his pretension and, later, as the source of ill luck for the ship. Withal, then, White-Jacket is stunned to find nothing more of the spirit of democracy among the crew than he had located in the institution. Much less does he discover the kind of broadly based context of community for which he had hoped, for he finds himself ostracized by the general crew for most of the voyage. With this compounding of the failure to discern a genuine democracy, he sees his chances for communal satisfaction shrink further still—to the smaller circle of the men "of the top" wherein, at last, he finds a measure of fellowship.[4]

The movement in White-Jacket's search for a meaningful context for himself, then, proceeds in terms of the failures of the contexts he enters to bring to life that which is commensurate for him with the necessities for his fullest selfhood. But, at the time, it was not a question of his surveying the failures so much as it was his inability, for whatever reason, to belong. In terms of the sizes of the contexts he attempts to inhabit, his eventual discovery of some community among the "men of the top" is significant, for he has moved from the largest available context to the smallest one: the community on the top is the closest thing aboard ship to being alone, both because this group is literally cut off from the ship below and because here is the realm of privacy. The man in search of community proves to be the *isolato* at last, for "aloft" men are alone with their reveries even when they are together. Whether progress or retreat, this movement from public forms to private reflection is not simply a matter of White-Jacket's inability to locate communality; indeed, the tension between the institution and the private man has been with the man from the first, and there have been moments when privacy was not only the negative result of the lack of community but was, rather, something White-Jacket sought out. For him, the "top" has special significance:

I am of a meditative humor, and at sea often used to mount aloft at night, and, seating myself on one of the upper yards, tuck my jacket about me and give loose to reflection. In some ships in which I have done this, the sailors used to fancy that I must be studying astronomy—which, indeed, to some extent, was the case—and that my object in mounting aloft was to get a nearer view of the stars, supposing me, of course, to be shortsighted. A very silly conceit of theirs, some may say, but not so silly after all; for surely the advantage of getting nearer an object by two hundred feet is not to be underrated. Then, to study the stars upon the wide, boundless sea, is divine as it was to the Chaldean Magi, who observed their revolutions from the plains. (*W*, 76)

Underneath the half-humorous tone of this passage, the narrator makes a serious point about the context which, on the voyage, he had been seeking. The privacy of the top—where one can "give loose to reflection"—nourishes one's sense of himself in ways not to be gained through community. As hungry as he might have been and might continue to be for human association, White-Jacket cannot, in retrospection, dispute the necessity of the personal context wherein reflection and meditation give him a fuller sense of himself.

But there is more here as well, for, ironically, what seemed the smallest conceivable context—the personal enclosure at the top—becomes the largest possible context, the universe of experience available to personal encounter and to reflection. It is this context, finally, which holds out the genuine democracy White-Jacket is seeking—the right and responsibility of every man to confront his experience for what it bears for him without the mediation by institutional authority or social pressure. The retrospective narrator seizes the meaning of democracy in terms of this largest context, as he recalls "getting nearer an object":

And it is a very fine feeling, and one that fuses us into the universe of things, and makes us a part of the All, to think that, wherever we ocean-wanderers rove, we have still the same glorious old stars to keep us company; that they still shine onward and on, forever beautiful and bright, and luring us, by every ray, to die and be glorified with them.

Ay, ay! We sailors sail not in vain. We expatriate ourselves to nationalize with the universe; and in all our voyages round the world, we are still accompanied by those old circumnavigators, the stars, who are shipmates and fellow-sailors of ours—sailing in heaven's blue, as we on the azure main. (W, 76–77)

In the face of the immensities, he concludes, all men stand as equals, and, with this recognition of what Ishmael will call "the spirit of democracy in all things," the narrator finds something of community—the accompaniment of the stars as "shipmates and fellow-sailors."[5] Thus, in his retrospective stage at least, White-Jacket at last locates the context which he can call *home*—the context of experience itself which feeds his reflections, which gives him both a sense of himself and a sense of democratic community. This discovery represents an alteration of large proportions in his attitude toward the realm of experience: earlier, he sought to have his experience mediated for him by the association with this context or that and, in such mediation, to find himself by finding a community; at the end of the narrative, he is confirmed in the realization that the question of selfhood in the largest democratic context, experience itself, is settled by way of a man's direct encounter with the context. He knows in retrospection that, once that context has been discovered, it *must* be encountered because in the discovery a man is thrown back on the resources of his own isolated interiority, his naked self, to face his experience without the intervention of others. In this context, he says, "each man must be his own savior" (*W*, 400).

If the retrospective narrator recognizes the necessity to draw on his own resources, however, the White-Jacket who moves and lives aboard the *Neversink* had first to be taught that necessity by force. It is not a lesson he learns in a moment of ocean revery or in an occasion for intellectual reflection; it arises, rather, in the profoundly existential moment in his experience during which he has no other recourse but his interior sense of himself, when, that is, he is threatened with a flogging. In recalling the incident, the narrator does not miss the point that the White-Jacket who sought so strenuously a locus for himself aboard the *Neversink* nearly gets himself flogged for not being in his dutiful place, a place about which he had not been informed. For not being properly placed, with respect to the institution, White-Jacket, in the horrifying moments during which he is arraigned before the mast, awaits the scourge which he feels will be the institution's ultimate demeaning of his humanity. But as he waits White-Jacket locates within himself the elements of those last resources which are brought to the fore by this threat to his sense of himself. Those last resources lie in his interiority, in "the privilege, inborn and inalienable, that every man has, of dying himself, and inflicting death upon another" (*W*, 280). In short, he grasps within him an inner democratic right which allows him to contemplate rushing the captain and carrying him overboard, a privilege which helps him to see that he can settle the question of justice by putting it in the larger democratic context wherein individual men face the immensities: "Locking souls with him," the narrator remembers, "I meant to drag Captain Claret from this earthly tribunal of his to that of Jehovah, and let Him decide between us" (*W*, 280).

In these brief moments, White-Jacket finds his new sense of democracy ratified; all men are expatriated in the experiential universe—equals in the sight of eternity—and their rights and responsibilities, and the judgments on them, will finally be set-

tled in that context. He now recognizes also how his own substance derives its significance from the context of a democratic
universe, as his description of this realization reveals:

> My blood seemed clotting in my veins; I felt icy cold at the tips of my
> fingers, and a dimness was before my eyes. But through that dimness
> the boatswain's mate, scourge in hand, loomed like a giant, and Cap-
> tain Claret, and the blue sea seen through the opening of the gangway,
> showed with an awful vividness. I can not analyze my heart, though it
> then stood still within me. But the thing that swayed me to my purpose
> was not altogether the thought that Captain Claret was about to de-
> grade me, and that I had taken an oath with my soul that he should not.
> No, I felt my man's manhood so bottomless within me, that no word,
> no blow, no scourge of Captain Claret could cut me deep enough for
> that. I but swung to an instinct in me—the instinct diffused through all
> animated nature, the same that prompts even a worm to turn under the
> heel. (W, 280)

At the very moment in which the officer of the perverse institution of democracy threatens to unman him, then, White-Jacket
gains his essential manhood as it is grounded in those instinctual
sources in the democracy of experience.[6] His identity is connected with rhythms of life below, and bottoming under, his
distinguishing humanness, and, finding the foundations of his
manhood there, he locates his sense of himself in an interior element of himself which is beyond the reach of the institution or
the people. If he did not recognize it at the time, White-Jacket,
as narrator, recalls the details and feelings of this moment so viv-
idly and powerfully that he surely recognizes it as a transfiguring
experience in his life. In recollection at least, it is like seeing himself born, for in this scene he seizes upon the immutable and in-
violable sense of himself and his place in the universe—a sense of
himself which was not supplied by institution or community and
which cannot be stripped from him by the "public" or "the people." He has founded his self-definition, in impulse at least, on a
prompt from his recognition of the large democracy of the universe, and, with this, the alteration of his definition of *home* is
nearly complete. He begins to see that the context which gives
him the most radical and significant sense of his life is the one in

which his interiority is brought into converse with those experiences in the universe which give him moments and meanings to possess for his manhood.

III

It is in terms of these considerations that the career of the jacket —the white duck "frock"—has its significance, for, throughout his questing after a locus for himself in an adequate community, the jacket which enfolds him has served as home when nothing else seemed to suffice. For much of the experience aboard ship, the jacket had been the most immediate context of his security and self-sufficiency and, at once, the distinguishing factor of his individuality. With his retrospection, the narrator recognizes the functions the jacket had served from the outset, for his description of it in the opening chapter reveals, in a preliminary way, the purposes he then had for it: "I employed myself, for several days," he recalls, "in manufacturing an outlandish garment of my own devising, to shelter me from the boisterous weather we were so soon to encounter" (*W,* 3). The initial intention for the jacket, then, like his attempts to enter a community, is to find in it refuge from the bitter elements of experience. How fully he seeks to have the jacket become a home for him is revealed in the trope he fancies to describe the self-sufficiency he wanted the jacket to give him:

I proposed, that not only should my jacket keep me warm, but that it should also be so constructed as to contain a shirt or two, a pair of trowsers, and divers knick-knacks—sewing utensils, books, biscuits, and the like. With this object, I had accordingly provided it with a great variety of pockets, pantries, clothes-presses, and cupboards.

The principal apartments, two in number, were placed in the skirts; with a wide, hospitable entrance from the inside; two more, of smaller capacity, were planted in each breast, with folding-doors communicating, so that in case of emergency, to accommodate any bulky articles, the two pockets in each breast could be thrown into one. There were, also, several unseen recesses behind the arras; insomuch, that my jacket, like an old castle, was full of winding stairs, and mysterious closets, crypts, and cabinets; and like a confidential writing-desk, abounded in snug little out-of-the-way lairs and hiding places, for the storage of valuables. (*W*, 36)

In short, the jacket is another of those contexts wherein White-Jacket the actor attempted to find his definition of himself. As the narrative continues, even the early White-Jacket, aboard the *Neversink,* finds that this home is no more meaningful a resource for his selfhood than the other contexts he tries on: it prevents his free and easy movement and, so, interferes with the sense of himself as ocean-rover, and, far from protecting him from the bitter elements, it soaks up those elements and keeps them longer near him. He must finally discard the jacket, as he had rejected the other unsatisfactory contexts, but his reasons for doing so stem less from his physical discomfort than from his growing awareness that the jacket stands between him and the experiences which are the indispensable resources for his selfhood. After his arraignment at the mast, after his ratification of the necessity to locate his "man's manhood" in relation to the tractless universe of experience, it is only a matter of time, he realizes in his retrospection, until he will have to shed that last intermediary between himself and his experience.

That moment comes when White-Jacket falls headlong from the mast and plunges, "straight as a die, toward the infallible centre of this terraqueous globe" (*W*, 392), and, with this moment, he gains a concentration of *self* as product of his experience: "All I had seen, and read, and heard, and all I had thought and felt in my life, seemed intensified in one fixed idea in my soul" (*W*, 392). The jacket which had caused the fall with its unwieldy character becomes the factor, once White-Jacket plunges beneath the surface, which threatens to keep him under, to annihilate him, and, in this sense at least, it is an enclosure which, like the institution and its threat to flog him, would unman him utterly. If the idea of his selfhood is intensified during his fall by the instantaneous concentration of what he had experienced, however, he recalls as well that, as "dense as this idea was, it was made up of atoms" (*W*, 392)—that is, experiences distinct and integral, compacted to make the whole of his identity. As he goes under, resigned to die with "thoughts [which] were unmixed with alarm" (*W,* 392), there remains one more fleet, atomist moment of experience which will give him back his life:

As I gushed into the sea, a thunder-boom sounded in my ear; my soul seemed flying from my mouth. The feeling of death flooded over me with the billows. The blow from the sea must have turned me, so that I sank almost feet foremost through a soft, seething, foamy lull. Some current seemed hurrying away; in a trance I yielded, and sank deeper down with the glide. Purple and pathless was the deep calm now around me, flecked by summer lightnings in an azure afar. The horrible nausea was gone; the bloody, blind film turned a pale green; I wondered whether I was yet dead, or still dying. But of a sudden some fashion-less form brushed my side—some inert, coiled fish of the sea; the thrill of being alive again tingled in my nerves, and the strong shunning of death shocked me through.

For one instance an agonizing revulsion came over me as I found my-self utterly sinking. Next moment the force of my fall was expended; and there I hung, vibrating in the mid-deep. (*W,* 393)

His life is returned to him, in effect, by experience itself, recalled in experiential, sensory terms: his side is "brushed"; his nerves "tingled"; his senses are "shocked"; he "found" himself while "vibrating in the mid-deep." Even the nausea and revulsion sig-nal his being alive. It was not the jacket which gave him his identity; it was the accumulation of atomist experiences, even White-Jacket the actor now realizes, which make up his self-definition.

The jacket, indeed, had imperilled his sense of himself by inter-posing itself between his man's manhood and the universe of experiences upon which that manhood bottoms. As he regains the surface, White-Jacket is now "conscious of a feeling like be-ing pinioned" by the jacket, and, as he then "burst out of it, and was free" (*W,* 394), as he discards the last of the inadequate con-texts within which he had hoped to secure himself, his redefini-tion of *home* is complete. In the last chapter of the narrative, the narrator can celebrate the home toward which his earlier career aboard ship had been tending, the one genuinely demo-cratic home, the place within which and in relation to which one's identity has its most significant context—the experiential world itself:

As a man-of-war that sails through the sea, so this earth that sails through the air. We mortals are all on board a fast-sailing, never-sinking world-frigate, of which God was the ship-wright; and she is but one craft in a Milky-Way fleet, of which God is the Lord High Admiral. The port we sail from is forever astern. And though far out of sight of land, for ages and ages we continue to sail with sealed orders, and our last destination remains a secret to ourselves and to our officers; yet our final haven was predestinated ere we slipped from the stocks at Creation. (W, 398)

In this recognition that no less a context than that of the created order will suffice to give a man his self-definition, the knowledge of White-Jacket the actor begins to catch up, as it were, with the knowledge of the retrospective narrator. Home is not a destination so much as it is a process of self-discovery amidst the experiential universe; one's citizenship refers less to his homeland than to his effort to nationalize with the universe. With this recognition, the narrator chooses to close his narrative "far out of sight of land"—on the tractless seas, the unbounded experiential space of the creation. He now realizes that there on the wide-rolling sea a man finds the ultimate context of his life in the encounter of his naked self with the immensities:

Let us leave the ship on the sea—still with the land out of sight—still with brooding darkness on the face of the deep. I love an indefinite, infinite background—a vast, heaving, rolling, mysterious rear!

It is night. The meagre moon is in her last quarter—that betokens the end of a cruise that is passing. But the stars look forth in their everlasting brightness—and *that* is the everlasting, glorious Future, forever beyond us. (W, 396)[7]

It is in this frame of mind that he cites the *sententia* which closes the narrative, for he has worked through to an awareness of the "final haven" of man in that which is everlasting. For him, now, it is possible to say that "Life is a voyage that's homeward-bound!" (W, 400) and to know that his self-definition is inextricably entangled with the experience of the voyage.

This is the drive which had motivated the narration itself, for

Democracy and Identity *in* White-Jacket

White-Jacket had discovered by the end of the cruise that his identity had been gained just by way of the experiential stuff he had undergone, and his retrospection occurs with the purpose of deciphering the pattern and meaning of the voyage of his self-discovery. Such intentionality accounts as well for the episodic construction of the narrative, for White-Jacket had learned, in his fall from the mast, that the experiences which compose him are atomistic and distinguishable and that, yet, they are compacted and coherent in making up his life. Among these experiences, he locates certain signal moments which, in retrospection at least, possess symbolic value for his selfhood because in the vivid memory of these moments, he seizes upon that which portends "an indefinite, infinite background—a vast, heaving, rolling, mysterious" context in which "fashionless forms" touch his life and, thus, give it to him. In this, *White-Jacket* culminates the organicist view initiated in *Redburn* with the narrator's recognition that his life occurs in vital symbiosis with the realm of experience. In the recovery of these episodically appearing moments in his experience—moments which allude to the everlasting—*White-Jacket* points toward *Moby-Dick,* whose narrator will want to plumb the metaphysical implications of that symbiosis. As with *Redburn,* Melville was not completely happy with *White-Jacket.* He wrote to his father-in-law that "I have felt obliged to refrain from writing the kind of book I would wish to." *White-Jacket* nonetheless moves forward decisively to his desired "kind of book" because, in its episodic construction and in its location of a "vast, heaving, rolling, mysterious" universe, there is that hint of the "wonder-world" which Ishmael will inhabit, in which "another world" converges profoundly on the world of human living and nurtures human identity at a deeper level still. And even Melville had to admit, in the same letter to Lemuel Shaw, that while *Redburn* and *White-Jacket* were "done for money" and were neither "the kind of book I would wish," still "I have not repressed myself much . . . but have spoken pretty much as I feel."[8]

PART TWO

Experience and Transcendence

CHAPTER FOUR

FLOOD-GATES OF THE WONDER-WORLD

Portents of the Transcendent and the Generic Question of Moby-Dick

Nearly two decades ago, in noticing the frequently pragmatic motives at the heart of American literature, Perry Miller observed that "on the whole, one is safe in saying, the literature of America is marked by its concern, often neurotic rather than sanative, that literature be not regarded as an end in itself, but that expression be put to work in the service of a creed, a career, a philosophy, a disgruntlement or a rage."[1] For Herman Melville, this "rule of efficiency," identified by Miller as the functional drive of the literary imagination, had been operative from the outset. In *Typee, Redburn,* and *White-Jacket,* Melville had pressed his creative expression into the two-fold service of testing some alternative models of perception in his age and of positing an idea of what would suffice for meaningful human life. This concern, however, did not stem ex post facto from any simple desires to evangelize a creed or to promulgate a career or to promote a philosophy which had been conceived and accepted before the author set his hand to the literary task. Rather, it began and continued to evolve from Melville's commitment to the idea that imaginative reflection on experience could function cogently in the clarification of the essential terms of human life. When Melville's early protagonists learned that they must respond forthrightly and directly to the world of experience and that they only achieved their selfhood in that world, Melville himself could not dismiss this discovery as a mere literary idea. He had created the necessity of this new awareness by exposing his protagonists to a world he understood to be the essential world of their existence, and he had guided and controlled the progress of this awareness both by stripping them of their beginning strategies of perception and by forcing them to reconceive the fundamental terms of their experience. With the cumulative lessons of his protagonists before him, Melville now faced a requirement which his own commitment to the validity of fictive ideas or knowledge would not allow him to refuse—namely, the necessity to use his art in the construction of a radically altered imagination of the world. In short, Melville had, in the context of experience imaginatively rendered, brought his early protagonists to the brink of that profound experience, that deeply shattering moment, in which old perceptions fail in the face of and are replaced by a new vision of reality. Now, with those protagonists, or at least for them, he had to present in *Moby-Dick* the nature and conditions of this new reality.[2]

In this sense, Herman Melville was distinctively a man who belonged to the age of Ralph Waldo Emerson, for no one was more haunted than Melville by the spirit of the question Emerson posed for his generation in *Nature* (1836): "why should not we have a poetry and philosophy of insight and not of tradition, and a religion by revelation to us and not the history of . . . [revelation to the foregoing generations]?" And no student of *Moby-Dick* has ever doubted that Ishmael's ocean reveries—his records of his passage through "the great flood-gates of the wonder-world" (*M*, chap. 1)—represent anything less than Melville's attempt to seek out what Emerson had called the necessary "original relation to the universe." If Melville had come to realize that full selfhood was to be achieved in relation to the world of experience, he realized as well that his fiction, as he conceived it, needed to present a world in which that full selfhood could be founded in rich and durable terms.

With *Moby-Dick,* then, Melville worked *from* the assumption that literature could "be put to work in the service of" investigations which traditionally belong to the offices of the theological intelligence, and, in this, he worked *toward* the possibility of defining the meaning of human experience in relation to what he understood to be its ultimate ground. Although Melville did not use his masterwork to derive any theological system or, like Emerson, to plead an ontology, *Moby-Dick* seems to locate and possess its final coherence in a complex of religious drive and fictive form; it wants "revelation to us," as Emerson put it, refracted through the language of the imagination. And, thus, Vincent Buckley is surely correct when he suggests that *Moby-Dick* "presents with unusual sharpness problems not merely of deciding its 'meaning' but also of discovering the terms appropriate to discussing it at all," for implicit in this comment is an awareness of the generic issue posed by the book.[3] The confluence of literary mode and religious motive is more, however, than a problem for the student of literature or of religion: it was, first, a problem of craft for Herman Melville, who knew that the radically original relation to the universe he sought in a fictive world would require his effort both to outstrip the orthodox sense of the perimeters of reality and to push the resources of fiction to their outer limits.

Initially at least, the most "appropriate" terms to bring to *Moby-Dick* are apparently the ones which will illumine Melville's sense of, and solution to, these generic requirements.[4] First, by way of some brief assessments of representative interpretations of Melville's religious "pessimism," it is possible to discern the ways in which Melville responded to and wanted to surpass the two major religious orthodoxies of the America of his day and in which, despite these unsatisfactory alternatives, Melville was compelled to search human experience for its indispensable condition. Then, by inquiring into Melville's deepening awareness of a transcendent dimension present to that world of experience, one can begin to locate the sources and terms of the author's own burgeoning religious imagination. Finally, by observing Melville's continuing mastery of the resources, functions, and possibilities of his art in relation to some of his contemporaries, there can be discerned his conviction that his fiction must articulate a vision of experience as conceived under the shadow of the ultimate, a vision crucial for human self-understanding.

Thus, the specific contentions here are that the motive behind the writing of *Moby-Dick* was to elicit a world brimming with portents of the transcendent, a motive whose energies and goals and whose consequences on the generic construction of the book cannot be fully understood apart from Melville's restiveness in the face of the regnant Protestant thought of his period, and that the presentation of the "wonder-world" which would finally invite and support Ishmael's inhabitancy was enabled by Melville's developing a genre fully commensurate with the oceanic revelations such a world contained.

I

Since 1851, when an early, anonymous reviewer recognized in *Moby-Dick* "pointed hints" of a "pregnant allegory, intended to illustrate the mystery of human life,"[5] critics have frequently sought to account for the religious thrust at the heart of the book, and by now, of course, it is practically an interpretive cliché to point out Melville's distrust of institutional Christianity by arguing that the white whale is a symbol of both a perverse deity and a despised orthodoxy or to enumerate the ambiguities in *Moby-Dick* as evidence of Melville's epistemological dilemma and religious despair by accepting Ahab's testimony about the limits of his "knowing" as universally conclusive for Melville. Critics have, in a variety of ways, been quick to follow the kind of lead provided, in one instance, by Henry A. Murray, whose interpretation of *Moby-Dick* is founded on Melville's confidence to Nathaniel Hawthorne, shortly after the book was written, that "I have written a wicked book, and feel spotless as the lamb."[6] "The implication is clear," Murray declares; "all interpretations which fail to show that *Moby-Dick* is, in some sense, wicked have missed the author's avowed intention."[7] The attempts to ratify viewpoints like this one have frequently led critics to conclude that Melville sensed the world to be abandoned by God and that this fact accounts for the deep disillusionment and skepticism and, indeed, satanism which, in their views, reside at the core of Melville's sense of life. It is this sort of God, these interpretations insist, which Melville understood to allow evil and suffering in the world, to constrict intolerably the efforts of human will and reason, and to permit history to follow a course of disaster. This conception of God, Murray and others argue, reigns over *Moby-Dick*—a fact which constitutes final proof that Melville wrote a "wicked book."

Three critical pieces, designed to expose the "wickedness" of *Moby-Dick,* are in many ways representative of those studies, too numerous to survey here, which want to isolate the fact of Melville's pessimism. Murray's view is that Melville, "through the mediumship of Ahab, 'burst his hot heart's shell' upon the sacrosanct Almighty and the sacrosanct sentiments of Christendom."[8] Lawrance Thompson argues that, by the time *Moby-Dick* was written, Melville's knowledge of evil in the world had increased to the extent that, "having started by loving God, he turned skeptically to hating God."[9] The author, according to Thompson, "was compelled to project the story of his own immediate disillusionment into the story of Captain Ahab's deep-sea adventures,"[10] and, thus, in *Moby-Dick,* Melville's "pleasure is to find symbolic forms for taunting God Almighty."[11] In another interpretation, William Braswell is persuaded that "Melville's inability to account for evil had made him conclude that the Christian concept of a wholly benevolent Deity is wrong, and [with *Moby-Dick* in 1851] he had arrived at the point where he could give full artistic expression to his heretical views without suffering pangs of conscience."[12] An instrumental factor in reaching this point, Braswell supposes, was the corroboration Melville found for his darker vision in skeptical and pessimistic writings like Bayle's *Dictionnaire historique et critique,* Hobbes's *Leviathan,* Montaigne's *Essays,* Schopenhauer's *Studies in Pessimism* and *The World as Will and Idea,* Shelley's *Essays,* and so on. In *Moby-Dick,* Braswell argues, Ahab's rage represents an enactment of the doubts Melville felt about the concept of divine goodness and about the validity of "Christian submissiveness."[13] Each of these interpretations possesses a measure of validity to the extent that each demonstrates Melville's aversion to the prevalent Protestant alternatives of his day.

In the face of enlightened and rationalist views, the strictest brand of Calvinism of Melville's age had turned into a vindictive

legal system which largely ignored, in its theological constructions, the graceful and redemptive work of God and which emphasized in extremis the innate depravity of man and the terrors
of imminent judgment. The promise of the Christ, the possibility of new righteousness, dropped into the background, and, in
its place, interpretations arose which attempted to demonstrate,
as Joseph Haroutunian has pointed out, "that the cross exhibited
the vindictive justice of God" [14] and that Christ had died not because "God so loved the world" but because a hateful God required his pound of flesh. As Haroutunian writes: "To the new
Calvinism, the life of Christ, apart from the agony of the Cross,
was theologically irrelevant. Christian living [on the basis of
such a theology] became identified with obedience to the moral
law of God as revealed to Moses, and the fear of God's vindictive
justice was made its foundation. All things revolved around the
'moral law.' God became the great Enforcer of the moral law,
the blood of Christ became the evidence that God will punish
transgression. Holy love faded into conformity to moral law,
and such conformity was now the measure and substance of
'true virtue.'" [15] The point of the final reference, of course, is to
indicate how far removed was this bleak legalism from the piety
of Jonathan Edwards, whose own definition of "true virtue"
began in faith and issued in worshipful "consent of being to
Being." Now, the malevolent and fearful God accepted by this
harsh remnant of Calvinism would surely have been despised by
Melville, for it is just this sort of God which not only permits
but indeed causes evil to exist in the world. [16] It is true that Captain Ahab extrapolates from his experience the validity of this
doctrine of God, and it is this God, "visibly personified, and
made practically assailable in Moby Dick," (M, chap. 41)
against whom Ahab releases his pent-up rage. And the heroic
proportions, the epic size, which Ahab achieves in his quest leave
little doubt about Melville's sympathies for his character against
the God foisted by this dark faith. [17]

But there was another, altogether benign alternative which
Melville reacted against as well. A more liberal strand of Calvinism had adapted in the early nineteenth century to the enlightened and hopeful thinking of the day. For a time, in fact, this

liberal faith walked apace with Unitarian views, without thought of heresy, because, as Haroutunian has remarked, "the humanitarians [liberal Calvinists] failed to see, or at least elaborate, the theological implications of their political and social views." [18] In short, the remaining thread of New England Calvinism had, almost unconsciously, adjusted its attitudes and beliefs to suit the temperament of postrevolutionary America. [19] While the split with the Unitarian tendencies was inevitable once theological disputations were begun, the hopeful strain of American Calvinism kept intact its liberal spirit—at least to the extent that it no longer bore any close resemblance to the doctrinal life of the Puritanism from which it stemmed. [20] Like the severe, legalistic Calvinism, this new orthodoxy cast up a brand of moralism; unlike the harsh Calvinism, however, its morality depended not on the prescriptions of Mosaic law but on the identification of religious morality with civic virtue. To all intents, obedience to the weal of God was converted into, and was considered the same as, assent to the rules of proper civil conduct, upon which hinged the righteous life of the nation and, thus, the redeemer destiny of the American people. [21] The religious community no longer assumed a prophetic stance in relation to the general society, no longer launched the old jeremiads against the ills in the nation or in its own internal life; rather, it set out to promote the religious reformation of individuals outside the pale of this moral community. [22] This hopeful brand of Calvinism was decidedly as repugnant to Melville, however, as the punitive Calvinism it had rejected. Here he found an obliviousness to the existence of evil in the world and nothing of that element he admired in Hawthorne, "that touch of Puritanic gloom" from which "no deeply thinking mind is always and wholly free" and without which "no man can weigh this world." [23] He had seen for himself the results of the redeemer moralism that missionaries of this outlook had practised in the South Seas. [24] Indeed, the blithely optimistic theology at the heart of this orthodoxy must have gravely troubled Melville, whose own deeply thoughtful mind could manage nothing like the presumption, certitude, and confident thoroughness with which these Calvinists "read" nature and history.

II

Even with these unsatisfactory orthodoxies before him, however, Melville continued to be driven by his need to locate human life in an original relation to the ultimate structures of reality. Nathaniel Hawthorne recorded something of the depth and form of this drive when, for 20 November 1856, he entered into his *English Notebooks* an account of his last meeting with Melville:

> He stayed with us from Tuesday till Thursday; and, on the intervening day, we took a pretty long walk together, and sat down in a hollow among the sand hills (sheltering ourselves from the high, cool wind) and smoked a cigar. Melville, as he always does, began to reason of Providence and futurity, and of everything that lies beyond human ken, and informed me that he had "pretty much made up his mind to be annihilated"; but still he does not seem to rest in that anticipation; and, I think, will never rest until he gets hold of a definite belief. It is strange how he persists—and has persisted ever since I knew him, and probably long before—in wandering to-and-fro over these deserts, as dismal and monotonous as the sand hills amid which we were sitting. He can neither believe, nor be comfortable in his unbelief; and he is too honest and courageous not to try to do one or the other. If he were a religious man, he would be one of the most truly religious and reverential; he has a very high and noble nature, and better worth immortality than most of us.

Perhaps as much as any of Melville's own writing, this single passage has worked to convince generations of critics that Melville could not reconcile his experience with religious faith. It does, to be sure, suggest his epistemic despair in the face of "everything that lies beyond human ken."

But the facts that Melville could not take shelter in common belief and could not dismiss a post-Kantian epistemological situation do not mean that he failed in what his Ishmael has succeeded: "Doubts of all things earthly," Ishmael admits, but he claims "intuitions of some things heavenly; this combination makes neither believer nor infidel, but . . . a man who regards them both with equal eye" (*M*, chap. 85). The point is that religious reflection does not, as Hawthorne's observations seem to suggest, belong only to the believer and does not always issue only from a certitude about matters of "Providence and futurity." As Nathan A. Scott, Jr. has recently argued in another context:

> The effort to think religiously about experience is not . . . an endeavor appropriate only to those who are members of a special sect or guild, such as churchmen or seminarians or professional theologians. On the contrary: the act of religious reflection is the act that all men are performing at whatever point they begin to search their experience, at the level of *theos* or of ultimate meaning, for the guaranty or sanction that finally gives warrant to human existence. Yet, in speaking of what authentic religious inquiry intends, to use a language (of "warrant" and "guaranty") whose flavor is moderately forensic is already somewhat to have falsified the case, since what is at issue is not matters of formal assurance but the question as to the possibility of a kind of Pascalian wager, that the world of our habitancy is so constituted as to be, in its basic tendency, supportive rather than spendthrift of the human enterprise.[25]

Thus, Hawthorne's understanding of what stands as religious reflection, at least in these remarks about Melville, is too narrowly circumscribed, for here he seems to have no sense at all that Melville's drive in these matters, his persistence for knowledge of "Providence and futurity," has as its method and its goal the searching of experience, at the level of ultimacy, for the possibility of the wager that the world supported the human self.[26]

Now, there is no gainsaying either the fact that Melville understood life to be an ambiguous affair or the fact that he came to realize that the deepest paradoxes in human experience resulted from man's inability to calculate the hidden character of the transcendent.[27] But the epistemological problem Melville encountered with respect to this imponderable transcendent element indicates only that it is hidden and not that it has stranded the universe. Signals appear in *Moby-Dick* that Melville has made the wager, that he can affirm the reality of an unearthly dimension which completely transcends human reason but which, yet, impinges powerfully on human life. In several respects, Melville's understanding of transcendence seems to have evolved in the afterglow of Jonathan Edwards's doctrine of a deity which, although manifesting evidence of itself in human history, remains finally hidden in a character whose meaning and motive cannot be discerned or at all accommodated by any human calculus. The deeply furtive character of this transcendent dimension did not, however, force Melville to relent to pessimism, for, also like Edwards, he realized a "revelation to us" (Emerson's phrase) which gifted life with the presence of spirit. He located the assurance, that is, that certain focal instances in human experience adumbrated their sources in the transcendent, that ordinary life, suddenly outstripping the banal and mundane, assumed startling and unaccustomed significance, and that, during these moments, another world, fecund with potency and meaning, had erupted into his own.[28] In short, Melville located in his experience moments which were, for him, unaccountable in any terms but the irreducibly spiritual—in the sense that he felt, in those moments, the power and mystery and demand of something "other than" the human which was penetrating into the world of the human.

With Ishmael, Melville could discover moments which signalled their transcendent sources. The "fountain," the spouting of the whale, is such a portent: "Rainbows do not visit the clear air; they only irradiate vapor. And so, through all the thick mists of the dim doubts in my mind, divine intuitions shoot, enkindling my fog with a heavenly ray. And for this I thank God; for all have doubts; many deny; but doubts or denials, few along with them, have intuitions" (M, chap. 85). The reflection stems from prolepsis; the rainbow of the whale's fountain, the visible image, contains its own allusiveness, its "heavenly ray," which in turn enables the intuition. Such intuitive moments, as Whitman knew, "pass all the argument of the earth"; they are beyond belief in the sense that they are filled with that which is uncanny and unintelligible, that which maintains its own separate logic beyond the rational, that which is not available to argumentation but only to wonder and awe in the domain of the affections. Rudolf Otto designates such moments as *numinous* and, in suggesting the varied responses their felt presence creates in the human, writes:

The feeling of it may at times come sweeping like a gentle tide, pervading the mind with a tranquil mood of deepest worship. It may pass over into a more set and lasting attitude of the soul, continuing, as it were, thrillingly vibrant and resonant, until at last it dies away and the soul resumes its "profane," non-religious mood of everyday experience. It may burst in sudden eruption up from the depths of the soul with spasms and convulsions, or lead to the strangest excitements, to intoxicated frenzy, to transport, and to ecstasy. It has its wild and demonic forms and can sink to an almost grisly horror and shuddering. It has its crude, barbaric antecedents and early manifestations, and again it may be developed into something beautiful and pure and glorious. It may become the hushed, trembling, and speechless humility of the creature in the presence of ... that which is a *mystery* inexpressible and above all creatures.[29]

What is at stake in *Moby-Dick* is not Melville's account of the motive force at work in these signal moments or, indeed, any specific content which could be gleaned from their appearance; his epistemology accepted limits on human intellection and thus allowed him no possibility of such an accounting. His attention was turned, rather, to an attempt to conceive the most radical meaning of the human in relation to a world in which such moments occurred. Any attempt to capture or contain the ultimate source hidden behind or within these portentous instances would have put him on the side of profanation, would, at least, have made him share the overconfident "God-language" which he had rejected as the most troublesome aspect of contemporary orthodoxy.[30]

It is in this context that Melville's continuous attempts to decipher the relations between man and the universe are, in several respects, comparable to the conclusions of Jonathan Edwards's "Dissertation Concerning the End for Which the World was Created," for Edwards speaks in that work to a habitual theological concern to plumb the relations between creature, creation, and creator. From the first, Edwards asserts that the nature and motives of the creator are not accessible to human reason in any full way; "indeed," he writes, "this affair seems properly to be an affair of divine revelations" and can only finally be settled by what "the Scriptures have truly revealed." But the scrutiny of biblical revelations is reserved by Edwards until the second chapter of the dissertation, while in the first chapter he would "soberly consider . . . what seems rational to be supposed concerning this affair."

In following the dictates of reason, Edwards surmises that the ultimate end for which God created the world was to express his own regard for himself, "that in delighting in the expression of his perfections, he manifests a delight in himself; and in making these expressions of his own perfections his end, *he makes himself his end.*" In this expression of himself, Edwards insists, God has no initial regard for man because, although it is "fit and desireable, that the glorious perfections of God should be known, and the operations and expressions of them seen by others besides himself," what moved God to create the world was this disposition to manifest his "glorious attributes"—a disposition which "must be [understood as] prior to the existence of [and regard for] the creature." Edwards writes:

This propensity in God to diffuse himself, may be considered as a propensity to himself diffused; or to his own glory existing in its emanation. A respect to himself or an infinite propensity to, and delight in his own glory, is that which causes him to incline to its being abundantly diffused, and to delight in the emanation of it. Thus that nature in a tree, by which it puts forth buds, shoots out branches, and brings forth leaves and fruit, is a disposition that terminates in itself. And so the disposition in the sun to shine, or abundantly to diffuse its fulness, warmth and brightness, is only a tendency to its most glorious and complete state. So God looks on the communication of himself, and the emanation of the infinite glory and good that are in himself to belong to the fulness and completeness of himself; as though he were not in his most complete and glorious state without it.

Thus, Edwards outlines his doctrine of the inviolably hidden God. But, while God has no initial motive in the creation to express himself to his creatures, and while he exercises a tendency which terminates in itself, one of the "consequences" of the created order, Edwards thought, was that there flows from this "emanation of divine fulness . . . the communication of virtue and holiness to the creature." However indirectly this occurs,

God takes pleasure in the goodness and happiness of the creature—not because the creature is the end for the creation but because "God, in seeking his glory, therein seeks the good of his creatures." His regard for the creature, however, must always be understood as subordinate to the ultimate end of the creation, which is only to reflect God's glory.

These consequences of the creation for human life arise again when Edwards turns, in chapter two of the dissertation, to what "the Scriptures have truly revealed" concerning God's end in creating and sustaining the world. He argues that the providential acts of God and the maintenance of moral government among men—both figured in the most decisive instance by the redemptive work of Christ—are ends in the creation which lead to the ultimate end of glorifying God. But these subordinate ends also work intentionally for good in the life of man because they open before man a world which reflects the transcendent fountain from which goodness originally flows. In this sense, the created order is a locus of continuing revelation of divine being for the possession of man: "As there is an infinite fulness of all possible good in God, a fulness of every perfection, of all excellency and beauty, and of infinite happiness; and as this fulness is capable of communication or emanation *ad extra;* so it seems a thing amiable and valuable in itself that it should be communicated or flow forth, that this infinite fountain of light should, diffusing its excellent fulness, pour forth light all around." Built into the very structures of the creation, then, were "streams" of spirit which both portended their original source and withheld for man the reconciliation of his own nature and meaning with the structures of that hidden ultimacy under the shadow of which he existed. Later in the dissertation, Edwards clarifies the conditions of that reconciliation: "In the creature's knowing, esteeming, loving, rejoicing in, and praising God, the glory of God is both exhibited and acknowledged; his fulness is received and returned. Here is both an *emanation* and *remanation.* The refulgence shines upon and into the creature, and is returned back to the luminary. The beams of glory come from God, and are something of God, and are refunded back again to their original. So that the whole is *of* God, *in* God, *to* God, and God is the beginning, middle and end in this affair." In short, the beneficent consequences of the creation demanded from man, in Edwards's conception, the acknowledgement of man's dependence for his fullest ontological life on the fulness of that divine being which "comprehends all entity . . . in his own essence . . . and is in effect, *Being in General.*" For Edwards, man's acknowledgement of his dependence, and his consent to it, represented "the nature of true virtue"—a virtue enabled by that principle of incarnation which presents to the creation, from the surplusage of transcendent being, emanations of spirit in a complex moral symbiosis, terminating in itself, and in which man participated only as a consequence.

The point that should not be missed here is that, with the original source of such emanations incalculably hidden, the world itself, portending its source, becomes, for Edwards, the context in which the meaning and possibility of man are defined, and it is this understanding of the world, charged beyond the imagination of contemporary Calvinism, which Melville wanted to reify in his master work. The world of *Moby-Dick* needed to be portrayed at "the level of *theos*"; it needed to resemble the world, its motive cause, and its human consequences, which were the results of Edwards's theological inquiries; it needed to contain, as its principle of coherence, a sequence of those momentous revelations, or emanations, which both adumbrated their transcendent source and were finally "refunded" to that source because their ultimate meanings were hidden there, past human knowing. In *Moby-Dick,* as in the "Dissertation Concerning the End for Which the World Was Created," these revelations to man will need, in the construction of the book, to be perceived and presented as self-creating and self-cohering, reflecting a "disposition that terminates in itself," but also as radiant and allusive, pouring "forth light all around." But, whatever particular illumination or benefit these enclosed and yet expansive moments might provide for the human in *Moby-Dick* or in Edwards's doctrine of the world, it was as true for Melville as for Edwards that these refulgences disclose above all else the presence of a *mysterium* not to be circumscribed by man. And yet, like Edwards, Melville was convinced that this transcendent dimension figured as the indispensable condition of human life, that, indeed, human being derived its meaning only in relation to a created order inspirited, and acknowledged, with these moments resonant with the presence of the hidden source.

Although Edwards's interpretation begins with God and then moves to a calculation of the nature and possibility of man, it is perhaps more likely that Melville's commitment to locate an original relation to the universe led him, first, to a deepening "anthropology" which in turn led him or forced him to acknowledge the reality of a transcendent factor as the final, crucial ground of human identity. As Carl Michalson has noted, this movement has been a characteristic, and perhaps inevitable, one for modern religious reflection:

Since Kant, anthropology has had more status than metaphysics. But anthropology in its radical interrogation of the meaning of man—what he can know, what he should do, what he may hope—has led philosophy to the very edge of nihilism, to the affirmation of the possible nonexistence of man. The question, "Why am I something and not nothing?" though initially anthropological has been the gateway to a revised and fundamental ontology. The data of common human experience, of experience as it faces the situations of life which draw most drastically upon man's resources, have become the object of philosophical analysis. Radical theology inevitably becomes anthropology by denying the self-sufficiency of man, but radical anthropology moves just as well in the direction of theology by that same denial. The question of the possibility of God's existence, once subordinated, re-enters the philosophical dialogue under the chastened conditions of man's self-analysis. For when it is suspected that man does not have within himself the resources by which his continued existence is rendered meaningful the question of the possibility of God's existence arises. God in this context is no longer, however, a theoretical possibility which one may affirm or deny. He is an existential requirement. The authenticity of man's life depends on God's reality. God is not a fact at the end of a line of reasoning, but a hope at the end of the rope of despair.[31]

But the point here is that, quite apart from the question of whether it stemmed from the existential necessity for God, or *theos,* or ultimate meaning, Melville had grown convinced of the reality of a transcendent factor which, even if finally hidden and impenetrable, figured for him, in the world of human experience, as what Edwards might have called "the real presence of the hidden God"[32] or, in less specifically theological vocabulary, as a dimension of ultimacy portended by certain focal and allusive moments in man's engagement with the world of his living. And the recognition of these moments, in their promise of a relationship of man with the deepest structures of experiential reality, had emerged more or less ineluctably from Melville's searching his experience, by way of the imagination, for the terms of a "radical anthropology"; in this search, he had discovered a world which fulfilled the Emersonian requirement of "revelation to us."

In aligning Melville's understanding with Edwards's doctrine of the creation and in identifying the form of Melville's religious drive with the movement from anthropology to theology, the purpose is not to suggest that Melville's thought is in every way coextensive with these patterns of theological interpretation but, rather, to demonstrate that his concerns occurred within the context of concerns which have frequently compelled the attention of the theological mind. If Melville failed to achieve the ontological convictions of an Edwards or if his assumptions and conclusions were not at numerous points continuous with the methods and bases of Protestant thought in his time, the fact remains that Melville wanted to depict a world in *Moby-Dick* which was brimming over with signals of the transcendent, the view of which, the generic intentionality of the book suggests, stands in continuity, at least with respect to "God-language," with a thoughtful and long-standing tradition of Christian theology.[33] And, finally, if the prevalent orthodoxies of his day did not appear to Melville to contain the element, or the possibility, of this genuine God-language, both enabled by and rooted in the world of experience to which the hidden God was present as emanation, it is not surprising that he would think of *Moby-Dick* —emerging from his own "deep-diving" interrogation of experience—as a "wicked book" designed, in intention and effect, to say "NO! in thunder" to the banal perceptions of the world with which, he thought, those orthodoxies were overlaid.[34]

III

By the time *Moby-Dick* was written, Melville had learned to expect in the world the appearance of these emanations, and he had begun to think of his fiction as an appropriate medium for the only God-language he could think genuine—namely, the imaging of the startling presence of these portents, the exploration of their astonishing effects, and yet, a poetry of restraint whose language of image and implication and allusiveness was nonetheless alert to its limits in knowing and naming the hidden source of these radiant moments. He reveals something of this idea of fiction in the famous "Agatha letter" to his friend Hawthorne on 13 August 1852, in which he relates the tale of a Nantucket woman and the husband who had deserted her.[35] What aroused Melville's "first spontaneous interest" in this experience, he wrote, were its "striking incidents" and some "tributary items" which are related to the "suggestiveness" of the scene and activity of the story: the sea has "an air of solemn . . . [and] elaborate deliberation . . . [and the] air is suppressedly charged with the sound of long lines of surf"; there is "a handful of cloud on the horizon, presaging storm" and the "strange and beautiful contrast . . . of the innocence of the land [a sheep] eyeing the malignity [of the continuous assault] of the sea." Melville's vocabulary—his notations of the "charged" and "strange" and "presaging" character of the ambience of the scene—reveals his orientation toward the mysterious and portentous elements he discovers in it. The experience, he tells Hawthorne, "is instinct with significance," and, in it, "you have a skeleton of actual reality to build about with fulness & veins & beauty." This letter discloses, in at least a preliminary way, Melville's fundamental commitment in his developed conception of prose fiction, for although he required the fictive world to be faithful to "actual reality," the experiential realm, he was primarily oriented toward those elements of the actual world which were instinct with echoes of the transcendent, which were charged with portents of an uncanny factor.

With these commitments before him, Melville required an art in *Moby-Dick* whose generic possibilities were commensurate with the imaging of common experience at its deepest or most ultimate levels of reality, and the Emerson of "The American Scholar" (1837) might have supplied Melville with the goal for his fiction when he wrote:

Give me insight into to-day, and you may have the antique and future worlds. What would we really know the meaning of? The meal in the firkin; the milk in the pan; the ballad in the street; the news of the boat; the glance of the eye; the form and gait of the body;—show me the ultimate reason of these matters; show me the sublime presence of the highest spiritual cause lurking, as always it does lurk, in these suburbs and extremeties of nature; let me see every trifle bristling with the polarity that ranges it instantly on an eternal law; and the shop, the plough, and the ledger referred to the like cause by which light undulates and poets sing.

Now, Melville was no Transcendentalist, a fact about which Ishmael is assured when he nearly gains the "final" knowledge by slipping off "The Mast-Head" (M, chap. 35), because he knew, with Edwards, that the epistemological gap between man and the transcendent remained; and he was no pantheist because he realized that, while the ultimate will momentarily present aspects of itself to the world of experience, the portents fade as suddenly as they come and that, far from residing in the created order, their "ultimate reason" was beyond human telling.[36] Still, even without Emerson's more confident epistemology, Melville might have learned from him both the locus of "revelation to us" in the realm of common experience and the notion of the poet as "visionary."[37]

But if Emerson might have taught Melville, as artist, to think of himself as responsible for a form of seeing, surely it was Hawthorne from whom he discovered, or confirmed, his own sense of how to see and what could be seen in the mode of fiction. In Hawthorne, Melville recognized the Emersonian double requirement to root the imagination in the everyday particularities and, at once, to relate those concrete forms to the overarching realm of the transcendent. But Melville found in Hawthorne not only the grand capacity to "soar to such rapt height, as to receive the irradiations of the upper skies" but also "the indispensable complement . . . [of] a great, deep intellect, which drops down into the universe like a plummet." [38] While Emerson seemed to Melville in danger of flying too quickly from the world of concrete experience, Hawthorne's plunging acts of artistic intellection took him more deeply into the world of the human and allowed him only "short, quick probings at the very axis of reality." And this consisted for Melville as the first of Hawthorne's lessons about the "great Art of Telling the Truth," the great art of how to see in fiction: "rich utterances of a great intellect . . . arterialized at his large warm lungs, and expanded in his honest heart." The artist is a profound thinker, even visionary thinker, and, yet, he has a heart connected. If his vision can soar, if one "may be witched by his sunlight," the artist should not soar past his "honest heart," the acknowledged limits of his humanity, should not and cannot see the "ultimate reason" of things Emerson more confidently pursued; the artist must make "those short, quick probings," but his "great intellect" cannot surpass its limits.

With this realization of how to see, then, Melville detected as well Hawthorne's exemplary articulation of what could be seen. Although with Hawthorne's vision one might be "transported by the bright glidings in the skies," or might soar with him "to receive the irradiations of the upper skies," Melville recognized that, for Hawthorne as for himself, there is "the blackness of darkness beyond" and that "even his bright glidings but fringe and play upon the edges of thunder-clouds." This "power of blackness" that Melville located in Hawthorne's work represents simultaneously the dark element of human interiority which Hawthorne apprehended with his "deeply thinking mind" and the transcendent stretches which outdistanced any human capacity of mind. In either case, it stems from Hawthorne's "touch of Puritanic gloom" because, in the first sense, it refers to "that Calvinistic sense of Innate Depravity and Original Sin" which Hawthorne could not elude and, in the second sense, it reflects the recognition of a hidden and, yet, ineluctable transcendent factor which furnished Hawthorne, as Melville wrote, with "the infinite obscure of his background." [39] The Hawthorne who "so fixes and fascinates" Melville, then, is the man who, evincing "the largest brain with the largest heart," attempts to tell the truth about human life in relation to the dark and impenetrable powers within that heart and beyond it. And in this attempt, Hawthorne can be esteemed by Melville for possessing "that lasting temper of all true, candid men—a seeker, not a finder yet."

Thus, the artist who earned Melville's admiration was the Hawthorne who pressed his fiction into the effort of penetrating into the meaning of human experience when perceived within the shadows cast by this infinite obscure, the Hawthorne who called his work "romance":

When a writer calls his work a Romance, it need hardly be observed that he wishes to claim a certain latitude, both as to its fashion and material, which he would not have felt himself entitled to assume, had he professed to be writing a Novel. The latter form of composition is presumed to aim at a very minute fidelity, not merely to the possible, but to the probable and ordinary course of man's experience. The former— while, as a work of art, it must rigidly subject itself to laws, and while it sins unpardonably so far as it may swerve aside from the truth of the human heart—has fairly a right to present that truth under circumstances, to a great extent, of the writer's own choosing or creation. If he thinks fit, also, he may so manage his atmospherical medium as to bring out or mellow the lights, and deepen and enrich the shadows, of the picture. He will be wise, no doubt, to make a very moderate use of the privileges here stated, and, especially, to mingle the Marvelous rather as a slight, delicate, and evanescent flavor, than as any portion of the actual substance of the dish offered to the public. He can hardly be said, however, to commit a literary crime, even if he disregard this caution.[40]

Here was a theory of fiction—and the promise of a genre—appropriate for Melville's religious interpretation of the created order: he could commingle the "marvelous" with the mundane; he could "deepen and enrich the shadows" of human experience in ways that alluded to the transcendent; he could seek the Emersonian "original relation to the universe" and still not "swerve aside from the truth of the human heart"; he could, in fact, use those intuitions which light Ishmael's "fog with a heavenly ray" to tell the truth about that heart understood in the most radical terms. If he dispensed with the "minute fidelity . . . to the probable and ordinary course of man's experience" in a way that trespassed Hawthorne's cautions for moderation, he did so because he was convinced that the truth was, at last, to be discerned and depicted in the heart's encounter with the elements of the marvelous present to it. The creation, the natural world of human experience, had not, he was certain, "been all over ransacked by our progenitors, so that no new charms and mysteries remain."[41] Melville had learned, with Jonathan Edwards and Nathaniel Hawthorne, that he could not penetrate to the source of these mysteries, but he knew as well, in the writing of *Moby-Dick,* that such mysteries and their sudden, tumultuous appearances figured vitally in the world he sought to recover, a world which, with this portentous character, provided the resource for the only meaningful God-language accessible to human utterance.

Regardless of where he learned the lessons, Melville absorbed this idea of fiction, and he returned to it, by way of homily, in three chapters of *The Confidence-Man.*[42] In his anticipating objections to inconsistencies of his characters in that book, Melville claims that, in these apparent contradictions, he is being "faithful to facts" because, "if reason be judge, no writer has produced such inconsistent characters as nature herself has" (C, 72). Human nature is not so transparent, he thinks, that a predictable and consistent character can be considered authentic: "Upon the whole, it might rather be thought, that he, who in view of its inconsistencies, says of human nature the same that, in view of its contrasts, is said of the divine nature, that it is past finding out, thereby evinces a better appreciation of it than he who, by always representing it in a clear light, leaves it to be inferred that he clearly knows all about it" (C, 73). And it is the ability to penetrate into the deepest and most mysterious elements of nature, without at all circumscribing the motive force at the heart of those elements, which Melville admires in "the great masters" because they "challenge astonishment at the tangled web of some character [by discovering] . . . the last complications of that spirit which is affirmed by its Creator to be fearfully and wonderfully made" (C, 73).

Although he refers specifically to the depiction of character in these passages, Melville was, concomitantly, adumbrating his understanding of the relationship between fiction and life. He wanted fiction to be faithful to reality, but he thought that it best fulfilled that requirement by grappling with reality "at the tangled web." In this way, the fiction possessed fidelity to the actual, but now the loyalty was, for Melville, to the actual apprehended at the level of ultimacy, the actual as charged and instinct with significance. Such fiction, Melville knew, needed readers who were "not unwilling to drop real life, and turn, for a time, to something different" because "they look not only for more entertainment, but, at bottom, even for more reality, than real life itself can show. Thus, though they want novelty, they want nature, too; but nature unfettered, exhilarated, in effect transformed. In this way of thinking, the people in a fiction, like the people in a play, must dress as nobody exactly dresses, talk as nobody exactly talks, act as nobody exactly acts. It is with fiction as with religion: it should present another world, and yet one to which we feel the tie" (C, 199). Thus, when Melville calls on his readers "to drop real life," he is not asking them to follow him into fantasy but, rather, to envision with him aspects of real life which orthodox habits of vision and imagination preclude. That other world is, for him, the real world; it is "nature unfettered, exhilarated," and, if that world seems "in effect transformed," it is only because it is seen now with eyes struck by its allusive quality—not new or transformed but newly seen, not "ransacked . . . so that no new charms and mysteries remain" but apprehended "at the level of *theos*." It is a world to which "we feel the tie," Herman Melville thought, because it is *the* world—at bottom the world of experience in which had to be answered the radical question of the human—entered at the point of "the last complications" and "affirmed by its Creator to be fearfully and wonderfully made."

Having discovered such a world, in which "the morning dew is as wet to my feet as Eden's dew [was] to Adam's," Melville knew that, in *Moby-Dick,* it would not at all do "to say that the world is getting gray and grizzled now, and has lost that fresh charm which she wore of old."[43] He wanted a world in his fiction as immediately portentous of its transcendent source as the world had been on the morning of the creation. But Melville knew, as well, that the wonder-world of Ishmael's inhabitancy must present itself to eyes unaccustomed to such a charged "atmospherical medium" and that, as author, he "must have plenty of sea-room to tell the Truth in; especially when it seems to have an aspect of newness."[44] In passing through the "great floodgates," then, Ishmael requires auditors willing to "turn, for a time, to something different" because the other, true world he will describe "challenges astonishment" and because, as he says, "in a matter like this, subtlety appeals to subtlety, and without imagination no man can follow another into these halls" (*M,* chap. 42). Ishmael can step forward as guide in *Moby-Dick* because he has experienced the world of the *Pequod*'s journeying, and he can tell the "truth" because Melville had discovered a genre—in which the literary and religious imaginations could conflow—to afford him the "sea-room" necessary for a metaphysics of this freighted and portentous world.

The answer to the generic question posed by *Moby-Dick,* then, lies in understanding the religious drive which brought Melville to a "strange Untried" world as the only articulation available to human expression of the god he sought and, as such, as the locus wherein the final question of man, in his "last complications," had to be answered. But this world was untried, Melville knew, only in the sense that it outreached in its "immense Remote" the imagination of experience possessed by his contemporaries. *Moby-Dick* stands as an imaginative jeremiad, a reformative document as the author himself understood it, which now characterizes that age in America not so much in its tendency to reflect the main currents or the central debate or the mind-set of the age as in its efforts to image for the cultural perception a world "to which we feel the tie" but which the age, Melville thought, had left untried.

CHAPTER FIVE

THE GROVES OF OUR THESSALIES
The Early Works and the Metaphysics of Moby-Dick

In a letter to Nathaniel Hawthorne in June of 1851, Herman Melville revealed his sense of the risks involved in "the great art of telling the truth" he wanted to tell in *Moby-Dick*—the very risks which, he was certain, required an amplitude of literary license, a huge "sea-room" for the telling of his tale. He lamented the fact that "Dollars damn me," that his most ambitious efforts, like *Mardi,* were bound to be scorned by the reading audience. Still, this financial risk only compounded Melville's deeper feeling that, in order for his literature to succeed with a common audience, he would need to compromise his vision of the truth:

Truth is the silliest thing under the sun. Try to get a living by the Truth —and go to the Soup Societies. Heavens! Let any clergyman try to preach the Truth from its very stronghold, the pulpit, and they would ride him out of his church on his own pulpit bannister. It can hardly be doubted that all Reformers are bottomed upon the truth, more or less; and to the world at large are not reformers almost universally laughing-stocks? Why so? Truth is ridiculous to men. Thus easily in my room here do I, conceited and garrulous, reverse the test of my Lord Shaftesbury.[1]

Even Solomon, whom Melville declares to be "the truest man who ever spoke," had compromised the truth, had, in Melville's sense of things, "*managed* the truth with a view to popular conservatism." These passages, written during the same period of Melville's final efforts to "slave on my 'Whale,'" indicate in a pointed way both his attempt to design an art which would stand prophetically in relation to common belief and his conviction that habitual perception would either be transformed by the new vision of reality or else be struck by its outlandish quality. In either case, Melville felt he had to proceed, for, like the reformer, he sensed he had "bottomed upon the truth"—had located an unwonted world which, charged with uncanny, transcendent resonances, must appear ridiculous to human logic. The promise of this logic to apprehend the truth had faded for Melville; realizing that wonder surpassed intellect in responding to these portents of "another world," he had learned that in the presence of these signal instances to human life consisted such truth as man could know: "I stand for the heart," he declared. "To the dogs with the head! I had rather be a fool with a heart, than Jupiter Olympus with his head." The head could tell him nothing of the hidden, and yet ineluctable, god at the source of these portentous moments; *Moby-Dick* will elaborate "the reasons of the heart" which beats and has its being in a world brimming with such moments of ridiculous ultimacy.

What is less pointed, but no less important, in this same letter to Hawthorne, is Melville's suggestion of how and when he had penetrated "more or less" to the truth. In his reflections on the "horrible" state of his literary reputation, he observes to his Berkshire friend that "I did not think of Fame, a year ago, as I do now":

My development has been all within a few years past. I am like one of those seeds taken out of the Egyptian pyramids, which, after being three thousand years a seed and nothing but a seed, being planted in English soil, it developed itself, grew to greenness, and then fell to mould. So I. Until I was twenty-five, I had no development at all. From my twenty-fifth year I date my life. Three weeks have scarcely passed, at any time between then and now, that I have not unfolded within myself. But I feel that I am now come to the inmost leaf of the bulb, and that shortly the flower must fall to the mould.

Although Melville's claim to have been completely dormant in his early life probably should not be taken seriously and although his pessimism about his literary future is only speculative at this point, these remarks to Hawthorne have the virtue of posing, in a reasonably direct way, Melville's understanding of when he had gained his vision of the truth. To date his development from 1844 is to locate the moment of his intellectual birth at the time he was picking up his pen to write *Typee,* and to rehearse his continuous "unfolding" from that moment to the present moment in 1851 is to suggest that his progress toward the "inmost bulb" or the "bottom" had been entangled with, and indeed had emerged from, the reflections on experience in the early works. The strong implication here, then, is that the early fictions represent in Melville's intellectual career not only a stage of sifting through and eliminating some inadequate responses to experience but, as well, a more positive progress toward the truth—the reality of the wonder-world—upon which he now felt himself, at the "moment" of *Moby-Dick,* to be uncompromisingly bottomed.

With this hint of Melville's earlier preparation in view and with the sources of his maturing vision as the issue, it is necessary to delineate the ways that the works preceding *Moby-Dick* lead toward the recognition of the wonder-world which orients Ishmael's retrospective account to the reader. Close scrutiny of the less spectacular worlds of *Typee* and *Redburn*—refracted through the consciousness of their respective narrators—suggests that the experience of those fictive worlds had contained or disclosed presaging and portentous moments but that such moments occur almost coincidentally, not commandingly, to the narrational memories: the moments do not come to be regarded, in recollection, as focally important and thus they fail to reorient either the narrator's perceptions or his presentation of the world.[2] This failure to give these moments any valuable interpretation in the narratives implies an axiology which assumes that, or at least operates as if, such moments are not significant. Still, if Tommo and Redburn do not recognize a dimension of ultimacy implicit in these resounding instances, their encounters with such moments are not forgotten in the course of their stories; their memories linger with, and their narratives record, spots of time in the midst of which each found himself confronted with some astonishing element looming through, and yet strangely beyond, the ordinary terms of human experience. While these moments are preserved in the narrational memory and presented to the reader only as "odd feelings" or "curiosities" or "inexplicable occurrences" whose implications are untold and whose dimensions are unexplored, their significance has not been lost upon Melville, who, in writing *Moby-Dick,* seeks the possibility of recovering a sense of the transcendent from and through the realm of experience.[3]

Building on the developing understanding of the early narrators, Melville can present an Ishmael who has learned that, in telling the truth, he can do no other than to explore those facets of life in which the finite bears signs of the infinite, and thus, in recounting his experience, he is oriented by what is at least an implicit metaphysics.[4] *Typee* and *Redburn* figure as propaedeutics for Melville's recognition of the wonder-world because they adumbrate, unknowingly for their narrators, the view of time and the conception of symbol which at once structure the narrative presentation and embody the substance of the world Ishmael will render. By the time Ishmael begins the telling of his tale, the content of his experience and the forms with which to articulate that content have become identical in the generic mode of the narrative. His yearning for the recovery of spirit has developed into a faith in experience itself to contain and to disclose the reality of a transcendent factor overarching it, and the perceptions of time and symbol which run throughout *Moby-Dick* are designed by Melville both to reflect the mode of Ishmael's visionary inquiry and to reflect substantively the realm of experience, in its metaphysical allusiveness, to which his faith refers.

I

Late in *Redburn,* the narrator attempts to present his feelings about Harry Bolton, whose image is recalled as "plain and palpable as in life" and who, yet, is also remembered as "mixed with a thousand strange forms, the centaurs of fancy; half real and human, half wild and grotesque." In his description of Harry, Wellingborough Redburn recognizes, at least retrospectively,

that Harry, apart from his or Redburn's own intending, represented one of those signal instances in human experience which
are both self-contained and allusive, which both occur in the
midst of the ordinary course of life and portend, in a startling
and profound way, the hand which created them: "Divine imaginings," Redburn concludes, "like gods, come down to the
groves of our Thessalies, and there, in the embrace of wild, dryad
reminiscences, beget the beings that astonish the world" (*R*,
252). It cannot be denied that Redburn is incapable of following
through on his brief insight into experience momentarily augur-
ing something beyond itself or that he fails to respond to Harry
in a way which is concordant with the religious demands implicit
in the insight. What is important in the consideration here, however, is not the discrepancy between Redburn's opportunities
and his actual gains but, rather, the appearance in this earlier
fiction of one of those portentous moments which will found the
wonder-world of Ishmael's living. Other such moments arise in
Typee and *Redburn* and, upon examination, yield a sense of
what Melville will require from Ishmael in his later, deeper encounter with them. In this context, the most important progres-
sion or movement from *Typee* to *Moby-Dick* is to be discerned
in the shifting conceptions of experience which characterize the
narrational postures of the works—from the positivism of Tommo, to the developing organicist attitudes of Redburn and
White-Jacket, to the metaphysical impulses of Ishmael.

Tommo's retrospective account of his career in the Marquesas
contains several of those charged and resonant moments which
might have prompted him to consider the allusiveness of his experience toward a dimension which overarched it, but his positivist attitude toward these moments, even in recollection, is
betrayed by the narrative presentation itself. After some time in
the valley of the Typee, Tommo wanders into an area which
houses the natives' monuments and which, he recalls, "reminded
me of Stonehenge and the architectural labors of the Druid" (*T*,
154). In this spot he encounters, among "a wilderness of vines
. . . [which makes] the stones lie half-hidden," a moment latent,
at least, with significance, because, although he shares nothing of

the Typee religion, he finds here that which astonishes him with its resonant character:

As I gazed upon this monument, doubtless the work of an extinct and forgotten race, thus buried in the green nook of an island at the ends of the earth, the existence of which was yesterday unknown, a stronger feeling of awe came over me than if I had stood musing at the mighty base of the Pyramid of Cheops. There are no inscriptions, no sculpture, no clue, by which to conjecture its history: nothing but the dumb stones. How many generations of those majestic trees which overshadow them have grown and flourished and decayed since first they were erected! (*T,* 155).

Although Kory-Kory suggests that the monuments "were coeval with the creation of the world; that the great gods themselves were the builders; and that they would endure until time shall be no more" (*T,* 154), and although Tommo himself is dumbstruck with awe about the "generations" of the monuments, this fortuitous encounter and the feeling of wonderment it evokes do not suggest to Tommo the presence of a transcendent dimension looming through the concrete elements of his experience. Indeed, Kory-Kory's remarks only lead him to be convinced that neither Kory-Kory "nor the rest of his countrymen knew anything about them." While the monumental remains "naturally suggest many interesting reflections," as Tommo allows, the moment itself gives rise, the narrative reveals, only to positivist speculations about the geological "age of the island," the architectonics of the monuments, and the tools and "mechanic arts" (*T,* 155) of the builders. Instead of being quickened by the extraordinary quality of this instance, and in spite of the feelings it inspired, Tommo subverts the moment just by the kind of imagination he brings to bear on it. When its mysteries are rendered ordinary by the character of his interpretation and presentation, the moment must fail to have for Tommo the commanding aspect which, even in retrospection, would occur to his consciousness in a more than coincidental and clinical manner.

A similar instance, in which the moment brims over with some profoundly arcane element only to be reduced by the terms of the narrative presentation, occurs as Tommo and Toby flee into the interior of the island. As they pursue the Eden which the island seems to promise, as they explore "the unknown regions" (*T*, 44), Tommo brushes aside a branch and gratuitously catches a glimpse of paradise: "In this direction, as far as our vision extended, not a sign of life, nor anything that denoted even the transient residence of man, could be seen. The whole landscape seemed one unbroken solitude, the interior of the island having apparently been untenanted since the morning of the creation; and as we advanced through this wilderness, our voices sounded strangely in our ears, as though human accents had never before disturbed the fearful silence of the place, interrupted only by the low murmurings of distant waterfalls" (*T*, 44). In the face of the primordial resonances which have their loci in this spot, Tommo is momentarily filled with wonder, and the astonishment created in him by this scene apparently stems from "the fearful silence" which connects this spot with "the morning of the creation." As he and Toby move about in this area, so radically demarcated from their ordinary experience, the rushing waterfalls "seemed to penetrate into the very bowels of the earth" (*T*, 45). In short, this interlude is charged with those elements which could refer to the disclosure of the holy in and through the stuff of palpable reality: the eternal is boded by the temporal to create in the human those feelings of allurement and rapture, awe and dread, which belong to the sudden encounter with the *mysterium tremendum et fascinosum*. To say that the moment might contain and disclose the transcendent is not, however, to say that Tommo either responds fully to or indeed even recognizes fully the presence to his experience of that wholly other. Rather, again, his first tendency is to survey the pragmatics of the matter instead of interpreting the allusiveness of the moment as portentous of the transcendent. Immediately upon glimpsing this scene, "untenanted" in its "unbroken solitude," Tommo expresses "our disappointment . . . in not finding the various fruits with which" (*T*, 44) he and Toby had intended to feast. Although Tommo pauses at one point to wonder how he was conducted to "so singular a place" (*T*, 46) and, a bit later, to think about "by what means I had thus suddenly been made a spectator of such a scene" (*T*, 49), he pushes aside any implications of the transcendent in this moment and begins, he says, "recovering from my astonishment" (*T,* 50), in order to take leave of this discomfiting spot and to continue the practical logistics of his journey.

Although Tommo recalls the strange and awestruck feelings these moments inspired, then, his habitual interpretation of experience precludes his searching out the dimensions of spirit a set of more religious eyes and sensibilities might have discovered in the encounter with these scenes. Indeed, even at those stages of his retrospection wherein he records experiences which apparently require the language of religious reflection, he seems signally unaware of the implications of his own vocabulary. As Tommo and Toby stop on their journey in order to restore themselves "to some degree by food and repose," the moment takes on a cathedral quietude: "We seated ourselves upon the least uncomfortable spot we could select, and Toby produced from the bosom of his frock the sacred package. In silence we partook of the small morsel of refreshment that had been left from the morning's repast, and without once proposing to violate the sanctity of our engagement with respect to the remainder, we rose to our feet, and proceeded to construct some sort of shelter under which we might obtain the sleep we so greatly needed" (*T,* 54–55). The moment, even in recollection, continues to have a special quality for Tommo which makes it discrete from other, more habitual elements in his experience. The depth of relation, the communion they achieve with one another in this instance, is clear: "perceiving in each other's countenances that desponding expression which speaks more eloquently than words" (*T,* 54), they break their bread together and consecrate the silent brotherhood beyond words. Tommo's diction seems curiously misapplied here, however, for terms like *sacred* and *sanctity* refer less to the character and depth of the human rapport of the moment than to the necessities of physical comfort. The implications of such a vocabulary are simply lost on Tommo: he fails altogether to imagine that his terms could refer to this deep instance of human reciprocity in which he has fortuitously participated and turns his attention instead to the decision about whether this "spot was better adapted to our purpose than the one in which we had passed the last wretched night" (*T,* 55). In short, he attends again to the practical exigencies of the moment and dismisses the considerations of depth and implication.

Now, the point is not to condemn Tommo for such failures of imagination; indeed, evaluating his frame of mind at all, apart from the question of the sources of Melville's later vision, is quite irrelevant. Given the consistency of the attitude toward experience that runs throughout the narrative—the attitude, characterizing the narrator, that events and objects and moments are simply events, objects, and moments, that they are without relation to each other and without reference to anything beyond themselves—it is inevitable that Tommo is wont to render the ostensibly presaging moments in his experience in the same way that he records the ordinary and banal moments. The more important point is that the naive romanticism which inspired the journey to Typee has, by the time of the retrospective account of it, turned into a virtually positivist attitude toward experience. Even so, the account contains a record of some of those resounding moments whose character and implications will be understood much differently by another narrator.

Such moments occur in *Redburn* as well, although again they are not regarded by the narrational memory with anything like the imagination Ishmael will bring to bear in *Moby-Dick.* Wellingborough Redburn's first "sight of the great ocean itself" is an experience in which "there was much to behold and wonder at" and here, cutting through the mild waves that "seemed all live things with hearts in them, that could feel" (*R,* 64), Redburn has an intuition that some prodigious dimension looms through the moment: "But what seemed perhaps the most strange to me of all, was a certain wonderful rising and falling of the sea; I do not mean the waves themselves, but a sort of wide heaving and swelling and sinking all over the ocean. It was something I can not well describe; but I know very well what it was, and how it affected me. It made me almost dizzy to look at it; and yet I could not keep my eyes off it, it seemed so passing strange and wonderful" (*R,* 64). In this instance, in which Redburn "expected to hear myself called to, out of the clear blue air" (*R,* 64), a man of different sensibility might have felt himself confronted with the "heaving and swelling and sinking" of an unseen but ineluctable current of being itself and might have found himself engaged in religious reflection, searching his experience "at the level of *theos* or ultimate meaning." Redburn himself, he remembers, "did not have much leisure to indulge in such thoughts" because his wonderment must give way to "getting some stun'-sails ready to hoist aloft" (R, 64). Still, the special tenor of the moment continues to lay hold on him:

Every mast and timber seemed to have a pulse in it that was beating with life and joy; and I felt a wild exulting in my own heart, and felt as if I would be glad to bound along so round the world.

Then was I first conscious of a wonderful thing in me, that responded to all the wild commotion of the other world; and went reeling on and on with the planets in their orbits, and was lost in one delirious throb at the center of the All. A wild bubbling and bursting was at my heart, as if a hidden spring had just gushed out there; and my blood ran tingling along my frame, like mountain brooks in spring freshets. (R, 66)

Having experienced what he thinks must be the "delirious throb" of the absolute in a strange, unloosed, and exultant moment, Redburn has encountered that which might have overturned his perceptions to create a new understanding of reality, that which, for another imagination, might have led to continuing metaphysical speculation. Again, however, he fails to grasp what is at least the potential significance of the experience and remarks instead "how soon these raptures abated" when he is "set to work" (R, 66).

Later in the book, Redburn finds, on the docks of Liverpool, the noble truck-horses whose "look, so full of calm intelligence and sagacity," presents an allusive reminiscence and momentarily portends another world:

There are unknown worlds of knowledge in brutes; and whenever you mark a horse, or a dog, with a peculiarly mild, calm, deep-seated eye, be sure he is an Aristotle or a Kant, tranquilly speculating upon the mysteries in man. No philosophers so thoroughly comprehend us as dogs and horses. They see through us at a glance. And after all, what is a horse, but a species of four-footed dumb man, in a leathern overall, who happens to live upon oats, and toils for his masters, half-requited or abused, like the biped hewers of wood and drawers of water? But there is a touch of divinity even in brutes, and a special halo about a horse, that should forever exempt him from indignities. As for those majestic, magisterial truck-horses of the docks, I would as soon think of striking a judge on the bench, as to lay violent hand upon their holy hides. (R, 197)

Yet again, however, readers of Melville's works are forced to await a later book in order to see what the metaphysical imagination of an Ishmael will discover in such a moment. For Redburn, this instance in which there is disclosed the hint of unknown worlds, a dimension of profound connection in the contours of life, becomes merely an accident of insight on which he cannot follow through. The narrative catalogues the moment in such a way as to betray that, for Redburn, the discovery is no more presaging than other, habitual moments in the round of his survey of the docks: his interest turns quickly to an account of the loads these truck-horses can draw.

As with the discussion of the wondrous moments in *Typee,* the point is not that these moments are hierophanous, that they are filled with the numinous. Rather, even were these moments brimming over with the wholly other, the perspectives which characterize the narrations of Tommo and Redburn would prevent these two from seeing such moments as disclosive of the holy. Ishmael, on the other hand, will feel warranted to develop a religious interpretation of them, and he will do so with some justice, for, as James Richmond has written in a different context:

When the metaphysical theologian is confronted by the sceptical empiricist what can he claim as empirical in this area of religious experience? Briefly, he can point to countless millions (of both past and present) claiming firmly that their consciousness has been impinged upon and their awareness enlarged by the uninduced pressure of something ultimate and transcendent. . . . It is perfectly true that the existence of such an empirical fact alone does not prove the truth of religion or that the interpretations put by religious subjects upon their experience are correct. But it does something else. It points us to a vast tract of experience of which we have to make sense, which we have to integrate into other areas of our experience. We can see it *as* a region of experience capable of being explained naturalistically or as an aspect of the world *contingent* upon the existence of the transcendent.[5]

If Tommo and Redburn are wont to view, or at least to render, their experiences "naturalistically" even in those moments during which they sense something arcane and powerful, this fact becomes all the more apparent and significant, with respect to the issue of Melville's increasingly religious interpretation of experience, in its continuity with the radically altered imagination Ishmael will develop. It is only that new explanation of experience, however, which makes the visions of Tommo and Redburn seem truncated by comparison. They nonetheless profit Melville in the sense and to the comparative degree that their narratives contain, even in an attenuated way, those moments which undergird Melville's idea of the wonder-world and in which Ishmael will locate something ultimate and transcendent.

Perhaps the signal appearance of an element of the wondrous occurs for Redburn in the figure of Harry Bolton, one of those "beings that astonish the world," one whose life alludes at moments to divine imaginings. Harry is no supernatural character; he is, in Redburn's view, a figurement which momentously presents, in "the groves of our Thessalies," the signal of an unearthly dimension. The strange behavior of Harry aboard the Highlander portends this presence, for Redburn, in a way which makes it clearly apart from Harry's intentionality:

But how was it that Harry Bolton, who spite of his effeminacy of appearance, had evinced, in our London trip, such unmistakable flashes of a spirit not easily tamed—how was it, that he could now yield himself up to the almost passive reception of contumely and contempt? Perhaps his spirit, for the time, had been broken. But I will not undertake to explain; we are curious creatures, as everyone knows; and there are passages in the lives of all men, so out of keeping with the common tenor of their ways, and so seemingly contradictory of themselves, that only He who made us can expound them. (R, 257–58)

In what Harry's ambiguous figure discloses, then, Redburn temporarily comes into encounter with what Ishmael will regard as "the real presence of the hidden God," to use Carl Michalson's phrase. The disclosures of this moment are not complete or final: they do not reveal the ultimate nature of the transcendent element resident in them; nor do they illuminate in any full and final way even the finite configuration of the Harry Bolton through whom that element looms. Rather, the discovery and the disclosures of such a presence reveal to Redburn a dimension of experience portentous of that which is beyond its phenomenal character. By this time, however, it is not surprising that this encounter, like others which have preceded it in the record of Redburn's career, stops short of reorienting the belief about experience which characterizes, and which is betrayed by, the narration: he turns his narrative attention, without pause, to observations about the "weather we experienced at sea" (R, 259)—experience which is apparently qualitatively equal, for Redburn, to the potentially transcendent resonances he had soon before located in Harry Bolton.

Now, despite the fact that Redburn does not develop the kind of imagination that would lead him to pursue the implications of such focal moments in his experience, the moments *do* occur to him and *are* placed, as it were, in his story. Even in view of the fact that Redburn fails to appreciate or even to recognize fully the promise and demand of these possible signals of the transcendent, he nonetheless advances Tommo's positivist attitude toward experience in *Typee* a step closer to Melville's perspective on experience in *Moby-Dick*. Redburn at least realizes, by the end of his journey and the beginning of his narrative, that an organic relationship exists between his self-definition and the experience he undergoes; he realizes, in short, that the self he has and will become has been nourished and shaped by the life in which he has suffered and acted. The retrospection itself figures as an attempt on his part to discern the pattern, depth, and meaning of his first voyage, for nothing else, he knows, will enable him to put the glass sailor and himself "on their feet."

Finally, however, Redburn's understanding of his experience makes him more nearly like Tommo than like Ishmael, for, although both he and Tommo have encountered and have recorded spots of time which filled them with wonderment, neither

has been seized—in heart and mind—by the element of the wondrous in human experience. It is Ishmael who is overtaken by
"the reign of wonder." [6] It is Ishmael whose imagination both
requires and is attuned to the experience of wonder. And it is
Ishmael whose entire perspective is controlled by Melville's
"imagination of wonder" [7] as it leads to metaphysics. As Paul
Weiss has written:

Metaphysics begins with the wondrous. Whatever awakens surmise as
to its ground or bearing on whatever else is or is known can prompt the
beginning of a long and hazardous dialectical journey. One knows that
one has come to the end of that journey and finally touched on an ultimate Being when, upon returning to the world of things, one finds that
everything has become wondrous—more wondrous even than the initial terms had been before—but more clearly demarcated and understood. Wonder does not disappear as a result of philosophic inquiry;
instead, it becomes manifest everywhere. Metaphysics does not dissolve
or solve problems. It traces them back to their origin, and thereby discovers why the problems arise and are always with us. [8]

While Ishmael does not undertake philosophic inquiry in any
strict sense of the term, the retrospective narration which he
presents to the reader has been prompted by his experience of the
wonder-world. After the encounter with such focal moments as
Tommo and Redburn have experienced, Ishmael, whose imagination cannot leave off, must begin the dialectical journey to
trace such moments back to their origin, back to their ground,
and thus, he must search his experience in its metaphysical
reaches.

II

If Melville's commitment in *Moby-Dick* was to "touch upon an
Ultimate Being," to "present another world, and yet one to
which we feel the tie," the formal impulse of the narrative was to
take shape around those focal moments which occurred periodically in the flux of ordinary experience but which were clearly
discrete from the mundane because of their prodigious transcendent dimensions. By the time the retrospective Ishmael recounts
his tale, he can tell the reader that, from the first, the hope for

such moments of wonder was what sent him to sea: "Chief among these motives was the overwhelming idea of the great whale himself. Such a portentous and mysterious monster roused all my curiosity. Then the wild and distant seas where he rolled his island bulk; the undeliverable, nameless perils of the whale; these, with all the attending marvels of a thousand Patagonian sights and sounds, helped sway me to my wish. With other men, perhaps, such things would not have been inducements; but as for me, I am tormented with an everlasting itch for things remote" (*M,* chap. 1). On the basis of this introduction, one might expect the remainder of the tale to become a flight into pure hallucination, and, indeed, the "Patagonian sights and sounds" in the book induced an early British reviewer to label *The Whale* a "rhapsody run mad." [9] Another early reviewer, however, realized that the rhapsodic segments of the book—the appearance of divine imaginings—do not depart from a world "to which we feel the tie": "We have occasional touches of the subtle mysticism, which is carried to such an inconvenient excess in Mardi, but it is here mixed up with so many tangible and odorous realities, that we always safely alight from the excursion through mid-air upon the solid deck of the whaler. We are recalled to this world by the fumes of 'oil and blubber,' and are made to think more of the contents of barrels than of allegories." [10] However precious this understanding of *Moby-Dick* might be, it serves at least to indicate Melville's double commitment in the book to reality and at once to a deeper reality "than real life can show." The world presented by Melville to conjoin these two realities— of common appearance and of ultimacy which seems ridiculous to common appearance—is founded upon a conception of time and symbol in human experience which bespeaks his yearning for such coinherence and, concomitantly, reflects the fundamental structures of experience as Ishmael's metaphysical search perceives them.

The episodic structure of *Moby-Dick* evinces the way time is perceived when one lives in anticipation of the convergence of another world upon his own. The tasks of finding lodging, of eating and drinking, and of earning money are not ignored, and the customary business of life aboard a whaler—of ropes and lines, of cisterns and buckets, of stowing down and clearing away—is chronicled as the homogeneous and mundane sense of time as mere duration. But periodically, and always temporarily, the elements and activities which belong to the habitual round of life, which mark the ordinary passage of time, are discovered suddenly to be leavened with the presence of something wholly other, and, during these moments instinct with power and mystery, chronological time is interrupted, displaced, by a presaging and portentous time which generates its own center of power and creates its own coherence apart from, and yet in the very stuff of, the ordinary pattern of time. Melville indicates his own desire to locate these singular and induplicable moments in experience by the language he uses to describe his "original character": [he] "is like a revolving Drummond light, raying away from itself all round it—everything is lit by it, everything starts up to it (mark how it is with Hamlet), so that, in certain minds, there follows upon the adequate conception of such a character, an effect, in its way, akin to that which in Genesis attends upon the beginning of things" (C, 261). While Melville is again speaking of character in this passage, he obviously wants his utterly original character to display the same sort of charged and imbued quality he seeks in experience generally. In short, he knows that the prepossessing quality of the singular character he desires is the one attribute of significance, an attribute related to, indeed shared by, those portentous moments in experience which become, however temporarily, powerful and commanding, which are self-contained, and which establish their own mysterious consonance with the transcendent.[11]

Ishmael inhabits a world in which these confluences of time and eternity, of the mundane and the *mysterium,* occur frequently and vibrantly. By the time of his narration, he has learned to discern these plenary elements in his experience and to anticipate, with hopefulness, the recurring profound moments of their appearance. For him, the routine business of "the first lowering" suddenly becomes an event which reifies a mysterious, transcendent element because he can perceive in the experience "a sight full of quick wonder and awe" (M, chap. 48). The slow and tedious passage of the *Pequod* "across four several cruising-

THE GROVES OF OUR THESSALIES

grounds" is abruptly interrupted by a vision of the spirit-spout which "mysteriously jetted into the clear moonlight," which allures the crew, and which, yet, creates "a sense of peculiar dread" (*M*, chap. 51). In the center of "The Grand Armada," as the mundane activity of whaling continues on the circumference, Ishmael, to his astonishment, finds within the churning circle of whales an "enchanted calm," a glimpse of new life among the newborn whales, suckling their mothers but "still spiritually feasting upon some unearthly reminiscence." In this sight, he is bathed with an "eternal mildness of joy" (*M*, chap. 87). Or, again, the ordinary experience of time as mere duration is suddenly displaced when Ishmael, working at the midnight helm, becomes "horribly conscious of something fatally wrong," as a "stark, bewildered feeling, as of death, came over me." Even in his retrospective rehearsal of the events of that dark night, the strange moment, he says, has been "ever since inexplicable" (*M*, chap. 96). As finally inexplicable as the moment might have been for him, however, Ishmael recognizes it, as he had with the other, less terrifying moments, as full of spiritual significance, as plenteous in presenting to him an element of the wondrous, even in dread form.

This understanding of time which characterizes the narrative perception is generically related to the religious idea of *kairos*. As Paul Tillich has explained, "'kairos,' the 'fulness of time,' . . . describes the moment in which the eternal breaks into the temporal, and the temporal is prepared to receive it." [12] In describing the imagination which has a readiness for this perception of time, Tillich writes:

An age that is turned toward, and open to, the unconditional is one in which the consciousness of the presence of the unconditional permeates and guides all cultural functions and forms. The divine, for such a state of mind, is not a problem but a presupposition. Its "givenness" is more certain than that of anything else. This situation finds expression, first of all, in the dominating power of the religious sphere, but not in such a way as to make religion a special form of life ruling over the other forms. Rather, religion is the life-blood, the inner power, the ultimate meaning of all life. The 'sacred' or the 'holy' inflames, imbues, inspires, all reality and all aspects of existence. [13]

In *Moby-Dick,* Ishmael is disposed toward just such an "openness to the unconditional," for he is allured by the wondrous to the extent that, as Weiss suggests, wonder "becomes manifest everywhere." And thus, the intermittent and portentous instances erupting out of, and for a moment suspending, the course of mundane, chronological time appear frequently and in a variety of forms. These forms may elicit in the human heart responses which range from "an eternal mildness to joy" to a frightening and "peculiar dread," from rapture to horror. Regardless of the emotion called forth, however, it remains only briefly, for there are ever new portents, which will inspire different feelings, arising before one. "Everything can be a vessel of the unconditional," Tillich writes, "but nothing can be unconditioned itself." In this, Tillich thinks, consists the "warning against the idolatrous elevation of *one* moment" [14] of *kairos,* for all such moments cast the preceding moments into relativity and any such moment is at best paradoxical because "what happens in the kairos should be absolute, and yet not absolute, but under judgment of the absolute." [15] The moments come and the moments fade; they are not created by man, and they cannot be sustained by man. What is sustained, rather, is the conception of time itself, the understanding for this kind of religious imagination that temporal life is infused, periodically, with an eternal element which transcends human possession but which, at once, proffers the presence of abundant moments.

This view of time is correlated with, and indeed enabled by, Ishmael's understanding that the world is to be seen symbolically. Confronting intermittent elements in experience which were charged with an allusiveness to something beyond themselves, Melville had himself come to rely, as the "Agatha letter" shows, on the symbolism he found inherent in the forms of the phenomenal world. With Ishmael, then, he could anticipate the sudden, tumultuous disclosures of these portents of the transcendent in just such an episodic fashion.

If Melville was convinced of the reality of these periodic, inspirited instances in the realm of experience, he knew as well that the presentation of their unique manifestations required, in his fictive world, a language capable of accommodating both the

concrete, empirical reality and the prodigious dimension looming through it. He needed, as with the rendering of the temporal
aspect of his book, to depict the disclosive element of another
world and, simultaneously, to establish its continuity with the
world of familiar experience. In filling the universe of *Moby-
Dick* with all the intractable materialities of whaling—with the
lengthy and involved descriptions of gear and mechanism, of the
ship's architecture, of duties and processes, of the whale's history and anatomy—Melville presents a world of unquestionable
density and detail, a world of sheer factuality and weight, a
world to which we feel the tie. Just this world of solid actuality
enables Ishmael, by the act of perception, to discover within its
precincts those elements which momentarily augur the presence
of something wholly other beyond themselves. In practising this
mode of symbolism, Melville realized, as did Henry James later,
that representation of the presence of the transcendent required
a language of symbolic forms, a language grounded in the tangible and concrete which could, yet, refer to a factor hidden beyond anything perceptible to sense or to intellection. James
writes that "prodigies, when they come straight, come with an
effect imperilled; they keep all their character, on the other hand,
by looming through some other history." [16] In *Moby-Dick,* these
portents of the transcendent issue up in the very midst, and out
of the very stuff, of palpable reality when instances of that reality
are apprehended as unfettered, when they are receptive to the
unconditional, when they, infused by some uncanny element,
appear commandingly as symbols.[17] In the "exhilarated" atmosphere of the *Pequod*'s voyage, time and space suddenly coalesce
to portend in otherwise ordinary moments and objects and activities the presence of the transcendent. For the man open to the
unconditional, the man who has a readiness for wonder, the man
perceptive enough to start with recognition, a common coin
becomes an irradiant object because of the significance it abruptly achieves in an altogether singular moment. The mechanism of
the weaving loom becomes a source for reflection and rhapsody
because its mundane and tedious functionings momentarily illumine the whole of life. The frenzied figure of Ahab himself inspires one of Ishmael's "furious tropes." The word *white* bears

an allusiveness, in the charged environs of the *Pequod*'s search, quite surpassing its ordinary usage. And, at last, the massive, rolling bulk of the whale, as an inclusive symbol for the creation itself in its awesome and majestic aspect, is the thing with which "you feel the Deity and the dread powers more forcibly than in beholding any other object in living nature." "It signifies," Ishmael emphasizes, "'God: done this day by my hand'" (*M*, chap. 79).

It is true, of course, that objects and events in *Moby-Dick* symbolize different things to the different characters who encounter them, but the characters' perceptions, including Ishmael's own as he well realizes, are not final in any sense. Beyond all the meanings located in the doubloon, for instance, is its own self-contained significance as symbol, a significance which human reason cannot grasp. The coin inspires different feelings and thoughts because, as symbol, it is opaque. It appeals as symbol because its singularly portentous character suddenly manifests itself in time and space and organizes life temporarily around itself. It is the Drummond light that Melville uses as analogue in *The Confidence-Man*: "raying away from itself all round it— everything is lit by it, everything starts up to it" (*C*, 261). Ishmael's description of the coin points to the same effect: "though now nailed amidst all the rustiness of iron bolts and the verdigris of copper spikes, yet, untouchable and immaculate to any foulness, it still preserved its Quito glow. . . . For it was set apart and sanctified to one awe-striking end; and however wanton in their sailor ways, one and all, the mariners revered it as the white whale's talisman" (*M*, chap. 99).

In Ishmael's view, the whale itself is the paradigmatic symbol because it stands as a figure for the tangible world which, in its rich density, casts up its own significances and because, as symbol for the created order, it bears the signature of the transcendent. In this second respect, in the understanding that prodigious elements in experience point beyond the palpable world to an ultimately hidden reality, Melville's conception of world as symbol in *Moby-Dick* is akin to Thomas Carlyle's version of the world in *Sartor Resartus*. Like Melville, Carlyle believed that certain moments and objects have intrinsic value and significance, "borrowing of the Godlike," because they appeal profoundly as "the wondrous agency of *Symbols*": "In the symbol proper, what we call a symbol, there is ever, more or less distinctly and directly, some embodiment and revelation of the Infinite; the Infinite is made to blend itself with the Finite, to stand visible, and as it were, attainable there. By Symbols, accordingly, is man guided and commanded, made happy, made wretched. He everywhere finds himself encompassed with Symbols, recognised as such or not recognised: the Universe is but one vast symbol of God."[18] If he discovered revelations of the infinite in symbols, however, Carlyle knew, as Melville did, that any account of the ultimate source of these revelations was impossible to construct. The final, incalculable center is hidden in silence, Carlyle writes, because "Silence is the element in which great things fashion themselves together; that at length they may emerge, full-formed and majestic, into the daylight of Life."[19]

It is just this element of silence which requires the religious symbol to possess its unique character, for, as Dorothy Emmet has explained, "in whatever sense religious symbols convey knowledge of the transcendent, it cannot be in the sense of literal and direct representation."[20] With its source and final meanings concealed as they must be, she writes:

The religious symbol has the peculiar function of having to convey its own questionable character. It must express something positively grasped, a significant relation in experience. And yet it must point not simply to the relation within experience but to something qualitatively other which stands beyond it. Hence the ambivalent and ambiguous character of religious imagery. Such ambiguity is not the result of pious vagueness or of confusion of thought (which are the hallmarks of sentimental religious imagery). It is a precise way of conveying the fundamental dilemma of religious symbolism, which presents an analogue of the transcendent in the forms of the phenomenal, of the infinite in the finite.[21]

Like the perception of the successive moments of *kairos,* then, the momentary and continuing symbolism encountered in the world represents a criticism on itself in the twofold sense that each symbol calls into question, into reinterpretation, all symbols which have preceded it and that any symbol remains only tenuous because it must be understood as pointing to a meaning which it cannot at all contain. Again, what is sustained is not the singular meaning, or the complex of meanings, to be discerned in any specific symbol. The elevation of a specific moment of *kairos* or of a single symbol to the height of final meaning— which fails to take into account the conditioned vessels of these portents and the fallibility of human perception—stands as a form of idolatry. As Melville well knew, "what plays the mischief with the truth is that men will insist upon the universal application of a temporary feeling or opinion." [22] Rather, what is sustained in such an ambiguously symbolic world and what can be affirmed is the continuously revelatory aspect of the world, the abundance such a world possesses, the commitment to the symbolic imagination.

For both Melville and Carlyle, then, the realization that the silence is finally indefinable was consoled by their convictions that the world is plenteous with portents, however opaque, of the infinite. As Carlyle writes: "Of kin to the so incalculable influences of Concealment, and connected with still greater things, is the wondrous agency of *Symbols*. In a Symbol there is concealment and yet revelation: here therefore, by Silence and by Speech acting together, comes a double significance. And if both the Speech be itself high, and the Silence fit and noble, how expressive will their union be!" [23] Thus, Carlyle required an understanding of the world which could comprehend the "double significance," which could both hear the high speech and sense in it the force and majesty of the silence behind it. "For is not a symbol ever," Carlyle asks, "to him who has eyes for it, some dimmer or clearer revelation of the Godlike?" [24] One man who has eyes for symbols, who believes momentous elements in experience will disclose a deep spiritual dimension, is Ishmael. His voyage on the sea was animated by his anticipation of a wonderworld there to be recovered, and he senses fulfilled "the long supplication of my youth" (*M*, chap. 111) as he recounts his entrance upon the Pacific Ocean:

There is, one knows not what sweet mystery about this sea, whose gently awful stirrings seem to speak of some hidden soul beneath; like those fabled undulations of the Ephesian sod over the buried Evangelist

St. John. And meet it is, that over these sea-pastures, wide-rolling watery prairies and Potters' Fields of all four continents, the waves should rise and fall, and ebb and flow unceasing; for here, millions of mixed shades and shadows, drowned dreams, somnambulisms, reveries, all that we call lives and souls, lie dreaming, still; tossing like slumberers in their beds; the ever-rolling waves but made so by their restlessness. (M, chap. 111)

Within the "millions of mixed shades and shadows," here "at the tide-beating heart of the world" (M, chap. 111), Ishmael seeks the element of spirit, for he senses that his own last complications must be seen in relation to that which transcends, and yet manifests itself in, the course of his finite life: for him, it will not do "to say that the world is getting gray and grizzled"; for him, the world stands as religious symbol, at least in the measure that he believes that, as Tillich suggests, "everything can be a vessel of the unconditional," in however temporary a moment; for him, the world is touched with wonder which challenges astonishment.

III

Ishmael, then, pulls into a wider ambit and pursues at greater depth those moments which had presented themselves to Tommo and Redburn. Unlike the clinical and positivist attitude of Tommo and unlike the attenuated organicism of Redburn, Ishmael responds in the metaphysical mode to such disclosive instances in the realm of experience because he is wont, in his retrospective account, to search each such instance for its implications about the holistic structure of experience itself and, further, to find revealed in each such instance those mysterious facets which portend a reality transcending human experience: "some certain significance lurks in all things," Ishmael believes; "else all things are little worth, and the round world itself but an empty cipher" (M, chap. 99). This statement issues from his engagement with experience, and it bespeaks convictions which have grown from his metaphysical speculations. Each element in the realm of finite experience has the potential at least to bear the infinite, he can affirm, because the world is so structured as to present to human experience moments which issue up their own profound symbolism—a symbolism which both hides and reveals that ultimate Being which is the ground of experience.

Finally, however, Ishmael's metaphysics must give way to a kind of faith, for, although he has discovered and can affirm the presence of the transcendent in "the groves of our Thessalies" as the agency which unites experience, his metaphysics has "touched upon an ultimate Being," whose character and motive are inviolably hidden from human knowing. His statement of metaphysical conviction—"significance lurks in all things" or "else the round world itself [is] but an empty cipher"—takes into account the nihilistic possibility that at the source of experience there might be nothing. Indeed, only faith can make the affirmation that the world of experience is revelatory in the face of such a possibility. Nonetheless, this faith is no mere soft-minded fideism; it comes only after the deepest searching of experience has proved to Ishmael that—despite the hidden character of the transcendent and despite the limits of his own epistemology—"wonder is [or can be] manifest everywhere." His faith arises not as a desperate leap across the epistemological chasm; rather, his faith refers to, and affirms, the realm of experience itself in its capacity to present to human life the portents of another world. Far from being only an intellectual assent to propositions, this faith is not exclusive of reason, however, for it comes just because Ishmael's metaphysical inquiries, which give him the wonder-world, have brought him to touch upon the hidden source of that world. It is not a faith against all evidence, for both his experience and his reflection on experience have taught him that he can say "yes" to the reality of the wonder-world, no matter how hidden the motive force of that world and no matter how ridiculous such a world must appear to common belief.[25]

Ishmael's faith finally refers to the patterns of revelation—the elements of *kairos* and symbol—which his metaphysics has informed him belong to the world of his living. Faith in the nature of experience after these patterns finally leaves the faithful with experience which is radically contingent, however, because no moment or symbol is final. All such moments and patterns appear in concrete forms which cannot themselves be uncondition-

THE GROVES OF OUR THESSALIES

al: the temporal stands under the judgment of the eternal; the vessel is repudiated by that which it cannot fully contain. Although Ishmael develops a faith in the capacity of experience to reveal the transcendent, then, this faith cannot end in certitude, for there is standing in and beyond the realm of experience which can elicit such faith the unknown ground of experience. Even with this ultimate contingency of experience so conceived, Ishmael does not fly from experience into other-worldliness. The fact that no aspect of human experience "can be unconditioned itself" does not, Tillich writes, "produce indifference to history; it creates an attitude [for the religious imagination] that takes history absolutely seriously."[26] History and experience cannot be dismissed when the groves of our Thessalies portend divine imaginings, for Ishmael has learned with the reasons of the heart that he must cling to those moments of wonder, in which he has bottomed upon the truth, in order to recover the sense of the transcendent for his life, in order at last to be able to place himself, as it were, in that universal home which *White-Jacket* began to adumbrate.

Thus, the retrospective narrative is the locus at which the forms and content of Ishmael's experience become identical for him. The structures of *kairos* and symbol which orient the fictive world *are* the substance of the world of experience about which his metaphysics has given him knowledge and to which his faith refers. Ishmael was not simply born with such knowledge, however; it came as a result of "a long and hazardous dialectical journey." Nor was he born with such faith; rather, it came in the midst of the encounter with the wholly other as Ishmael increasingly inculcates the integral posture for human living in this contingent world of revelations with all its promise and demand. And Ishmael's retrospective account in *Moby-Dick* issues not only in the acknowledgment and affirmation of the "Thessalies" he inhabits: it is also a record of his growing imagination of experience—a record of his own course of self-transcendence—as he comes into encounter with the terrain of wonder.

CHAPTER SIX

THE SPAN OF PORTENTS
The Career of Ishmael's Self-Transcendence

In the opening chapter of *Moby-Dick,* Ishmael, whose very name refers to the "outcast," presents himself to the reader as a more desperate orphan than the young Wellingborough Redburn ever considered himself. For Redburn, hearth and home, mother and sisters, await him at the end of the journey, and the journey itself is undertaken at what is a more or less characteristic stage in an adolescent process of maturation. For Ishmael, the sea voyage is the only logical sequel except for suicide to a life which seems to be getting "gray and grizzled":

> Whenever I find myself growing grim about the mouth; whenever it is a damp, drizzly November in my soul; whenever I find myself involuntarily pausing before coffin warehouses, and bringing up the rear of every funeral I meet; and especially whenever my hypos get such an upper hand of me, that it requires a strong moral principle to prevent me from deliberately stepping into the street, and methodically knocking people's hats off—then, I account it high time to get to sea as soon as I can. This is my substitute for pistol and ball. With a philosophical flourish Cato throws himself upon his sword; I quietly take to the ship. (*M,* chap. 1)

As Tommo came slowly to learn in *Typee,* then, the world of human life is radically fallen, and Ishmael inherits this fallen condition from his predecessor not as a doctrine to which he gives intellectual assent but as a fact of experience itself, felt in the "drizzly November in my soul." Severed from the kind of experience which would support and enrich his life, he remembers, in his retrospection, having been pulled toward the sea, having himself been one of those "thousands upon thousands of mortal men fixed in ocean reveries," and having been brought by adversity and woe to "the extremest limit of the land" (*M*, chap. 1).

In its continuity with the lives portrayed in the early works, then, Ishmael's life, while it cannot refuse the "fall" finally recognized by Tommo, also inherits the possibility of reconciliation with experience hypothesized, if not fully possessed, by young Redburn. For Ishmael, "grim about the mouth" as he recalled himself to be, the sea withholds such a promise to redeem life for him; why go to sea to avoid "pistol and ball," he asks rhetorically:

Why did the poor poet of Tennessee, upon suddenly receiving two handfuls of silver, deliberate whether to buy him a coat, which he sadly needed, or invest his money in a pedestrian trip to Rockaway Beach? Why is almost every robust healthy boy with a robust healthy soul in him, at some time or other crazy to go to sea? Why upon your first voyage as a passenger, did you yourself feel such a mystical vibration, when first told that you and your ship were now out of sight of land? Why did the old Persians hold the sea holy? Why did the Greeks give it a separate deity, and make him the own brother of Jove? Surely all this is not without meaning. (*M*, chap. 1)

Having suffered experience which has blighted and scarred him, Ishmael is allured, even driven, to "water gazing": "as every one knows," he says, "meditation and water are wedded for ever" (*M*, chap. 1). His voyage is for recuperation: he wants not to recover from some physical ailment but, rather, to recover himself in relation to the holy by meditating on oceanic revelations. However, despite the assertive tone of voice—"as every one knows"—Ishmael, as he presents himself in the early pages of his narrative, can only hope for such a recovery of spirit for his life, can only hope when the flood-gates are swung open to him that he will find in all that sea-room the exhilarated world of wonder which will answer to the need of his life. He searches for the portents of the transcendent which had earlier presented themselves to the experience of Tommo and Redburn, but he is a seeker and not a finder yet.

Now, Ishmael's fallen situation, his previous buffeting at the hands of experience, and, indeed, the fact of his seeking, figure cumulatively as the crucial condition of his self in the opening chapters of the narrative—the condition which he hopes will be surmounted by his passage through "the great flood-gates of the wonder-world" (*M*, chap. 1). He wants to meditate on the world of experience in its strange, unloosed, and allusive quality— wants to seize "the image of the ungraspable phantom of life" (*M*, chap. 1)—and, in these meditations, to find that which will enable him to reconcile himself to life. By searching his experience at "the level of *theos*, or ultimate meaning," he hopes to transcend the condition of woe which hems him in, and his seeking, definitive as it is of his fallen life, is the first stage in the career of his self-transcendence. His hope for the wonder-world will, by the end of the narrative, become a faith in the truth of such a revelatory world, and Ishmael, in a slow and frequently halting way, will have learned how to respond commensurately to the promise and demand of such a world, will have learned how to experience it fully. In the portentous world, such a version of full experiencing—of self-transcendence—is achieved by taking "the span of portents" as Melville's persona expresses it in the poem "In a Bye-Canal" (1891):

> Fronted I have, part taken the span
> of portents in nature and peril in man.
> I have swum—I have been
> 'Twixt the whale's black flukes and the white shark's fin.

The "span" includes a process or pattern of expectation, discovery, scrutiny, and possession of the "portents in nature"— a process, for Ishmael, which issues in the location of a context of ultimacy wherein to find new meaning for his life.[1] But a part of this pattern includes Ishmael's assessing the "peril" in himself and in other men which stands, in its variety of forms, as an obstacle to full experiencing and self-transcendence.

If the retrospective narrator of *Moby-Dick* presents an un-accustomed world, his account also records the version of self-transcendence which is defined by the course of Ishmael's active progress in the narrative from hope in the reality of such a won-der-world to faith in the truth of such a world discovered as *kairos* and symbol. The narrative opens, however, with Ish-mael's false starts into the watery groves of our Thessalies and the ways in which he overcomes these initial perils as he encoun-ters a variety of those abundant moments, which become the objects of his "gazing," and the spirit portended by them, which is the goal of his questing. These early encounters stand as pro-paedeutics, for their deep resonances teach him what will be necessary for his stance in relation to the great whale whose "island bulk"—whose "portentous and mysterious" aspect—makes it a symbol of the created order itself. In his metaphysical searching of the whale, the active Ishmael discovers both the limits on his epistemology and the real presence of the hidden God. Finally, in the attempt to possess the significance of his experience—by means of the narrative itself—Ishmael learns that life has, within its own keeping, a redemptive element for the man who has eyes for it, and in this he learns also how to transcend "the fine hammered steel of woe" (*M,* chap. 96).

I

As Ishmael prepares to embark on his "voyage of recovery," he runs immediately against two "perils in man" which stand as obstacles to the full experience of the wondrous—the temptation to mediate experience through secondhand authorities and the narcissistic impulse to project himself on his experience. The etymological account of the word *whale* and the extracts on the subject of the whale both precede the narrative proper and pres-ent—in coming to terms with the portentous whale—a hurdle to the direct encounter which enables the most integral response to the whale itself. As means for deciphering the mysterious riddle of the whale, the etymology points out the relativity of language, and the extracts suggest the ambiguity in relative human per-ceptions. Both figure as confidence-dissolving elements which leave the figure of the great whale even more arcane than before. In the face of such an enigmatic figurement—which was, Ishmael recalls, chief among his motives for going to sea—Ishmael inclines for a time to the second peril. When all meaning appears to be relative, when the possibility of objective knowledge seems lost, it is not surprising that knowledge, for Ishmael, comes to be understood as self-projection onto what is essentially indeterminate ground.[2] His gazing into the water reflects only his self-image: he can become Narcissus, "who because he could not grasp the tormenting, mild image he saw in the fountain, plunged into it and was drowned" (*M,* chap. 1). Ishmael himself finds in his water-gazing what seems to be "the ungraspable phantom of life," his own reflection, and thinks for a time that "this is the key to it all" (*M,* chap. 1). These perils, then, are also elements of the condition of the self, for each points toward an ambiguous reality, and the second, narcissism, represents a potentially self-destructive alternative in the face of such a reality. But Ishmael indicates in the first two chapters of *Moby-Dick* that he quickly surmounted each of these hurdles to his full experiencing.

Dealing with experience in a secondhand way is simply not an alternative for Ishmael. He tells the reader that he never goes to sea as a passenger who has the experience of the journey mediated by the crew of the ship but, rather, prefers to treat the voyage firsthand before the mast. With bluff tone, he jokes about his reasons for travelling as sailor and not as officer: "I always go to sea as a sailor, because of the wholesome exercise and pure air of the forecastle deck. For as in this world, head winds are far more prevalent than winds from astern (that is, if you never violate the Pythagorean maxim), so for the most part the Commodore on the quarter-deck gets his atmosphere at second hand from the sailors on the forecastle. He thinks he breathes it first; but not so. In much the same way do the commonalty lead their leaders in many other things, at the same time that the leaders little suspect it" (*M,* chap. 1). The maxim, of course, is to avoid eating beans which cause flatulence, but regardless of his reasons for wanting to be upwind, to meet the elements of the sea directly, he fulfills the necessity to "front" his life as the persona of "In a Bye-Canal" recalls having done. It was Henry Thoreau, of course, who fleshed out the notion of "fronting" a few years later in *Walden*. In a memorable passage about his motives, he wrote:

I went to the woods because I wished to live deliberately, to front only the essential facts of life, and see if I could not learn what it had to teach, and not, when I came to die, discover that I had not lived. I did not wish to live what was not life, living is so dear; nor did I wish to practise resignation, unless it was quite necessary. I wanted to live deep and suck out all the marrow of life, to live so sturdily and Spartan-like as to put to rout all that was not life, to cut a broad swath and shave close, to drive life into a corner, and reduce it to its lowest terms, and, if it proved to be mean, why then to get the whole and genuine meanness of it, and publish its meanness to the world; or if it were sublime, to know it by experience, and be able to give a true account of it in my next excursion.[3]

Ishmael is similarly, if more desperately, motivated. He has no choice in the matter; indeed the very disinheritance signalled by his name precludes his relying on anyone but himself to encounter and to possess the realm of his experience.

Ishmael as quickly eludes the second peril of narcissism. In his insistence on fronting his experience, the portentous whale becomes the paramount element to be encountered. His own self-image—reflected by the water, that which he thinks is the key to it all in the first chapter—presents him with the image of the "ungraspable phantom of life." By the third chapter, however, this ungraspable phantom is not his own image simply mirrored back to him; it is, rather, that which he discovers "in the unequal cross-lights" and within the "unaccountable masses of shades and shadows" of the painting in The Spouter-Inn:

But what most puzzled and confounded you was a long, limber, portentous, black mass of something hovering in the centre of the picture over three blue, dim, perpendicular lines floating in a nameless yeast. A boggy, soggy, squitchy picture truly, enough to drive a nervous man distracted. Yet was there a sort of indefinite, half-attained, unimaginable sublimity about it that fairly froze you to it, till you involuntarily took an oath with yourself to find out what that marvellous painting meant.

Ever and anon a bright, but, alas, deceptive idea would dart you through.—It's a Hyperborean winter scene.—It's the breaking-up of the ice-bound stream of Time. But at last all these fancies yielded to that one portentous something in the picture's midst. *That* once found out, and all the rest were plain. But stop; does it not bear a faint resemblance to a gigantic fish? even the great leviathan himself? (*M*, chap. 3)

It is at this point that Ishmael takes the oath "to find out what that marvellous painting meant" and that he begins to recognize that it will be plain only when he has once found out about great leviathan himself. The painting and that "something hovering in the centre" of it do not return to Ishmael only his own reflection; he fails to find himself in the picture and his projections onto the picture, his fancies, finally must yield to the recognition of the unknown and portentous other, the sublimity of which "fairly froze you to it." The whale itself portends the ungraspable phantom of life and toward the whale Ishmael directs his metaphysical energies. His temporary narcissism, like his momentary reliance on secondhand accounts, has been overcome: he needs to front the whale and to do so in a way which is alert to the whale's distinctive otherness.

Now, Ishmael will encounter other perils in man as the course of his voyaging continues, but, for a time at least, he has achieved the openness to encounters with the portentous which will enable him to embark on the watery wonder-world. Embark Ishmael *must*, for he soon learns in confronting the symbolic figurement of Bulkington's refusal of the lee shore that "all deep, earnest thinking is but the intrepid effort of the soul to keep the open independence of her sea" and that "in landlessness alone resides the highest truth, shoreless, indefinite as God" (*M*, chap. 23). It is better, Ishmael learns, to front "that howling infinite, than be ingloriously dashed upon the lee" (*M*, chap. 23). This is also one of the lessons Father Mapple extrapolates from his sermon on Jonah: one can refuse the whale only at the risk of being "swallowed up" by it. The second lesson, of course, is the one Ishmael has taken to heart in his telling of his tale: "'To preach the Truth to the face of Falsehood'" (*M*, chap. 9), a lesson commensurate with Melville's sense of the reformative document he wanted *Moby-Dick* to be. Embark Ishmael *can,* for he has been touched in his bosom by Queequeg in another of those strange, portentous moments:

As I sat there in that now lonely room; the fire burning low, in that mild stage when, after its first intensity has warmed the air, it then only glows to be looked at; the evening shades and phantoms gathering round the casements, and peering in upon us silent, solitary twain; the storm booming without in solemn swells; I began to be sensible of strange feelings. I felt a melting in me. No more my splintered heart and maddened hand were turned against the wolfish world. This soothing savage had redeemed it. There he sat, his very indifference speaking a nature in which there lurked no civilized hypocrisies and bland deceits. Wild he was; a very sight of sights to see; yet I began to feel myself mysteriously drawn towards him. And those same things that would have repelled most others, they were the very magnets that thus drew me. (M, chap. 10)

Ishmael begins to learn the reasons of the heart in the embrace of this "savage," begins to develop the receptivity to wonder which reason cannot completely fathom, and begins to find a principle of redemption within the precincts of experience. He sets sail aboard the *Pequod* on Christmas day in his pursuit of a new life, and he hears in Bildad's song, as they approach the "wintry ocean," words of "hope and fruition": "Never did those sweet words sound more sweetly to me than then. They were full of hope and fruition. Spite of this frigid winter night in the boisterous Atlantic, spite of my wet feet and wetter jacket, there was yet, it then seemed to me, many a pleasant haven in store; and meads and glades so eternally vernal, that the grass shot up by the spring, untrodden, unwilted, remains at midsummer" (M, chap. 22). When he is "boldly launched upon the deep" and "lost in its unshored, harborless immensities," (M, chap. 32) Ishmael will realize that the wonder-world is not only a "pleasant haven" in "midsummer" but the world as *kairos* and symbol, and he will learn in the face of these oceanic revelations to prepare for the promise and demand of the whale.

Receptive to wonder, Ishmael finds that portents of the transcendent come frequently and vibrantly in the course of the ordinary duration of time and profoundly displace that time. As he stands his dutiful and mundane round on the masthead, as he details its construction, history, lack of convenience, and so on, he finds himself living through a plenary moment, fecund with a symbolism which alludes to another dimension and with which he is allowed a glimpse into the heart of being itself:

Lulled into such an opium-like listlessness of vacant, unconscious reverie is this absent-minded youth by the blending cadence of waves with thoughts, that at last he loses his identity; takes the mystic ocean at his feet for the visible image of that deep, blue, bottomless soul, pervading mankind and nature; and every strange, half-seen, gliding, beautiful thing that eludes him; every dimly-discovered, uprising fin of some undiscernible form, seems to him the embodiment of those elusive thoughts that only people the soul by continually flitting through it. In this enchanted mood, thy spirit ebbs away to whence it came; becomes diffused through time and space; like Wickliff's sprinkled Pantheistic ashes, forming at last a part of every shore the round globe over.

There is no life in thee, now, except that rocking life imparted by a gently rolling ship; by her, borrowed from the sea; by the sea, from the inscrutable tides of God. But while this sleep, this dream is on ye, move your foot or hand an inch; slip your hold at all; and your identity comes back in horror. Over Descartian vortices you hover. And perhaps, at mid-day, in the fairest weather, with one half-throttled shriek you drop through that transparent air into the summer sea, no more to rise for ever. Heed it well, ye Pantheists! (*M*, chap. 35)

In this instance, erupting out of the stuff of chronological time, the signals of the presence of the transcendent appear in a form which commingles rapture and horror, which at once promise a blending with being, threaten to annihilate human being, and return "your identity . . . back in horror."

Later in the narrative, the habitual passage of time is again displaced by a period which is abundant with spirit and which, again, fills the heart with dread: after "days, weeks passed, and under easy sail, the ivory Pequod had slowly swept across four several cruising-grounds," the ship enters an area of wonder, there allured by "The Spirit-Spout": "It was while gliding through these latter waters that one serene and moonlight night, when all the waves rolled by like scrolls of silver; and, by their soft, suffusing seethings, made what seemed a silvery silence, not a solitude: on such a silent night a silvery jet was seen far in advance of the white bubbles at the bow. Lit up by the moon, it looked celestial; seemed some plumed and glittering god uprising from the sea" (*M*, chap. 51). But the "flitting apparition" disappears as quickly as it had come—"the silvery jet was no more seen that night" and "every sailor swore he saw it once, but not a second time" (*M*, chap. 51)—and ordinary time resumes, only again to be displaced:

This midnight-spout had almost grown a forgotten thing, when, some days after, lo! at the same silent hour, it was again announced: again it was descried by all; but upon making sail to overtake it, once more it disappeared as if it had never been. And so it served us night after night, till no one heeded it but to wonder at it. Mysteriously jetted into the clear moonlight, or starlight, as the case might be; disappearing again for one whole day, or two days, or three; and somehow seeming at every distinct repetition to be advancing still further and further in our van, this solitary jet seemed for ever alluring us on. (*M*, chap. 51)

The alluring aspect, however, also evokes "a sense of peculiar dread . . . as if it were treacherously beckoning us on and on" in order to "rend us at last in the remotest and most savage seas" (*M*, chap. 51). Indeed, "the Cape winds began howling around us, and we rose ànd fell upon the long, troubled seas . . . [and] sharply bowed to the blast, and gored the dark waves." The spirit-spout presides over the period—"calm, snow-white, and unvarying; still directing its fountain of feathers to the sky; still beckoning us on from before, the solitary jet would at times be descried" (*M*, chap. 51). Here, then, Ishmael is presented with a time with its own special and self-contained periodicity, pregnant with its own resonance and implications. It is a time which supersedes his ability to devise it or even to evoke; he can neither create nor fully contain it. It is both disclosive and furtive, and he can only receive it and attempt to place himself in relation to it.

Such portentous moments do not always present themselves in dread guise to Ishmael's experience, however, for they come intermittently in forms which give rise to ecstasy and peace. Spotting and pursuing a nation of whales herding together, Ishmael finds his low boat pulled into the innermost of the concentric circles they have formed, wherein are kept the cows and calves of the herd:

These smaller whales—now and then visiting our becalmed boat from the margin of the lake—evinced a wondrous fearlessness and confidence, or else a still, becharmed panic which it was impossible not to marvel at. Like household dogs they came snuffling round us, right up to our gunwales, and touching them; till it almost seemed that some spell had suddenly domesticated them. Queequeg patted their foreheads; Starbuck scratched their backs with his lance; but fearful of the consequences, for the time refrained from darting it.

But far beneath this wondrous world upon the surface, another and still stranger world met our eyes as we gazed over the side. For, suspended in those watery vaults, floated the forms of the nursing mothers of the whales, and those that by their enormous girth seemed shortly to become mothers. The lake, as I have hinted, was to a considerable depth exceedingly transparent; and as human infants while suckling will calmly and fixedly gaze away from the breast, as if leading two different lives at the time; and while yet drawing mortal nourishment, be still spiritually feasting upon some unearthly reminiscence;—even so did the young of these whales seem looking up towards us, but not at us, as if we were but a bit of Gulf-weed in their new-born sight. (M, chap. 87)

The moment, like the water of this central lake, is "exceedingly transparent," for in it the finite augurs a glimpse of the infinite: "another and still stranger world" is in part disclosed in the figurement of the newborn, "still spiritually feasting upon some unearthly reminiscence," not yet completely severed from that world into which they gaze. Ishmael realizes that, paradoxically, the world of frights and fears also contains peace and bliss, "as if from some mountain torrent we had slid into a serene valley lake" (M, chap. 87).

Further, in this moment, he says, "some of the subtlest secrets of the seas seemed divulged to us in this enchanted pond. We saw young Leviathan amours in the deep." This instance, instinct with significance like the moment on the masthead, also gives him something of himself: "And thus, though surrounded by circle upon circle of consternations and affrights, did these inscrutable creatures at the centre freely and fearlessly indulge in all peaceful concernments; yea, serenely revelled in dalliance and delight. But even so, amid the tornadoed Atlantic of my being, do I myself still for ever centrally disport in mute calm; and while ponderous planets of unwaning woe revolve round me, deep down and deep inland there I still bathe me in eternal mildness of joy" (*M,* chap. 87). Such moments, and the allusiveness they bear, are induplicable and impermanent, Ishmael has discovered; they contain and portend an uncanny element, and yet, as they converge on the life of man, they throw light all around, creating their own magnetism and demanding a wonderment appropriate for the transcendent dimension which imbues them. Such a distinctively religious view of time is also dramatized in Henry Thoreau's poem "Within the Circuit of This Plodding Life" (1842) as the persona articulates his sense of some "moments of an azure hue" which, for a time, displace plodding, mundane, ordinary time and stand as their "own memorial." He recalls, among others, "How in the shimmering noon of summer past / Some unrecorded beam slanted across / The upland pastures where the Johnswort grew," and he realizes that, "by God's cheap economy made rich," the world discloses itself in such moments of abundance. As Giles Gunn has written in another context, moments such as these make it possible "to recover a sense of that radiance which temporarily redeems life even as the flow of life itself bears it away."[4]

Now, these luminous moments occur over and over again in *Moby-Dick,* and they both enable Ishmael to work through to a faith in the reality of the wonder-world and prepare him, though not in any consecutive way, to approach the great whale which is the paradigmatic symbol of such a world. From the frequent portents, he has learned by the time of his retrospective account that he can depend on the creation to appear to him in portentous form, as *kairos* and symbol, but he has learned as well that such a world is radically contingent because, although anything may become a vessel of the transcendent, the vessels themselves are not holy. He has discovered that, while the portents fade, their momentary presence has a commanding aspect which he cannot refuse. He has found that the forms of such presence can evoke in him feelings which range from dread and horror to rapture and peace, that such presence is wholly other than the human and does not necessarily come in images which satisfy the human senses of mercy and compassion. The fact that the portents in *Moby-Dick* occasion, at times, feelings of fear and dread only makes Ishmael's responses concordant with the aspect of the *tremendum* present in these instances. As Rudolf Otto writes, the manifestations of the holy never completely lose the element of "awe-fulness" and sublimity and the human encounter with this attribute can result in a deep shudder, as the soul, "held speechless, trembles inwardly to the farthest fibre of its being."[5] Nonetheless, Ishmael has recognized that despite their profound otherness, which might at times call his being into question or might threaten to annihilate him, these revelatory moments can give him back his essential being by enabling him to situate himself more fully in relation with the mysterious contours of this transcendent dimension. In order for this relation to occur, he must, in short, respect the integrity of the other, must maintain his essential self, and must bring the two into full encounter by the interpretation of symbols. This is the function of symbolism, as Paul Ricoeur describes it, when the "symbol gives reason to think that the *Cogito* is within being, and not vice versa." He writes: "Every symbol is finally a hierophany, a manifestation of the bond between man and the sacred. Now in treating the symbol as a simple revealer of self-awareness, we cut it off from its ontological function; we pretend to believe that 'know thyself' is purely reflexive, whereas it is first of all an appeal by which each man is invited to situate himself better in being—in Greek terms, to 'be wise.'"[6] And thus, Ricoeur suggests, "the symbol gives rise to thought"; thought, or interpretation, allows one to situate himself deeper in being, and this wisdom calls for a "second naiveté" in the sense that the thinking self discovers that its thinking does not make it "cease to share in the being that challenges it in every symbol."[7] Melville recognized this function of the symbol and its possibilities of a reconciliation with being, for certainly Ishmael will achieve such a "second naiveté" after thoughtful interpretation of the symbolic world which everywhere encompasses him. The lesson will be taught to Ishmael by the encompassing wonder-world through which he moves and will be confirmed when he engages and attempts to decipher the whale. Indeed, that portentous and mysterious monster will teach him further lessons still.

II

From first to last, Ishmael's narrative seeks to possess the significance of the whale, for, in order to decipher the "marvellous painting," the object toward which he "involuntarily took an oath," he must grasp "that one portentous something in the picture's midst," for "*that* once found out, and all the rest were plain" (*M*, chap. 1). He bends all his energies to the scrutiny of the whale and entertains all the varieties of inquiry which, cumulatively, he thinks will illumine the phantom of life by explicating that which resides at its center. The etymological tracings and the extracts which precede the narrative stand as the mode of inquiry which will give him understanding of what others have done by way of understanding the whale, and the cetology he rehearses is added to this as an attempt to decode the creature in "some systematized exhibition of the whale in his broad genera" by citing what "the best and latest authorities have laid down" (*M*, chap. 32). All of these forms of scientific inquiry— linguistic, bibliographical, and naturalist—are finally failures, "the classification of the constituents of a chaos," and he must finally own, with one of the authorities he quotes, that there is an "'impenetrable veil covering our knowledge of the cetacea'" (*M*, chap. 32). These intellectual, academic assaults on the whale, however, come "ere the Pequod's weedy hull rolls side by side with the barnacled hulls of the leviathan" (*M*, chap. 32). Before the direct encounter with any whale, before "the first lowering" (*M*, chap. 48), Ishmael is introduced to the idea of the whale of whales, Moby Dick, the figurement of which will finally present to him the paradigmatic symbol of the created order. He is pulled toward the moment of this presentation, and for the

response to that moment, all his "whale-hunting"—all his inquiries into the whale—will prepare him.

From the moment of his encounter with the "marvellous
painting" in which the whale presents itself to him as the paramount figurement of the wonder-world, and especially after "the
first lowering" which is "a sight full of quick wonder and awe"
(*M,* chap. 48), Ishmael attempts to survey the whale and all—
the spirit-spout, the doubloon, the ambergris, the brit—that
seems to refer to it. He inquires into the "monstrous pictures of
whales" (*M,* chap. 55), into the "less erroneous pictures of
whales" (*M,* chap. 56), and into what seem to his sense of things
to be "the true pictures of whaling scenes" (*M,* chap. 56). He
assays "whales in paint; in teeth; in wood; in sheet-iron; in
stone; in mountains; in stars" (*M,* chap. 57). Each of these attempts, however, takes him away from the whale—into folklore,
into scholarship, into art, into astrology—in the sense at least
that, with these methods, he cannot front the whale in its proper
element, the great seas of life. And, thus, he begins more fully to
employ his senses in his grappling with the idea of the whale as
he discusses "the whale as a dish" (*M,* chap. 65) for Stubb and
for the sharks (*M,* chap. 66). Finally, he turns his attention to the
whale proper with discussion of "that not unvexed subject, the
skin of the whale" (*M,* chap. 68), the Sphynx-like head of
the whale (*M,* chap. 70), in its contrasted views and double vision (*M,* chaps. 74 and 75). In these discussions, Ishmael plies
the methods of physiology, and in succeeding chapters (77–80)
in which he explores the face, skull, and brain of the whale, he
employs the phrenological method which requires a figurative
neural and spinal surgery. As the course of the narrative journey
continues, Ishmael successively seeks to "dissect" the whale in
order to uncover the source of his spouting—"the fountain"—
in the "remarkable involved Cretan labyrinth" (*M,* chap. 85) of
the heart and lungs and in order to explain "the sole means of
propulsion"—"the tail"—and the "great motions . . . peculiar
to it" (*M,* chap. 86). When he turns to the life and habits of the
whale, Ishmael involves himself in dissertations on "leviathan
amours" (*M,* chap. 87), the social covenant of the whale (*M,*
chap. 87), the whale as "school-master" (*M,* chap. 88), the cul-

tural condition of the whale in the face of the whaling industry (*M*, chaps. 89 and 90), the social uses of the whale's ambergris, "a very curious substance" (*M*, chap. 92), the sperm, "that inexpressible sperm" (*M*, chap. 94), and the more frivolous uses of the whale's penis (*M*, chap. 95). Having "chiefly dwelt upon the marvels of his outer aspect . . . [or] upon some few interior structural features," Ishmael has the opportunity in "a bower in the Arsacides" to study the whale "in his ultimatum; that is to say, in his unconditional skeleton" (*M*, chap. 102), and there he attempts a "measurement of the whale's skeleton" (*M*, chap. 103). The anatomical research of the bones of the whale leads Ishmael, in turn, to consider the geological remains of "the fossil whale" (*M*, chap. 104), which themselves force him to ponder the generation of the whale species. "Does the whale diminish?" Ishmael asks himself; "will he perish?" (*M*, chap. 105). He has seen "the dying whale" (*M*, chap. 116), but the generic whale, Ishmael must conclude, must be considered "immortal in his species, however perishable in his individuality" (*M*, chap. 105): "this Leviathan comes floundering down upon us from the headwaters of the Eternities" and "the eternal whale will still survive" (*M*, chap. 105) when the generations of man have passed. Utilizing every method at its disposal, then, Ishmael's rationality has inquired into the whale's external and internal aspect and has followed the whale from birth in "The Grand Armada" to his "perishable individuality" in "The Dying Whale." He has aimed at a "thorough sweeping comprehension" (*M*, chap. 102) of the whale; and it is perhaps no accident that the chapter at the very center of the book is entitled "Cutting in" (*M*, chap. 67). But for all his rational inquiry, Ishmael finally reaches the nonrational conclusion that the whale is eternal, that it cannot be fathomed by reason, that he cannot "contain" the whale.

The conclusion of his rational inquiries—the discovery by way of his reasoning of the limits of reason—is not the end of the matter, for, concurrent with his more or less systematic and analytical inquiries into the whale, Ishmael has developed a progressive imagination of the whale as the paradigmatic element of the wonder-world to which the transcendent is episodically and symbolically present. In virtually every rational encounter with the whale, Ishmael finds in it that which is allusive of a dimension overreaching its concrete and palpable form and yet adhering to that form. In this portentousness both the revelation and the concealment, the high speech and inestimable silence, belong to the manifestation of the holy. In these manifestations Ishmael recognizes that which, if it cannot be contained, cannot at all be refused in its implications for his life. As he and Queequeg "were mildly employed weaving what is called a sword-mat" and as Ishmael finds the workings of this "Loom of Time" (*M*, chap. 47) a source for his metaphysical speculations, as it implies the interweaving of necessity and free will, the entire speculation must be dropped because of the cry of the whale. The moment of the first lowering—of Ishmael's first direct encounter with the whale—surpasses all else in its demand as symbol. The ultimatum of the whale is that of direct encounter, not of perusing his "unconditional skeleton." After he has measured the skeleton of the whale, Ishmael has owned: "How vain and foolish, then, thought I, for timid untravelled man to try to comprehend aright this wondrous whale, by merely poring over his dead attenuated skeleton, stretched in this peaceful wood. No. Only in the heart of quickest perils; only when within the eddyings of his angry flukes; only on the profound unbounded sea, can the fully invested whale be truly and livingly found out" (*M*, chap. 103). Having vowed in the third chapter to "find out" the whale, then, Ishmael must take the span of the whale's portentousness by swimming "'Twixt the whale's black flukes." The wonder of the whale has awakened in Ishmael surmise as to its origin, and it is to the origin of its symbolic figurement that he wants to trace it.

From his first direct fronting of the whale in his proper element, however, Ishmael begins to suspect that, scientific inquiry having everywhere brought him to the conclusion that the whale is allusive of the eternal, he must approach the whale with eyes prepared for the whale's inherent symbolism. He must develop a special sort of vision:

To a landsman, no whale, nor any sign of a herring, would have been visible at that moment; nothing but a troubled bit of greenish white water, and thin scattered puffs of vapor hovering over it, and suffusingly blowing off to leeward, like the confused scud from white rolling billows. The air around suddenly vibrated and tingled, as it were, like the air over intensely heated plates of iron. Beneath this atmospheric waving and curling, and partially beneath a thin layer of water, also, the whales were swimming. Seen in advance of all the other indications, the puffs of vapor they spouted, seemed their forerunning couriers and detached flying outriders. (M, chap. 48)

Here, during "The First Lowering," Ishmael's initial encounter with the whale in the midst of "the profound unbounded sea" presents him with the elusiveness of the whale and with the hazardous aspect of "the vast swells of the omnipotent sea" (M, chap. 48). After this beginning, with all its luminous atmosphere which "vibrated and tingled," he confirms that the whale inhabits the center of the wonder-world within which he must ply reasons of the heart: "Not the raw recruit, marching from the bosom of his wife into the fever heat of his first battle; not the dead man's ghost encountering the first unknown phantom of the other world;—neither of these can feel stranger and stronger emotions than that man does, who for the first time finds himself pulling into the charmed, churned circle of the hunted sperm whale" (M, chap. 48). In the course of the narrative which follows from this first encounter, the whale will intermittently present to Ishmael moments to be encountered as *kairos* and symbol, and the nascent responses to the whale which he experiences in this, his first, encounter will grow until his recovery of the transcendent is complete.

In each encounter with the whale, Ishmael recognizes, after the assays of rational inquiry have run their course, that the whale, the singular grand analogue, the wonder-world itself, portends the transcendent. When he contemplates "The Great Heidelberg Tun of the Sperm Whale," he sees that "as that famous great tierce is mystically carved in front, so the whale's vast plaited forehead forms innumerable strange devices for the emblematical adornment of the whale's fluids." The great tun becomes, for Ishmael, "the secret inner chamber or sanctum sanctorum of the whale" (M, chap. 78). When he muses on the spouting of the whale—his fountain—Ishmael again finds the presaging aspect which brims over with the presence of the transcendent:

And how nobly it raises our conceit of the mighty, misty monster, to behold him solemnly sailing through a calm tropical sea; his vast, mild head overhung by a canopy of vapor, engendered by his incommunicable contemplations, and that vapor—as you will sometimes see it— glorified by a rainbow, as if Heaven itself had put its seal upon his thoughts. For, d'ye see, rainbows do not visit the clear air; they only irradiate vapor. And so, through all the thick mists of the dim doubts in my mind, divine intuitions now and then shoot, enkindling my fog with a heavenly ray. And for this I thank God; for all have doubts; many deny; but doubts or denials, few along with them, have intuitions. Doubts of all things earthly, and intuitions of some things heavenly; this combination makes neither believer nor infidel, but makes a man who regards them both with equal eye. (*M*, chap. 85)

He continues to develop his "intuitions of some things heavenly" when he encounters both the "graceful flexion" and the "Titanism of Power" which are disclosed in the whale's mighty tail:

Excepting the sublime *breach*—somewhere else to be described—this peaking of the whale's flukes is perhaps the grandest sight to be seen in all animated nature. Out of the bottomless profundities the gigantic tail seems spasmodically snatching at the highest heaven. So in dreams, have I seen majestic Satan thrusting forth his tormented colossal claw from the flame Baltic of Hell. But in gazing at such scenes, it is all in all what mood you are in; if in the Dantean, the devils will occur to you; if in that of Isaiah, the arch-angels. Standing at the mast-head of my ship during a sunrise that crimsoned sky and sea, I once saw a large herd of whales in the east, all heading towards the sun, and for a moment vibrating in concert with peaked flukes. As it seemed to me at the time, such a grand embodiment of adoration of the gods was never beheld, even in Persia, the home of the fire worshippers. (*M*, chap. 86)

In these and other instances, then, Ishmael discovers the uncanny revelations of the wholly other in his experience, for the symbolic vestigium of the whale gives off mystic references, transcendent allusions, signals of another world. The whale is revelatory, and Ishmael has eyes for such a symbol, instinct with significance. As a singular symbol of the wonder-world, the whale, like that unfettered and charged world, signals the hand of the creator, as Ishmael suggests after his scrutiny of the "sublime" brow of the whale:

Few are the foreheads which like Shakspeare's [sic] or Melancthon's rise so high, and descend so low, that the eyes themselves seem clear, eternal, tideless mountain lakes; and all above them in the forehead's wrinkles, you seem to track the antlered thoughts descending there to drink, as the Highland hunters track the snow prints of the deer. But in the great Sperm Whale, this high and mighty god-like dignity inherent in the brow is so immensely amplified, that gazing on it, in that full front view, you feel the Deity and the dread powers more forcibly than in beholding any other object in living nature. For you see no one point precisely; not one distinct feature is revealed; no nose, eyes, ears, or mouth; no face; he has none, proper; nothing but that one broad firmament of a forehead, pleated with riddles. (M, chap. 79)

If in profile the forehead's "grandeur does not domineer upon you so," nor "does this wondrous brow diminish" (M, chap. 79). When fronted, however, this "mystical brow," for Ishmael, "signifies—'God: done this day by my hand'" (M, chap. 79). Bearing the signature of the transcendent, then, the world is revelatory: it contains, and discloses, in the midst of the world of human experience, the momentary but continuing portentousness of the ground of all experience in and through what Carlyle called "the wondrous agency of symbols."

If the whale reveals as a symbol, however, it also conceals as a symbol; the concrete realm may present signals of the presence of the wholly other but such signals—looming through finite forms—can never fully manifest the transcendent, as Ishmael learns in his reflections on the symbolism of the whale. The "Heidelberg Tun" of the whale might present to his contemplations a mystical and emblematic aspect, but the interiority of the whale's tun—its "sanctum sanctorum" (M, chap. 78)—can only be entered, as in the case of Tashtego's falling there, at the risk of perishing. The fountain of the whale, revelatory as it is in "enkindling my fog with a heavenly ray," presents, finally, only "incommunicable contemplations"—a vapor which recedes almost at the moment of its appearance (M, chap. 85): "And as for this whale's spout," he must finally allow, "you might almost stand in it, and yet be undecided as to what it is precisely" (*M,* chap. 85). Again, although the whale's tail discloses itself in gestures "snatching at the highest heaven," Ishmael cannot explain its meaning:

The more I consider this mighty tail, the more do I deplore my inability to express it. At times there are gestures in it, which, though they would well grace the hand of man, remain wholly inexplicable. In an extensive herd, so remarkable, occasionally, are these mystic gestures, that I have heard hunters who have declared them akin to Free-Mason signs and symbols; that the whale, indeed, by these methods intelligently conversed with the world. Nor are there wanting other motions of the whale in his general body, full of strangeness, and unaccountable to his most experienced assailant. Dissect him how I may, then, I but go skin deep; I know him not, and never will. But if I know not even the tail of this whale, how understand his head? much more, how comprehend his face, when face he has none? Thou shalt see my back parts, my tail, he seems to say, but my face shall not be seen. But I cannot completely make out his back parts; and hint what he will about his face, I say again he has no face. (*M,* chap. 86)

Unable to "dissect" the tail completely in order to fathom the ultimate meaning of its disclosures, he cannot either "read" the final character and motive of the whale's brow. Although that brow signifies God, Ishmael's attempts to contain it are failures: "for you see no one point precisely; not one distinct feature is revealed; no nose, eyes, ears, or mouth; no face; he has none, proper; nothing but that one broad firmament of a forehead, pleated with riddles" (*M,* chap. 79). Without obtaining an answer, he is left with a rhetorical question—"how may unlettered Ishmael hope to read the awful Chaldee of the Sperm Whale's brow?" (*M,* chap. 79)—the answer to which is that no amount of tutoring will enable such a reading. The whale does not appear to him after the images of the human; it has no face which will mirror back a recognizable and apprehensible form: it comes to Ishmael, rather, only as a "broad firmament"—as that which is nonhuman and which presents the wholly other in its dense and opaque and finally furtive reality. Ishmael's encounter with the hidden God is strongly reminiscent of the poem by

Emily Dickinson beginning "My period had come for Prayer" (c. 1862) as the persona finds that her artful "tactics" of prayer fail to recover for her the "Creator." She searches for this rudiment among the domestic images familiar to her—a house, a chimney, a door—only to find herself confronted with "Vast Prairies of Air / Unbroken by a Settler" which are equivalent to the "broad firmament" Ishmael finds on the whale's brow. Just as Ishmael declares then that the whale "has no face," the persona of the Dickinson poem asks "Infinitude—Had'st Thou no Face / That I might look on Thee?" Finally, she discovers in the midst of the vast, silent creation that she is "awed beyond my errand" and that she "worshipped—did not 'pray.'" Ishmael, too, will learn that in the "Afric Temple of the Whale" his tactics are not sufficient. Although the whale portends the presence of the transcendent, it also leaves Ishmael with the intractable reality of the hidden transcendent.

III

Understood in this way, then, Ishmael follows a course of inquiry with respect to the whale—and the mysterious world it symbolizes—which finally ends without his having penetrated to its final meaning. He begins with a rationality which seeks a "thorough and sweeping comprehension" (*M*, chap. 102) of the whale, but this form of inquiry fails him when it broaches on the whale as symbol. He then plies the reasons of the heart to find the truth of the symbols, but this method also fails him, for although he locates revelation in symbols he discovers concealment as well. The whale might allude, in abundant moments, to the transcendent, but the allusion is finally a riddle which hides its transcendent source:

In life, the visible surface of the Sperm Whale is not the least among the many marvels he presents. Almost invariably it is all over obliquely crossed and re-crossed with numberless straight marks in thick array, something like those in the finest Italian line engravings. But these marks do not seem to be impressed upon the isinglass substance above mentioned, but seem to be seen through it, as if they were engraved on the body itself. Nor is this all. In some instances, to the quick, observant eye, those linear marks, as in a veritable engraving, but afford the ground for far other delineations. These are hieroglyphical; that is, if you call those mysterious cyphers on the walls of pyramids hiero-glyphics, then that is the proper word to use in the present connexion. By my retentive memory of the hieroglyphics upon one Sperm Whale in particular, I was much struck with a plate representing the old Indian characters chiselled on the famous hieroglyphic palisades on the banks of the Upper Mississippi. Like those mystic rocks, too, the mystic-marked whale remains undecipherable. (M, chap. 68)

Inquire how he will—by way of rationality or by way of the imagination of symbol—Ishmael's inquiries end in, are pre-vented by, the opaque character of the symbols themselves: he is left facing the hieroglyphic whale—the riddle of the wonder-world—with all its immense and fecund, but finally clouded, presentations of itself. He can front the whale, but what he finds there are the "mysterious cyphers" of a transcendent presence. He has confirmed what he had earlier suspected:

For all these reasons, then, any way you may look at it, you must needs conclude that the great Leviathan is that one creature in the world which must remain unpainted to the last. True, one portrait may hit the mark much nearer than another, but none can hit it with any very con-siderable degree of exactness. So there is no earthly way of finding out precisely what the whale really looks like. And the only mode in which you can derive even a tolerable idea of his living contour, is by going a whaling yourself; but by so doing, you run no small risk of being eter-nally stove and sunk by him. Wherefore, it seems to me you had best not be too fastidious in your curiosity touching this Leviathan. (M, chap. 55)

These reflections suggest both the necessity of the direct encoun-ter with the marvelous aspect of the whale and the idea of the dread power of the whale as a portent of the transcendent which retains the *mysterium* and *tremendum* belonging to the wholly other. Since the whale figures forth the created order itself, Ishmael has learned that he must acknowledge the radical other-ness of the transcendent dimension which looms up in his expe-rience, must admit finally that the ground of experience will "remain unpainted to the last." A portrait of the whale is impos-sible because "I say again he has no face" (M, chap. 86).

The reasons of the heart do not end here, however, for, despite the ambiguity of the whale's revelations and despite Ishmael's inability to penetrate to the final character of the transcendent ground of the wonder-world, he has touched upon the dimension of ultimacy in his experience and in this has recovered the sense of the transcendent which animated his searching. What was at stake for him, from the outset, was not the solution to the final character and motive of the transcendent. What he sought, rather, was the truth of the human heart, and he bottoms upon that truth only after he has traced his initial wonderment to its source and, there, has encountered the whale which signifies God. After touching on the source of wonder, even if he cannot decode its riddles, he returns to the world to find wonder manifest everywhere. And this is the meaning of the transcendent for Ishmael: although he cannot fully know the transcendent, he knows that it enables his self-transcendence by presenting him with a world brimming with spiritual resonance, a world touched by wonder, a world containing the possibility for him to conceive his life within the mixed shades and shadows of ultimacy. The epistemological dilemma he confronts in the whale does not end in despair: if there is concealment, there is revelation. The issue of knowing, rather, returns him, by the reasons of the heart, to the world of the human, redeemed by wonder. In attempting to seize the precious fluids of the whale, he receives "a squeeze of the hand":

I squeezed that sperm till a strange sort of insanity came over me; and I found myself unwittingly squeezing my co-laborers' hands in it, mistaking their hands for the gentle globules. Such an abounding, affectionate, friendly, loving feeling did this avocation beget; that at last I was continually squeezing their hands, and looking up into their eyes sentimentally; as much as to say,—Oh! my dear fellow beings, why should we longer cherish any social acerbities, or know the slightest ill-humor or envy! Come; let us squeeze hands all round; nay, let us all squeeze ourselves into each other; let us squeeze ourselves universally into the very milk and sperm of kindness.

Would that I could keep squeezing that sperm for ever! For now, since by many prolonged, repeated experiences, I have perceived that in all cases man must eventually lower, or at least shift, his conceit of attainable felicity; not placing it anywhere in the intellect or the fancy; but in the wife, the heart, the bed, the table, the saddle, the fire-side, the country; now that I have perceived all this, I am ready to squeeze case eternally. In visions of the night, I saw long rows of angels in paradise, each with his hands in a jar of spermaceti. (*M,* chap. 94)

If his "attainable felicity" had been centered for a time around the final explication of the character and meaning of the transcendent, if he has craved that truth, Ishmael has proved that he craves the human even more. His epistemological dilemma in the face of the inviolably hidden transcendent reaches its denouement in his reconciliation with the world of his living. Had he not undertaken his inquiries and had he not encountered the real presence of the hidden God, he might have returned to the world of "the table, the saddle, the fire-side" without any sense of its wonder. Having discovered such a presence, he can find all his experience charged and resonant and instinct with significance.

The shift of "his conceit of attainable felicity," then, represents to Ishmael not an end in despair but a beginning in piety. He has encountered the whale which stands symbolically at the center of the creation, and he has seen that, although the whale and the creation must remain unsolved to the last, the creation is plenteous, that it contains those radiant moments, abundant with spirit, which are redemptive. As a figure for the wonder-world, with its transcendent allusiveness and profundity, the whale evokes from Ishmael a *sursum corda;* after attempting to measure the whale, after the failure to decipher its hieroglyph, and after "the squeeze of the hand," he encounters "the fossil whale"—the whale as old as the earth, built into and preserved in the very terrain of the earth—and "in this Afric Temple of the Whale I leave you, reader, and if you be a Nantucketer, and a whaleman, you will silently worship there" (*M,* chap. 104).

Thus, in the figure and career of Ishmael, Melville plots the integral response to a world freighted with significances of a spiritual presence, and this response issues in the deepest kind of reconciliation with the terms of experience. Ishmael had been committed, from early in his questing, to seek out an exhilarated world and to explore its resonances in relation to the tangled web at the center of his own heart. The final implications of his humanity, he senses, can only be settled in the context of, and in an authentic response to, that encompassing symbolic world which rises up around him. In the process implied by taking the span of portents—that is, in the process of expecting a full-freighted world, of discovering in it portents of a transcendent dimension, of scrutinizing the contours of these portents, and of possessing their significance for his life—Ishmael learns of the last complications of human life, learns of the revelatory, but ultimately opaque, character of life in history, and learns that his mortal condition derives its own significance only in an integral response to the immense mystery which is intermittently present to him.

Because he understands the objects and activities of common life to be endowed, episodically, with resonances of a transcendent factor, because he is convinced that "some certain significance lurks in all things," Ishmael enters the exhilarated world of *Moby-Dick* with expectancy and receptivity. Having suffered the experience of the *Pequod,* having encountered before the mast and "boldly launched upon the deep" the "unshored, harborless immensities" (*M,* chap. 32) of the mysterious creation, he tells his tale retrospectively, attempting to rehearse those moments instinct with significance which loomed up before him. He goes to sea, he remembers, in order to surmount the "damp, drizzly November of my soul" (*M,* chap. 1) by discovering the world which awaits him once embarked on that watery element. This expectant entry into the realm of spirit, his passage through the flood-gates of the wonder-world, had been his "substitute for pistol and ball" in the senses both that it staved off the suicidal woe hemming his life and that he anticipated gaining from it the vision of a new life. Later in the book, as Ishmael muses about the blacksmith, who likewise "went a-whaling" to shake off his mortal despair, he describes his own escape from his initial situation of "pausing before coffin warehouses, and bringing up the rear of every funeral" (*M,* chap. 1):

Death seems the only desirable sequel for a career like this; but Death is only a launching into the region of the strange Untried; it is but the first salutation to the possibilities of the immense Remote, the Wild, the Watery, the Unshored; therefore, to the death-longing eyes of such men, who still have left in them some interior compunctions against suicide, does the all-contributed and all-receptive ocean alluringly spread forth his whole plain of unimaginable, taking terrors, and wonderful, new-life adventures; and from the hearts of infinite Pacifics, the thousand mermaids sing to them—"Come hither, broken-hearted; here is another life without the guilt of intermediate death; here are wonders supernatural, without dying for them. Come hither! bury thyself in a life which, to your now equally abhorred and abhorring, landed world, is more oblivious than death. Come hither!" (*M,* chap. 112)

The allurements of the "immense Remote" in "the hearts of infinite Pacifics" beckon to the man who yearns for the presence of spirit in his life, and the hope that this area of "new-life adventures" was abundant with "wonders supernatural" had animated Ishmael's attempt to escape the condition which finds him "growing grim about the mouth" (*M,* chap. 1) as the result of some nameless woe.

Although he anticipates a full-freighted and charged world, Ishmael never fails to be astonished and awed when he discovers, intermittently, the prodigious manifestation of the holy in the orbit of human experience. Although the numinous stirrings create in him feelings which range from rapture and ecstasy to repulsion and dread, he approaches these profound moments with a piety commensurate with the existence of the wholly other portended in them. Even his familiar friend Queequeg can suddenly become the element through which the transcendent dimension looms, for in seeing "Queequeg in His Coffin" Ishmael senses the reaches of infinity and responds with reverence:

How he wasted and wasted away in those few long-lingering days, till there seemed but little left of him but his frame and tatooing. But as all else in him thinned, and his cheekbones grew sharper, his eyes, nevertheless, seemed growing fuller and fuller; they became of a strange softness of lustre; and mildly but deeply looked out at you there from his sickness, a wondrous testimony to that immortal health in him which could not die, or be weakened. And like circles on the water, which, as they grow fainter, expand; so his eyes seemed rounding and rounding, like the rings of Eternity. An awe that cannot be named would steal over you as you sat by the side of this waning savage, and saw as strange things in his face, as any beheld who were bystanders when Zoroaster died . . . So that—let us say it again—no dying Chaldee or Greek had higher and holier thoughts than those, whose mysterious shades you saw creeping over the face of poor Queequeg, as he quietly lay in his swaying hammock, and the rolling sea seemed gently rocking him to his final rest, and the ocean's invisible flood-tide lifted him higher and higher towards his destined heaven. (*M*, chap. 110)

This resonant instance provides "intimations of some things heavenly" for Ishmael because he has eyes for the allusiveness the moment bears. In surveying the figure of the dying Quee-queg, however, Ishmael realizes as well that the ultimate character and meaning of this presaging moment are clouded because there is "a last revelation, which only an author from the dead could adequately tell" (*M*, chap. 110). Nevertheless, Ishmael sustains his capacity for astonishment and wonder with respect to the portents, despite their finally hidden source; he has learned that if there is concealment there is also revelation and that the disclosures of the transcendent dimension, however furtively they manifest themselves in finite history, enable him to conceive his own life under the shadow of ultimacy.

The capacity for symbolic perception which now characterizes Ishmael allows him to discern in the portents the "high Speech" which withholds significance for human life and yet to refrain from extracting any final significance from them because of the "fit and noble Silence" he intimates behind them. This sensibility of Ishmael's is evident when he scrutinizes Queequeg's tatooed body:

This tatooing had been the work of a departed prophet and seer of his island, who, by those hieroglyphic marks, had written out on his body a complete theory of the heavens and earth, and a mystical treatise on the art of attaining truth; so that Queequeg in his own proper person was a riddle to unfold; a wondrous work in one volume; but whose mysteries not even himself could read, though his own live heart beat against them; and these mysteries were therefore destined in the end to moulder away with the living parchment whereon they were inscribed, and so be unresolved to the last. (*M*, chap. 110)

The finally incalculable character of Queequeg's riddle is not nearly as important to Ishmael as the mystery and allurement it proffers, and the same is true when, at last, Ishmael fronts the great white whale—the whale of whales—who is rumored ubiquitous and immortal and who, like the generic whale Ishmael has interrogated throughout, broods over the seas of life with a revelatory but finally inscrutable countenance. Moby Dick comes as a symbol—"the portentous something in the picture's midst"—which "once found out, and all the rest were plain" (*M,* chap. 1). By now, however, Ishmael knows that, like the creator who made him, Moby Dick is "past finding out" and that the whale, and the world he symbolizes, have depths he cannot plumb. If this paragon of whales, like the generic whale, is too dense to be penetrated, too immense to be measured, too "hieroglyphic" (*M,* chap. 68) and furtive to be puzzled out in its final significance, if, in short, the whale does not diminish, neither does Ishmael suffer any diminution in his inability to measure its immensity and to sound its fecund depths. As Melville observed in a letter to Hawthorne of 29 June 1851, he knew, with Ishmael, that a certain strength resided in the recognition and acknowledgment of one's dependence: "Let us speak, though we show all our faults and weaknesses,—for it is a sign of strength to be weak, to know it, and out with it,—not in [a] set way and ostentatiously, though, but incidentally and without premeditation."[8] Far from reducing Ishmael, the portentous character of the creation presents him with the reality of a grandeur and power and mystery, "the whole bulk of leviathan," his "Titanism of power" (*M,* chap. 86), and bulwarks the value and significance of Ishmael's life by introducing to it a dimension of spirit on which he realizes his fullest sense of himself depends. This is literally saving knowledge for Ishmael, for with it he can possess the ubiquitous whale without capturing the whale, as Ahab attempts, or being captured by the whale, as Jonah is in refusing its demand. Ishmael cannot contain the whale but, with piety, he can recover from it the sense of the transcendent which opaquely inspirits it.

The possibility of finding for his life a reservoir of spirit was the factor which enabled Ishmael's quest from the first, and it is this possibility that his retrospective rehearsal of his experience is designed to possess. In the manner of his quest, Ishmael maintains the integral posture a man must assume in relation to the portentous aspects of life conceived in its exhilarated form: he anticipates with faithfulness a world freighted with significance; he brings awe and astonishment, a kind of reverence, to his sudden discoveries of the charged moments; he both has eyes for scrutinizing the manifestations of the wholly other and has the piety to prevent any attempt on his part to calculate its final hiddenness; and he yearns to possess what he can of the spiritual dimension which converges on his life. He has taken the full span of portents, has revolved "at the axis of that slowly wheeling circle" at the heart of the creation, and if he considers himself an orphan in the epilogue, it is only in the sense he knows all men to be orphans, for in "The Guilder," Ishmael has already realized that "our souls are like those orphans whose unwedded mothers die in bearing them: the secret of our paternity lies in their grave, and we must there to learn it" (M, chap. 114). If the ultimate father of the human spirit is finally hidden, however, Ishmael has at least caught a glimpse of the portents and seized the significance of his reality.

That significance resides in the fact that he can return to a world imbued with wonder. After visiting for a time the "Afric Temple of the Whale," after being presented with the plenitude of spirit in the creation which allows him to reconcile himself to experience, he knows that hereafter he "will silently worship there" (M, chap. 104). He can consent to life because he inhabits a wonder-world which contains within its precincts those moments of opportunity to establish one's self more deeply in being itself. Like Carlyle's Teufelsdröckh, Ishmael is overtaken by the command of the mysterious creation and the transcendent dimension which inspirits it: "For the rest, as is natural to a man of this kind, he deals much in the feeling of Wonder; insists on the necessity and high worth of universal Wonder; which he holds to be the only reasonable temper for the denizen of so singular a Planet as ours. 'Wonder,' says he, 'is the basis of Worship: the reign of wonder is perennial, indestructible in Man; only at certain stages (as the present), it is, for some short season, a reign *in partibus infidelium.'"* [9] If in his retrospective narration Ishmael is insistent about the necessity of wonder, it is because he knows that his reason can carry him no further and need not carry him further; it is because, as he says, "in a matter like this, subtlety appeals to subtlety, and without imagination no man can follow another into these halls" (*M,* chap. 42). Melville knew full well that, although his Ishmael has eyes for the wonder-world and has been ruled by it, the reign, for many another, was *in partibus infidelium,* lost to the peril in man to which, for a time, Ishmael had himself surrendered.

PART THREE

Trials of Transcendence

CHAPTER SEVEN

DAMNED IN THE MIDST OF PARADISE
"Peril in Man" *in* Moby-Dick *and* Pierre

Intentionally or not, Melville's early fictions had the effect of testing, and finding inadequate, several major sets of perceptions of experience in his time. The whole of *Typee* had worked to expose the frail romantic undergirding of a predilection for innocence in mid-nineteenth-century America. The thrust of *Redburn* was from beginning to end to explode a similarly powerful appeal to tradition. In *White-Jacket,* the celebration of the forms of nationalistic democracy is called radically into question, and, as described in the fourth chapter above, the vision of *Moby-Dick* must have appeared wicked indeed to the forms of religious sensibility in response to which, at least in part, it developed. *Moby-Dick* represents more than a deep-diving reaction to what Melville sensed to be banal and incorrect alternatives, however, because he had pressed this fiction into the further tasks of presenting a new perception of the world of human experience and of articulating the most integral response to that world. Further, the effort had not ended there, for Melville realized that Ishmael was not the only inhabitant of the wonder-world. If the promise and demand of such a world stood as a trial for Ishmael in his quest for self-transcendence, and if Ishmael is, on Melville's behalf, insistent finally about the reign of such a world over the human heart, the literary tests are now juxtaposed: the fiction now tests not the human perception of the world but, rather, presents a world which itself adjudicates all human responses; Melville's inquiries begin now not with this or that attitude toward the world but, instead, with a world in which, he is convinced, man must recover his fullest sense of himself.

Ishmael's ability to take "the span of portents" is ratified by the test of the wonder-world and its demands—validated at least in the senses that he can reconcile himself to experience and that, within the context of ultimacy ineluctable in his experience, he can transcend the condition of woe which at first had hemmed him in. This does not mean, of course, that he will not have time and time again to be tested by those moments of *kairos* and symbol which loom up before him; what he has been able to affirm is not a final idea of meaning but, rather, the special form of response, of vision, which gives to his life, even if in a radically contingent manner, a plenitude of spirit. Nor does the ratification of his posture mean that he had not, for a time, succumbed to those perils in man which prevented his full experience of the strange, unloosed, portentous moments presented to him. Even after shaking off the initial misapprehensions of dealing in secondary authority and of succumbing to narcissism, he encounters, and occasionally submits to, additional threats to his achieving his self-transcendence, his full humanity, and, as is the case with the portents in nature, his developing mode of integral response to experience requires him to take "the span of . . . peril in man" —the peril in himself and in others. The voyage aboard the *Pequod* has afforded Ishmael ample occasion for scrutinizing the hazards accompanying the entrance into the wonder-world and the dangers in man himself in responding to that world in ways which are not concordant with its portentous character.

In the progress from *White-Jacket* to *Pierre*, there is a shift from first- to third-person narrators which suggests that the vision of experience cumulatively achieved by the labors of the first-person narrators from *Typee* through *Moby-Dick* belonged now to Melville himself, thus making the quests of the narrator-protagonists no longer necessary. In a sense, the narrational technique of *Moby-Dick* prepares for this shift because the Ishmael aboard the *Pequod* frequently falls completely out of sight from the reader. With each of these disappearances, the narration takes on a decidedly third-person cast: the retrospective Ishmael comes to the fore not in person before the readers' eyes but as a voice with increased omniscience and authority. He arbitrates the world within which the other characters, now under his larger view, enact their responses, and his arbitration of the world figures as a criterion against which to judge those other responses. In this respect, Walter E. Bezanson, who writes about Ishmael's narrational control of the book, observes that "it is wonder that lies at the center of Ishmael's scale of articulation, and the gamut runs out either way toward fear and worship." [1] But Bezanson does not pursue the fact that this "scale of articulation" is not only moored in Melville's metaphysics but also implies an axiology in which Ishmael's integral response to the wonder-world figures as a standard against which to see other, less satisfactory, responses.

These incommensurate responses—the failures to see and to engage a world instinct with significance—take a variety of forms as Ishmael records them, but in each case those who enact such failures are, like Ahab, "damned in the midst of paradise." Ishmael sees, if the others do not always, that failure to discern and to posses those moments of abundance is to fail to recover what is possible for earthbound man for his selfhood in its relations to that context of ultimacy which is the ground of experience. He cannot and does not judge such characters; they are, in fact, judged by the unfettered world of the *Pequod*'s journeying. If Ishmael alone is saved at the end of the narrative, if he is buoyed up by a "dirge-like main" when others have been pulled down by its deadly undertow, if he floats among "unharming sharks . . . with padlocks on their mouths" and under "savage sea-hawks . . . with sheathed beaks" when others have been annihilated by the demonic element, it is because he has answered to the exactions of the wonder-world and is protected by his reconciliation. He cannot judge the others; he can only learn from them: the perils to which they are prey are themselves portentous, stemming as they do from the tangled webs of beings who are affirmed by the creator to be "fearfully and wonderfully made"; the final meaning of the perils and the persons who enact them are, like the hand which created them, past finding out. If they are portents, however, their span can be taken, their significance possessed to shore up one's life.

In *Moby-Dick* and later fictions, there are various forms of what Ishmael has learned represents peril in man in the encounter with a world which contains moments of *kairos* and symbol. Queequeg and Starbuck—whose perilous responses to the portentous world which surrounds them are virtually accidental in their simple unknowing—make responses which simply cannot accommodate the complex requirements of the symbolic ambience within which they move. In contrast, Captain Ahab is more like Ishmael, in the one sense at least that he sees life "strongly and metaphysically." Ahab's responses to the encompassing wonder-world are self-conscious and studied; he is fully aware of the hazards he himself embodies, and although he regrets his postures at times, the nature of his vision renders change impossible. His failures and his final peril, however, spring just from the nature of this vision and his refusal to accept any limits on it. From his perusals of these failures, Ishmael is able to avoid similarly flawed responses to the portents and, in part, to frame a more concordant response to the presence of the wholly other which manifests itself in his experience. He learns especially to develop a genuinely human alternative to the epistemological barriers which make Ahab groan and chafe about the confined condition of human life. Still another character, Pierre, the title character of the book which follows *Moby-Dick,* inherits something of Ahab's dark vision and enacts, without any of Ahab's epic size, his own peril in man. Inhabiting a world which the third-person narrator assures the reader is similar in construction and in demand to the wonder-world of *Moby-Dick,* Pierre responds to it in a way which simply cannot obtain. He thinks himself master of the rule of wonder, but he is finally enslaved by the ambiguous and contingent experience with which the mysterious portents leave him. He cannot imagine the ways that "the groves of our Thessalies" might be understood to support his passage, and, thus, he cannot stave off the suicidal woe which Ishmael had earlier transcended. Now, of course, the responses of these characters, which are hazardous and ultimately fatal, make Ishmael's more integral manner of dealing with experience all the more impressive, and the fact that he survives, when others perish, seems to represent Melville's final critique of *all* modes of response which his fictions bring before the reader. But this large array of failures, successively presented, is less significant as an indication of any moral judgments on individuals on Melville's part than as a signal of the author's historical realism about the world of human perception to which his vision of the wonder-world would be making its appeal for accreditation.

I

Queequeg and Starbuck both have some sense of the reality of the wonder-world, if neither of them ever becomes fully aware of its implications for his life. They recognize the charged environs of the voyage of the *Pequod* in their proximity to Ahab's epic size and to his furious pursuit of the white whale, if not always in other instances, and each responds to the pregnant and mysterious quality of their experience in ways which stem from and are definitive of their more or less singular characters. Each of them is a static character in the course of the narrative Ishmael presents; they are without, or at least do not demonstrate, the capacity to change—despite the evidence of experience which convinces Ishmael that the wonder-world requires different responses than either of them is wont to muster. This static quality which characterizes each is the first symptom of the failure of each, for the intermittent presence of the wholly other does nothing if it does not demand a man's altered vision of his life in relation to the immensities. But Queequeg and Starbuck each inculcate, in their unchanging figurements, perils which belong uniquely to each and which Ishmael's narration brings to the fore.

Early in the book Ishmael learns from Queequeg, "this soothing savage" in whom "there lurked no civilized hypocrisies and bland deceits" (*M,* chap. 10), the necessity to maintain an openness to all forms of being. When they are "married"—"bosom friends"—and when Ishmael casts off "those old rules" of human distrust, he finds that "no more my splintered heart and maddened hand were turned against the wolfish world . . . [for Queequeg] had redeemed it" (*M,* chap. 10). Throughout the journey as Ishmael records it, Queequeg acts without reserve, full of instinct and honest reflexes, indiscriminate in his "heart's honeymoon" with the world. After the native's brush with the bumpkin who has offended him and after saving the same green-horn from death in the deep, Queequeg's unstudied, savage grace is something which makes Ishmael marvel: "Was there ever such unconsciousness? He did not seem to think that he at all de-served a medal from the Humane and Magnanimous Societies. He only asked for water—fresh water—something to wipe the brine off; that done, he put on dry clothes, lighted his pipe, and leaning against the bulwarks, and mildly eyeing those around him, seemed to be saying to himself—'It's a mutual, joint-stock world, in all meridians. We cannibals must help these Chris-tians'" (*M,* chap. 13). Queequeg continues to teach Ishmael such lessons of the heart as he plunges into the great Heidelberg Tun to rescue the fallen Tashtego and as he holds up his end of "The Monkey-Rope" to enact, for Ishmael, a scene which be-tokens deep human interdependence. In all such situations, Queequeg responds with a kind of animal reflexiveness to the needs of the moment; ambiguity, fear, beauty, pain, are all the same to him as he follows the currents of his instincts, regardless of how they pull him along. If Tashtego needs saving, Queequeg leaps to the rescue; if the white whale needs killing, Queequeg will dip his harpoon into the fire; if the moment afflicts him, Queequeg prepares to be "in his coffin" (*M,* chap. 110). When he remembers that he has unfinished business, he simply changes his mind about dying, for "it was Queequeg's conceit, that if a man made up his mind to live, mere sickness could not kill him" (*M,* chap. 110).

As much as Ishmael gains from him of the reasons of the heart, however, Queequeg's preconscious responses to experi-ence are not, finally, a viable option, for the harpooner's pos-tures, were they to be taken on by modern man, would imperil one in the ways Tommo finally recognized himself to be endan-gered by the narcotic life of the Typee. Queequeg's indifference and indiscrimination with respect to experience make him act on the basis of the whimsical instinct which Melville thought belonged to the primitive mentality. Queequeg is not so much open to being as he is acquiescent to situations. He cannot recover himself in relation to the context of ultimacy presented by the wonder-world, for he simply blends in with the world, thus forfeiting that requirement of consciousness which Tommo had earlier struggled to achieve and which Ishmael realizes is indispensable. When he asks the question begged by Queequeg's selflessness—"Was there ever such unconsciousness?"—he does so with genuine admiration, but he comes to recognize on "The Mast-Head" that the unconsciousness which characterizes Queequeg, even if it permits a merging of self and world, must issue for modern man in "an opium-like listlessness of vacant, unconscious reverie . . . [in] the blending cadence of waves with thoughts . . . [and in which] at last he loses his identity" (*M,* chap. 35). The merger of the self with the object of its reflection can be achieved only with self-annihilation, and, thus, however much Ishmael can appreciate Queequeg's broad, savage humanism and can return to it in a different form, he cannot adopt the strategy of Queequeg's naive vision, which comes to the savage not as a tactic at all but as an instinct. Ishmael seeks self-recovery, not self-loss, and such recovery requires that he encounter and interpret the portentous aspect of the world, not that he acquiesce to and blend with it. His own reconciliation with the ground of being will come in relation, not in merger. Queequeg's primitive and untutored mysticism, maintained throughout, will not suffice as a mode of response to the complex demands of the wonder-world without the complete merger of himself with the hidden other when he takes "his last long dive" (*M,* chap. 13) of self-loss as the *Pequod* goes down.

Starbuck, like Queequeg, remains consistent throughout the narrative in his attitude toward the experiences of the exhilarated world, and for a time his quiet piety seems to represent a viable alternative to meet the promise and demand of such a world. The first mate is introduced to the reader in the first of the "Knights and Squires" chapters as a "staid, steadfast man" of "hardy sobriety and fortitude" who is "endued with a deep natural reverence." If he is aware of "outward portents and inward presentiments," however, he cares less about tracing them to their sources and exploring their implications than about dwelling on "far-away domestic memories of his young Cape wife and child" (*M*, chap. 26). Starbuck is everywhere to be defined by his prudence and caution, just because hearth and home are the central concern of his "deep natural reverence." His faith refers to, and reposes in, the comfortable orthodoxies of decent family life and "right-mindedness," and the sources of this faith are nowhere more apparent than in Starbuck's interpretation of the doubloon: "'No fairy fingers can have pressed the gold, but devil's claws must have left their mouldings there since yesterday,'" murmured Starbuck to himself, leaning against the bulwarks.... "'I have never marked the coin inspectingly. He [Ahab] goes below; let me read. A dark valley between three mighty, heaven-abiding peaks, that almost seem the Trinity, in some faint earthly symbol. So in this vale of Death, God girds us round; and over all our gloom, the sun of Righteousness still shines a beacon and a hope'" (*M*, chap. 99). Starbuck's placid faith develops in relation to the sunlight God who answers easily to his hope, and the mate is secure in his convictions because the evidence of his family life bears out for him the possibilities of this "attainable felicity." "Sweetness and light" stem from the simple righteousness of lifting his eyes upward to the "God [who] girds us round," and, on the basis of such an apparent ratification of his piety, Starbuck attempts to build that "stubbornness of life" (*M*, chap. 36) which will see him through all the gales at sea and allow him to return home. It is he who will, for a time, confront Ahab with the need to retain his "humanities," for Starbuck's God is fashioned after the images of human good and compassion, peace and contentment, which belongs to his Cape hearthside.

After "a squeeze of the hand," of course, Ishmael himself finds redeemed the mortal happinesses of "the bed, the table, the saddle, the fire-side," but the course of events and reflection which brings him to the point at which he can say "now . . . I perceive all this" (*M*, chap. 94) has been much different than the stance in which Starbuck is secured and the piety with which his life is anchored. Ishmael recognizes that the first mate's sun-

shine affirmations have been achieved only at the cost of ignor-
ing the demands of the wonder-world and that such affirmations
are founded on perilous ground. Starbuck's uncritical orthodoxies of mind are too easy, for they do not mount up from the
full encounter with "the dark valley between [the] three mighty,
heaven-abiding peaks"; he refuses the experience and the implications of the dark night horrors of the world in order to keep
his gaze fixedly upon "the sun of Righteousness." As he reveals
in his interpretation of the doubloon: "'If we bend down our
eyes, the dark vale shows her mouldy soul; but if we lift them,
the bright sun meets our glance half way, to cheer. Yet, oh, the
great sun is no fixture; and if, at midnight, we would fain snatch
some sweet solace from him, we gaze for him in vain! This coin
speaks wisely, mildly, truly, but still sadly to me. I will quit it,
lest Truth shake me falsely'" (*M,* chap. 99). Starbuck is aware
of the "dark vale" but averts any encounter with it—substitut-
ing, instead, the faith in "the bright sun." His faith is a faith
against evidence, for there are some aspects of the truth which
he simply prefers not to know.

The peril in such willing refusal of the dark element of the
wonder-world will come to Starbuck when the mate finds himself "with soul beat down and held to knowledge" on which the
sun casts no light. This moment comes in the chapter entitled
"Dusk," when at last Starbuck can no longer fail to be aware of
Ahab's "impious ends" and the captain's rule over "a heathen
crew that have small touch of human mothers in them":

Foremost through the sparkling sea shoots on the gay, embattled, ban-
tering bow, but only to drag dark Ahab after it, where he broods within his sternward cabin, builded over the dead water of the wake, and
further on, hunted by its wolfish gurglings. The long howl thrills me
through! Peace! ye revellers, and set the watch! Oh, life! 'tis now that I
do feel the latent horror in thee! but 'tis not me! that horror's out of me!
and with the soft feeling of the human in me, yet will I try to fight ye, ye
grim, phantom futures! Stand by me, hold me, bind me, O ye blessed
influences! (*M,* chap. 38)

Thus, at the very moment Starbuck feels the "latent horror" of
life, he refuses to acknowledge its implications; he evokes, instead, "the soft feeling of the human," the "blessed influences"

of home, all that remains to him after the sun has gone down. He believes against knowledge, posits faith simplistically against experience, and thinks that, with the reappearance of his sunlight deity, "yet is there hope" for yet "God may wedge aside" Ahab's "heaven insulting purpose" (*M,* chap. 38).

The retrospective Ishmael has known from the outset of the narrative that Starbuck's daylight affirmations contain their own peril because, after the experience of the voyage, Ishmael knows that such affirmations, when they are possible at all, are founded on the encounter with the full range of experience and not in spite of that range. Ishmael has learned that if he cannot push aside the "gentle joyousness" (*M,* chap. 133) he descries in the white whale neither can he ignore the presence of the beast. He can only affirm the perception of value and significance achieved with "a squeeze of the hand" after seeing, in the chapter immediately preceding it, the results of Pip's plummet to the bottom of the sea. Or, again, when he affirms the existence of "The Lamp"—"so that in the pitchiest night the ship's black hull still houses an illumination" (*M,* chap. 97)—he does so in full view of the fact that he had experienced, in the chapter immediately before, the darkest and most ghastly night of his life. If he can think, after his experience at the midnight helm, that "tomorrow, in the natural sun, the skies will be bright," he must own as well that "the sun hides not Virginia's Dismal Swamp, nor Rome's accursed Campagna, . . . [nor] the ocean, which is the dark side of this earth, and which is two thirds of this earth" (*M,* chap. 96). For Ishmael, then, Starbuck's faith is imperilling because, refusing two-thirds of the truth, it is not formed in the forge of experience and cannot withstand the test of experience.

But Starbuck's simple faith leads him further into harm's way, Ishmael thinks, because it stymies moral action. Refusing the knowledge of the dark world, trusting that "God may wedge aside" evil, Starbuck is "morally enfeebled . . . by [his] mere unaided virtue and right-mindedness" (*M,* chap. 41). His domestic pieties, which issue in one kind of fortitude, the "stubbornness of life" that takes him home again, will find no abetment in the confrontation with darkness, and, if worshipping at the sunlight altar he will never be seized by the "wisdom that is woe" (*M,* chap. 96), nor will he be able to grapple with the "lurid woe" (*M,* chap. 38) he finds in dark Ahab's eye. Starbuck's hopeful fortitude, which relies exclusively on the "heaven-abiding peaks," will quail, Ishmael senses, before the intrepid and menacing "brow of an enraged and mighty man" (*M,* chap. 26). When faced with the knowledge of the "darkest gorge" (*M,* chap. 96)—the knowledge Ahab contains and presents—Starbuck cannot meet it; he can only attempt to displace it with his own more comforting knowledge. When faced with Ahab's disclosures of his dark mission, all "three mates quailed before his strong, sustained, and mystic aspect. Stubb and Flask looked sideways from him; the honest eye of Starbuck fell downright" (*M,* chap. 36). In short, Starbuck's habitual upward gazing, with which "the bright sun meets our glance half way," fails him here, and he knows that "if we bend down our eyes," seeking "sweet solace, . . . we gaze for him [the sunlight God] in vain" (*M,* chap. 99). Here, then, Starbuck acknowledges the peril in him, for under Ahab's powerful sway he sees:

My soul is more than matched; she's overmanned; and by a madman! Insufferable sting, that sanity should ground arms on such a field! But he drilled deep down, and blasted all my reason out of me! I think I see his impious end; but feel that I must help him to it. Will I, nill I, the ineffable thing has tied me to him; tows me with a cable I have no knife to cut. Horrible old man! Who's over him, he cries;—aye, he would be a democrat to all above; look, how he lords it over all below! Oh! I plainly see my miserable office,—to obey, rebelling; and worse yet, to hate with touch of pity! For in his eyes I read some lurid woe would shrivel me up, had I it. (*M,* chap. 38)

Having refused the wisdom that could have come from integral encounter with the dark two-thirds of the world of experience, Starbuck lacks the critical tools to cut himself from Ahab's mesmerizing gaze. Ill equipped to face the reality of evil with the simple right-mindedness which represents his sanity, he can only succumb to the force of Ahab's insanity.

If the mate fancies that he will mix his obedience with rebellion, the forms of that rebellion appear as nothing more, finally, than his continual evocation of his compassionate God to illumine the dark field onto which he has been dragged to combat.

Confronted by darkness, he waits, hoping for the light, and his incapacity to change is complete, his peril, accomplished. Faced all around by Ahab's madness, he attempts to the last to displace that presence with the images of peace and contentment which reach him from home:

"Oh, my Captain! My Captain! noble soul! grand old heart, after all! why should anyone give chase to that hated fish! Away with me! let us fly these deadly waters! let us home! Wife and child, too, are Starbuck's —wife and child of his brotherly, sisterly, play-fellow youth; even as thine, sir, are the wife and child of thy loving, longing, paternal old age! Away! let us away!—this instant let me alter the course! How cheerily, how hilariously, O my Captain, would we bowl on our way to see old Nantucket again! I think, sir, they have some such mild blue days, even as this, in Nantucket." (M, chap. 132)

Starbuck refuses to change, for he fears the woe that is madness; he cannot face Ahab's black, vengeful soul any more than he can face the memory of the "doom" of his father and "the torn limbs of his brother" lost "in the bottomless deeps" (M, chap. 26). He dares look down at the dark two-thirds of the earth only on a sunlit day which makes it reflect and, therefore, answer to the hue of his conception of the merciful heavens:

And that same day, too, gazing far down from his boat's side into that same golden sea, Starbuck lowly murmured:—
    "Loveliness unfathomable, as ever lover saw in his young bride's eye! —Tell me not of thy teeth-tiered sharks, and thy kidnapping cannibal ways. Let faith oust fact; let fancy oust memory; I look deep down and do believe." (M, chap. 114)

Whelmed by Ahab, Starbuck cannot but obey; presented with the presence of the beast, Starbuck lets "faith oust fact." Instead of fronting his experience, instead of acknowledging the radical otherness portended by it, instead of accepting its promise and wrestling with its demand, Starbuck displaces it with "the soft feeling of the human" which is the mode and issue of untested piety. Ishmael has learned that, to be true, such soft feelings must be forged, in the fire, out of the harder knowledge of "the fine hammered steel of woe" (M, chap. 96). Starbuck, resisting the fires of experience, securing himself in the placid humanisms founded on his daylight deity, will find himself "'fixed at the top of a shudder'" with "'all the past . . . grown dim.'" The image of wife and child "'fadest in pale glories behind me,'" as he lowers at last into the "swarming seas" (*M,* chap. 135) which he can no longer dispel.[2]

II

In one sense at least Ahab's peril can be understood as the obverse, the opposite form of extremity, to the comfortable pieties which are Starbuck's peril. If Starbuck clings desperately to hearth and home in a refusal to acknowledge and to grapple with the existence of evil in the world, Ahab sheds himself of all his "humanities" just because he has not only acknowledged the beast but vows to master it. Just as Starbuck evades the dark two-thirds of the earth, and does so to his ultimate hazard, Ahab is so ruled over by his dark perception that he cannot grant—or at least grasp—the well-lit, supportive element of the world. Analogously to Starbuck, who elevates one part of experience to be regarded as the truth about life, Ahab refuses the existence and the implications of the full range of experience and swears that what he has seen and felt is absolute and universal. If Starbuck's optimistic pieties immobilize him, enfeeble him for moral action, Ahab conversely embodies, as a part of his dark vision, that which can allow him no repose until what he considers the proper moral combat has been completed. Finally, if Starbuck evades the wisdom that is woe but finds peril in his daylight sanities, Ahab begins with such wisdom and its accompanying woe and finds peril in the woe that is madness.

Thus, there is also a sense in which Ahab's peril can be comprehended in the light of Pip's career into madness, for Ahab enacts, in front of a much larger canvas and in a hue of different tone, Pippin's figurative descent to the bottom. When Pip jumps for the second time, when he becomes "castaway," he experiences what, from that moment, renders him mad:

The sea had jeeringly kept his finite body up, but drowned the infinite of his soul. Not drowned entirely, though. Rather carried down alive to wondrous depths, where strange shapes of the unwarped primal world glided to and fro before his passive eyes; and the miser-man, Wisdom, revealed his hoarded heaps; and among the joyous, heartless, ever-juvenile eternities, Pip saw the multitudinous, God-omnipresent, orbs. He saw God's foot upon the treadle of the loom, and spoke it; and therefore his shipmates called him mad. So man's insanity is heaven's sense; and wandering from all mortal reason, man comes at last to that celestial thought, which, to reason, is absurd and frantic; and weal or woe, feels then uncompromised, indifferent as his God. (*M,* chap. 93)

Pip's encounter with the wondrous occurs in a moment during which, at least by intimation, he is brought face to face with the wholly other in images horrifying to him. He has seen a portent of "heaven's sense," the compacted and "multitudinous" inter-weaving of joy and heartlessness, created by "God's . . . loom," but it is not the ambiguity of the "primal world"—rather, it is its sheer depth and immensity—which blasts Pip's mind away. Made a castaway by the indifferent Stubb, Pip can only under-stand this portent as a cipher of his being reduced to nothing by the size of the creation, of his being cast away by an indifferent God. Submerged to "wondrous depths," he has wandered away "from all mortal reason," and, regarding the disclosures of this moment as ultimate revelations, final truths, he will never return to anything resembling human reason. His already meager self-esteem thrown into doubt by Stubb, Pip's sense of himself is simply abolished by what he perceives as heaven's sense—an abolishment revealed in his inability to locate his own gram-matical perspective before the doubloon: he runs the course of pronouns, seeking a place for himself to stand and see: "'I look, you look, he looks; we look, ye look, they look'" (*M,* chap. 99).

During a moment antecedent to the opening of the narrative, Ahab has likewise been maimed in an encounter with the dread element in the creation: like Pip, he has, from that moment, re-garded the disclosures of that moment to be final and absolute and,. with "that celestial thought," he wanders from mortal reason. Having been "where strange shapes of the unwarped primal world glided to and fro," having encountered the immen-sity of the white whale, the "hoarded heaps" of Moby Dick, and having found in that moment what he thinks is a signal of the dark, indifferent visage and nature of the creator, Ahab will forever after elevate the woe of that insight to the level of ultimate truth, an elevation which, like Pip's similarly singular and momentary intuition, will lead him to madness. Any contradictory insight to be gained in the experience of other, less dreadful portents, is precluded for Ahab because he cannot now see past or through the woe which hems him in. His dark vision is riveted to, and controlled by, the universally demonic element he is convinced he has discerned; as Ishmael understands it:

Small reason was there to doubt, then, that ever since that almost fatal encounter, Ahab had cherished a wild vindictiveness against the whale, all the more fell for that in his frantic morbidness he at last came to identify with him, not only all his bodily woes, but all his intellectual and spiritual exasperations. The White Whale swam before him as the monomaniac incarnation of all those malicious agencies which some deep men feel eating in them, till they are left living on with half a heart and half a lung. . . . All that most maddens and torments; all that stirs up the lees of things; all truth with malice in it; all that cracks the sinews and cakes the brain; all the subtle demonisms of life and thought; all evil, to crazy Ahab, were visibly personified, and made practically assailable in Moby Dick. He piled upon the whale's white hump the sum of all the general rage and hate felt by his whole race from Adam down; and then, as if his chest had been a mortar, he burst his hot heart's shell upon it. (*M,* chap. 41)

Ishmael sees that, in Ahab, "his special lunacy stormed his general sanity" (*M,* chap. 41). Like Pip, Ahab becomes what he is because, from the full range of the wonder-world, he lives within the experience of *one* incredibly intense moment during which the menace of the creation and the creator were disclosed to him.

Unlike Pip, however, Ahab undergoes no annihilation of the self; the consequence in his case is, rather, to find a new self within him "deepeningly contracted," Ishmael thinks, out of Ahab's "full lunacy," now "transfigured into some still subtler form" (*M,* chap. 41). It is this maddened, wolfish self which rules Ahab and which, Ishmael concludes, tears away the captain's humanities. This lunatic, cerebral Ahab runs to exhaustion and impotency the Ahab with a heart, for, as Ishmael sees:

The latter was the eternal, living principle or soul in him; and in sleep, being for the time dissociated from the characterizing mind, which at other times employed it for its outer vehicle or agent, it spontaneously sought escape from the scorching contiguity of the frantic thing, of which, for the time, it was no longer an integral. But as the mind does not exist unless leagued with the soul, therefore it must have been that, in Ahab's case, yielding up all his thoughts and fancies to his one su-preme purpose, that purpose, by its own sheer inveteracy of will, forced itself against gods and devils into a kind of self-assumed, independent being of its own. Nay, could grimly live and burn, while the common vitality to which it was conjoined, fled horror-stricken from the un-bidden and unfathered birth. Therefore the tormented spirit that glared out of bodily eyes, when what seemed Ahab rushed from his room, was for the time but a vacated thing, a formless somnambulistic being, a ray of living light, to be sure, but without an object to color, and therefore a blankness in itself. (*M,* chap. 44)

The "frantic thing," then, becomes Ahab's self or at least be-comes the driving inveterate will, and its characterizing mind, which scorches and finally burns out Ahab's former being. Ish-mael realizes that it was not the "strange shapes of the unwarped primal world" that gave rise to this "self-assured, independent being" in Ahab: he knows that this "unfathered birth" occurred only because Ahab cleaved exclusively to "the truth with malice in it" and refused all other forms of the truth; he knows that Ahab contained "a globular brain and a ponderous heart" (*M,* chap. 16) which found affinity with the disclosures of malice. "It is not probable," Ishmael thinks, "that this monomania in him took its instant rise at the precise time of his bodily dismem-berment" (*M,* chap. 41). Ishmael hints, rather, that Ahab, even before the first encounter with Moby Dick, possessed something of that "half-wilful over-ruling morbidness at the bottom of his nature" (*M,* chap. 16), something of that "characterizing mind" (*M,* chap. 44), which becomes the dark monomaniac self only after Ahab has interpreted, in a kind of delirium, the symbolism of the whale as "visibly" personifying "all evil" (*M,* chap. 41). But whatever its sources and whatever its enraged countenance, Ahab's ruling self has come fully to birth: he is not, like Pip, lost in the grammatical maze; he is the inveterate "I," the assertive ego, the intrepid and incorrigible self, and its "narrow-flowing monomania" has, by the opening of the narrative, "turned all its concentrated cannon upon its own mad mark; so that far from having lost his strength, Ahab . . . did now possess a thousand fold more potency than ever he had sanely brought to bear upon any one reasonable object" (*M,* chap. 41).

Now, although it sheds light on the sources and nature of Ahab's character to compare and to juxtapose him with Starbuck and Pip, it is in relation to the wonder-world and its demands that the peril Ahab embodies comes fully to the fore.[3] If Starbuck and Pip run into hazard and are overtaken by the swarming seas, it is because neither ever fully understands the requirements of integral experience in such a world. The similarities—even the juxtapositions—end here, for Ahab is fully aware that he lives in an encompassing symbolic world, that the mixed plenitude of this world withholds for him the possibility of self-transcendence, and that, despite all this, he willfully remains "madness maddened" (*M,* chap. 37). He recognizes the promise of the wonder-world, and he knows that to refuse it is to leave its demand unfulfilled. He reveals his sense of this knowledge in his sunset soliloquy as he sees, rejects, and regrets that which makes him reject the peaceful, radiant sunset moment disclosed to him:

Yonder, by the ever-brimming goblet's rim, the warm waves blush like wine. The gold brow plumbs the blue. The diver sun—slow dived from noon,—goes down; my soul mounts up! she wearies with her endless hill. Is, then, the crown too heavy that I wear? this Iron Crown of Lombardy. Yet is it bright with many a gem; I, the wearer, see not its far flashings; but darkly feel that I wear that, that dazzlingly confounds. 'Tis iron—that I know—not gold. 'Tis split, too—that I feel; the jagged edge galls me so, my brain seems to beat against the solid metal; aye, steel skull, mine; the sort that needs no helmet in the most brain-battering fight!

Dry heat upon my brow? Oh! time was, when as the sunrise nobly spurred me, so the sunset soothed. No more. This lovely light, it lights not me; all loveliness is anguish to me, since I can ne'er enjoy. Gifted with the high perception, I lack the low, enjoying power; damned, most subtly and most malignantly! damned in the midst of Paradise! (*M,* chap. 37)

With this consciousness, Ahab is fully confirmed in "the fine hammered steel of woe," for his skull has indeed taken on that aspect; he cannot put down the iron crown which wearies his soul. He cannot even concentrate on the sunset because he is forever pulled back—as the movement of the soliloquy betrays—to the burden of woe he carries, to the pulsing of his own "globular brain," and to the "brain-battering fight" which is his sole purpose. Even ruled by the frantic thing which came to unfathered birth in him, Ahab can recognize that the wonder-world, in forms other than malicious, is all that is possible of paradise, but what he thinks is that his "high perception" will not permit him to relent to the "lovely light," to overcome the "self-assumed" and "unbidden" will which makes him "a mighty pageant creature, formed for noble tragedies" (M, chap. 16). Despite the grandeur—or at least the huge scale—of his exertions, however, Ahab's responses, like those of the other characters, are brought under judgment by the character of the wonder-world he recognizes but refuses. What imperils him—what damns him in the midst of paradise—is, finally, the incorrigible rule of the self which has overtaken him and the nature of the vision which is that self's characterizing mind.

If Ishmael has learned that the full-freighted world of wonder must be entered with expectancy and receptivity, Ahab's posture remains rigidly projective throughout. Far from passing through the floodgates with any expectation of surprise, Ahab begins the voyage inflexibly persuaded by an a priori notion of what he *wills* to encounter. He cannot be receptive to infusions of spirit into the world because his sheer inveteracy of will prescribes what will be found there. In describing Ahab's first appearance on deck, Ishmael's portrayal of the captain's physical stance suggests his commensurately projecting attitude: "I was struck with the singular posture he maintained. Upon each side of the Pequod's quarter-deck, and pretty close to the mizen shrouds, there was an auger hole, bored about half an inch or so, into the plank. His bone leg steadied in that hole; one arm elevated, and holding by a shroud; Captain Ahab stood erect, looking straight out beyond the ship's ever-pitching prow. There was an infinity of firmest fortitude, a determinate, unsurrenderable wilfulness, in the fixed and fearless, forward dedication of that glance" (*M,* chap. 28). Even Ishmael's alliterative interests in the final sentence present an Ahab who is not open to experience but who is, rather, thrusting his way through it to reach the preconceived object he seeks. And the entire passage has the virtue of posing the incorrigibly rigid narrowness of vision which only looks forward and will not be distracted by the wondrous as it is disclosed on either side of the "ever-pitching prow." Time and time again, Ahab walks to the auger hole, and if the "posture he maintained" there is "singular" in the sense that it is unique or unusual, it is also singular in the sense that it figures as his sole stance in the face of experience. He will not be dissuaded: if "envious billows sidelong swell to whelm my track; let them," he says, "but first I pass" (*M,* chap. 37). The "great gods" themselves cannot knock him off course, he avers: "No, ye've knocked me down, and I am up again, but *ye* have run and hidden. Come forth from behind your cotton bags! I have no long gun to reach ye. Come, Ahab's compliments to ye; come and see if you can swerve me. Swerve me? ye cannot swerve me, else ye swerve yourselves! man has ye there. Swerve me? The path to my fixed purpose is laid with iron rails, whereon my soul is grooved to run. Over unsounded gorges, through the rifled hearts of mountains, under torrents' beds, unerringly I rush! Naught's an obstacle, naught's an angle to the iron way!" (*M,* chap. 37).[4] Mad for the encounter, Ahab rushes through his experience along an undeviating "iron way," and the sense of himself which he brings to his experience stems from all the "concentrated cannon" of his woe-ridden and tormented brain. He cannot accept the soothing light of the sunset, for he has allowed himself to be defined by one portentous moment during which he had been "knocked down" by a truth he regards as absolute—a truth "with malice in it."

If Ishmael has learned that the full encounter with the signals of the transcendent requires that the human self must both recognize and respect the otherness portended in such radically profound moments, Ahab succumbs utterly to the very narcissistic mode of vision which Ishmael had earlier surmounted. Just as Ahab's fixed purpose hurls him like a projectile through his experience, the captain projects himself on his experience; meaning, for him, is not substantive to the events, objects, and persons he encounters but is, rather, adjectival, and Ahab himself is the modifying agent. Everywhere he turns, he finds his own maddened self or his own deep woe or his own outraged purposefulness mirrored back to him. The engravings on the doubloon image only Ahab to Ahab, and his response indicates that the entire phenomenal world does nothing else: "'There's something ever egotistical in mountain-tops and towers, and all other grand and lofty things; look here,—three peaks as proud as Lucifer. The firm tower, that is Ahab; the volcano, that is Ahab; the courageous, the undaunted, and victorious fowl, that, too, is Ahab; all are Ahab; and this round gold is but the image of the rounder globe, which, like a magician's glass, to each and every man in turn but mirrors back his own mysterious self'" (*M,* chap. 99). Although he thinks life is symbolic, then, Ahab has lost the ability to see things symbolically. He fails to realize that the symbol is opaque, that it contains its own meaning apart from the human assignment of meaning to it, and that he must search it for its resonances of the other instead of the narcissistic attraction it withholds for him. Because he cannot seize the symbolic value of experience which lies hidden from his assignments to it, because he is wont always to locate one value, himself, in the symbolic forms which arise, Ahab is precluded from envisioning the ways that the plenteously portentous world could support his life. In the hieroglyphic Queequeg, who presents Ishmael with a living, breathing, "wondrous work in one volume," Ahab can only find another example of his outraged predicament: "this thought," Ishmael surmises, "it must have been which suggested to Ahab that wild exclamation of his, when one morning turning away from surveying poor Queequeg —'Oh, devilish tantalization of the gods!'" (*M,* chap. 99). With his monistic, egotistical vision, Ahab reads the volume that is Queequeg only as an exposition of his own woe. The signal example of Ahab's narrow-flowing vision, of course, occurs in his interpretation of the white whale. By the time Ishmael actually encounters Moby Dick, he has learned of the compacted ambiguity of the whale and has learned that the whiteness of the

whale presents that ambiguity symbolically to portend the creation, with the element of spirit looming opaquely through it. In
its symbolical whiteness, then, Moby Dick bodes, for Ishmael,
that which is appalling and that which is beautiful, that which
fills one with dread and that which gives one peace, the presence
of the beast and the gentle joyousness of "the Grand Armada."
He has learned, in short, that the whale is abundant in its ambiguity. For Ahab, however, the whiteness of the whale presents only a huge, blank canvas on which to paint the image of Ahab, the
image constructed on the basis of his absolute truth with malice
in it. Far from interpreting the richness of the whale's symbolism, Ahab imposes on it, ascribes to it, the malice he himself
bears toward it. His great "globular brain" having transferred
his own fury to the whale, Ahab's "thoughts," Ishmael recognizes, "have created a creature in thee; and he whose intense
thinking thus makes him a Prometheus; a vulture feeds upon that
heart for ever; that vulture the very creature he creates" (*M*,
chap. 44).[5]

If Ishmael has learned that the final character and meaning
of the portents will remain inviolably hidden and, yet, that the
presence of the transcendent in them permits him to "shift his
conceit of attainable felicity" to a local world touched by wonder, Ahab runs defiantly into the epistemological dilemma which
arises when he cannot see beyond himself. Because his rigidity
of self and fixity of purpose prevent his openness to the full ambience of the wonder-world, he is left solely with the concentrated cannon of his own woe. Because he projects himself out of
that woe, he can only find his tormented self mirrored back to
him and cannot, in turn, seize the significance of the presence of
the other to him. What he seeks is hidden, he thinks, behind a
blank, indifferent wall which his narcissistic mode of vision cannot pierce, and this thought maddens him further still, as he tells
Starbuck:

"All visible objects, man, are but as paste-board masks. But in each
event—in the living act, the undoubted deed—there, some unknown
but still reasoning thing puts forth the mouldings of its features from
behind the unreasoning mask. If man will strike, strike through the
mask! How can the prisoner reach outside except by thrusting through

the wall? To me, the white whale is that wall, shoved near to me. Sometimes I think there's naught beyond. But 'tis enough. He tasks me; he heaps me; I see in him outrageous strength, with an inscrutable malice sinewing it. That inscrutable thing is chiefly what I hate; and be the white whale agent, or be the white whale principal, I will wreak that hate upon him. Talk not to me of blasphemy, man; I'd strike the sun if it insulted me. For could the sun do that, then I could do the other; since there is ever a sort of fair play herein. Who's over me? Truth hath no confines." (*M,* chap. 36)

The malicious great gods Ahab seeks, however, continue to elude him, and he has "no long gun" to reach them. But the particular nature of his vision—that fixed and determinate gaze—will not be imprisoned, he swears, for if "truth hath no confines," nor will Ahab. Like the riddle of Queequeg, the elusive, furtive thing that inspirits Moby Dick seems the "devilish tantalizations of the gods" which Ahab wants to put to rout, and, with this, Ahab refuses the last of the lessons Ishmael learns. When Ishmael's metaphysics are brought up short by the finally incalculable character of the transcendent, his symbolist understanding allows him to accept a squeeze of the hand, a shift to the reasons of the heart, a return to a world redeemed by its pervasive wonder. In contrast, Ahab cannot acknowledge the final hiddenness of God, cannot accept any limitation on his vision, and, so, must pursue "the gliding great demon of the seas of life" (*M,* chap. 41) which is, at last, but the projection of his own mad, demonic woe. He would, as Starbuck observes, "be a democrat to all above" (*M,* chap. 38), but Ahab cannot, Ishmael knows, live out the lifetime of his God. When the possibility comes for a squeeze of the hand for Ahab, he will not accept Pip's offer because he cannot accredit the efficacy of the reasons of the heart. He relinquishes the offer of the human and continues to chafe defiantly under the limitations of the human. He rails at the sky as he is pulled into the deep.

III

In *Pierre,* the book which followed *Moby-Dick,* the early chapters present the title character in a scene which reifies all the idyllic domestic bliss Starbuck had insisted belonged to hearth and home, and those chapters come as close, perhaps, as anything Melville ever wrote to portraying an unfallen situation for modern man. They offer up to the reader just exactly that which Melville had promised Mrs. Hawthorne, as he feared for her tender sensibilities in reading *Moby-Dick: Pierre,* he wrote to her, will be a "rural bowl of milk."[6] This picture of Edenic bliss in the early chapters is called into question, however, almost simultaneously with its presentation because the reader soon realizes that, although the narration is in the third-person, the point of view and its tone belong completely to a sophomoric young Pierre who is excessively sentimentalist and optimistic, who finds life with his honorable mother and his blessed fiancée one long round of country rapture. The third-person narrator seems to reside within this adolescent outlook in the early chapters for reasons of parody—that is, to explore this point of view in order to expose it, to employ the young Pierre's eyes in order to explode their naiveté. Both the point of view and the vision of life in which it takes its bearings are soon qualified in a radical way by Pierre's introduction to "the ambiguities" (the subtitle of the book) of the wonder-world which had been heretofore unknown to him. That Pierre inhabits a world resounding intermittently with portents of the transcendent there can be little doubt after the opening paragraph of the book—one which belongs to the omniscient narrator: "There are some strange summer mornings in the country, when he who is but a sojourner from the city shall early walk forth into the fields, and be wonder-smitten with the trance-like aspect of the green and golden world. Not a flower stirs; the trees forget to wave; the grass itself seems to have ceased to grow; and all Nature, as if suddenly become conscious of her own profound mystery, and feeling no refuge from it but silence, sinks into this wonderful and indescribable repose" (*P,* 3). The Pierre who sallies forth in this "green and golden world" is not, however, the man, recently from the city, who will be "smitten" by the wondrous scene. For him, the "trance-like" quietude does not evoke bafflement; he regards it, if he considers it at all, as a birthright. With the arrival of the letter from Isabel, however, Pierre will encounter a dark portent in the wonder-world which will blast away his already attained and juvenilely assumed "felicities" and will locate him, after his own fashion, in the orbit of misery and epistemological despair characteristic of Ahab's peril.

Until Isabel makes her disclosures, and becomes herself the form through which loom irradiant disclosures of another world, the youth had worshipped at the shrine of his father which, for Pierre, "supported the entire one-pillared temple of his moral life" (*P*, 68). The inheritance from the father, "now incorruptibly sainted in heaven," is the figurement of purity: "In this shrine, in this niche of this pillar, stood the perfect marble form of his departed father; without blemish, unclouded, snow-white, and serene; Pierre's fond personification of perfect human goodness and virtue. Before this shrine, Pierre poured out the fullness of all young life's most reverential thoughts and beliefs. Not to God had Pierre ever gone in his heart, unless by ascending the steps of that shrine, and so making it the vestibule of his abstractest religion" (*P*, 68). On the basis of these "images of the past" (*P*, 69), Pierre has fashioned a vision of experience as the goodness and beauty and serenity which are commensurate with and ostensibly validated by the blissful situation of his present.

Such a vision is in peril immediately, according to Ishmael's final vision of the wonder-world, because it has not yet fronted and will not wash in its ignorance of the dark, watery "two-thirds of this earth" which have more of sorrow than joy in them. Here, the third-person narrator of *Pierre,* now pulled away from the point of view of Pierre, shares Ishmael's understanding as he forewarns the reader about the hazardous course the title character will run:

So choicely, and in some degree, secludedly nurtured, Pierre, though now arrived at the age of nineteen, had never yet become so thoroughly initiated into that darker, though truer aspect of things, which an entire residence in the city from the earliest period of life, almost invariably engraves upon the mind of any keenly observant and reflective youth of Pierre's present years. So that up to this period, in his breast, all remained as it had been; and to Pierre, his father's shrine seemed spotless, and still new as the marble of the tomb of him in Arimathea.

Judge, then, how all-desolating and withering the blast, that for Pierre, in one night, stripped his holiest shrine of all overlaid bloom, and buried the mild statue of the saint beneath the prostrated ruins of the soul's temple itself. (*P,* 69)

Although the narrator suggests here the juxtaposition of the "rural bowl of milk" from which Pierre presently drinks to the "city of sorrows" he will come to inhabit, the equation does not hold steadfastly.[7] The city becomes a veil of tears for Pierre, at least in part, because he takes to it eyes which are filled with tears, a soul which is full of woe, and there is evidence to suggest that the wonder-world of the countryside does not present only peace and delight but a deeper and more ambivalent aspect than the fatuous Pierre has cared to pursue. There are opportunities, in the midst of all his country optimism, which Pierre never seizes but which might have taught him the efficacy of a less superficial vision: he fails to see the "double" quality of his dead father, imaged in the two portraits; he fails to see the crass pride and pretension which are the underside of his hearth and home; he will not leave the well-travelled trail in the woods to enter the ambiguities of the deeper forest he senses are there. But the point is that, city or country, the early Pierre is not "keenly observant and reflective" and is, therefore, prey to that "all-desolating and withering" portent which, as a matter of fact, blasts him in the rural setting in a form he cannot refuse.

The signal portent in Pierre's experience looms through the form of Isabel, the heretofore secret half-sister whose appearance exposes the infidelity and shame of Pierre's revered father, and Isabel comes with all the accoutrements which belong to the symbolic resonance of the wonder-world. Even before he sees her in propria persona, Pierre has a presentiment of Isabel which painfully interrupts his unvarying round of country sunshine:

So far as this girl lies upon the common surface, ineffable composure steeps her. But still, she sideways steals the furtive, timid glance. Anon, as yielding to the irresistible climax of her concealed emotions, whatever they may be, she lifts her whole marvelous countenance into the radiant candlelight, and for one swift instant, that face of supernaturalness unreservedly meets Pierre's. Now, wonderful loveliness, and a still more wonderful loneliness, have with inexplicable implorings, looked up to him from that henceforth immemorial face. There, too, he seemed to see the fair ground where Anguish had contended with Beauty, and neither being conqueror, both had laid down on the field. (*P*, 46–47)

This prescient moment reaches Pierre after the fashion of the spirit-spout in *Moby-Dick:* it is furtive even in its disclosiveness; it is ambiguous and inexplicable; it allures and yet fills one with dread; it presents the supernatural in the forms of the natural suddenly made irradiant. If for a time Pierre is seized by this portent, if he is struck with "a wild, bewildering, and incomprehensible curiosity" (*P*, 47) in the face of this wondrous instant, he attempts nonetheless to dismiss it as a "harmless temporary aberration" (*P*, 48). Still, although wanting to reject that which will fill him with woe, Pierre finds himself "bewilderingly allured . . . by its nameless beauty, and its long-suffering, hopeless anguish" (*P*, 49).

The letter from Isabel verifies the vision, and Pierre's first encounter with her verifies for him Isabel's portentousness: on the threshhold "and holding the light above her supernatural head, Isabel stands before him" and Pierre is "overpowered with bodily faintness and spiritual awe" (*P*, 112). In Isabel's countenance, Pierre discovers the "death-like beauty" and "immortal sadness" (*P*, 112) which make her belong to another world, and the history of herself which Isabel recites enforces all the resonances of grief and darkness which are boded by her symbolic figurement. She is the wild and tumultuous sea, the insane and dark night, the insulted outcast groping for home, the child of the "deep stunted pine woods" (*P*, 114) which "hummed with unconjecturable voices of unknown birds and beasts" (*P*, 115); she is, she tells Pierre, a person who "'never knew a mortal mother'" (*P*, 114) and who can recall her life only in "'dim images'" (*P*, 115). She is, in all of these disclosures, the very incarnation of that darker world which is opposite to anything Pierre has ever lived and which seems to call all his previous experience into question. She brings him a hint of the unrecoverable past—a shadowy recollection of his father—which countervails the immobile image of his father Pierre has secured in the present, and thus she is for Pierre the "all-desolating" agency which undermines the "central pillar" of his green and golden world. Above all else, however, Isabel is, as symbol, the essence of mystery—portending the transcendent and hiding its source and motive in her own opaque and impenetrable form. Pierre now sees, he thinks, "the complex web of life" which no system can clarify:

In her life there was an unraveled plot; and he felt that unraveled it would eternally remain to him. No slightest hope or dream had he, that what was dark and mournful in her would ever be cleared up into some coming atmosphere of light and mirth. Like all youths, Pierre had conned his novel-lessons; had read more novels than most persons of his years; but their false, inverted attempts at systematizing eternally un-systematizable elements; their audacious, intermeddling impotency, in trying to unravel, and spread out, and classify, the more thin than gos-samer threads which make up the complex webs of life; these things over Pierre had no power now. Straight through their helpless miser-ableness he pierced; the one sensational truth in him, transfixed like beetles all the speculative lies in them. He saw that human life doth truly come from that, which all men are agreed to call by the name of *God;* and that it partakes of the unravelable inscrutableness of God. By infal-lible presentiment he saw, that not always doth life's beginning gloom conclude in gladness; that wedding-bells peal not ever in the last scene of life's fifth act. (*P,* 141)

With this Pierre confirms what his presentiments of Isabel had led him to suspect—that in her image is to be located something which "almost unmans me with its wonderfulness" and that in her story is to be found something which, "by a silent and tyran-nical call, [is] challenging him in his deepest moral being, and summoning Truth, Love, Pity, Conscience, to the stand" (*P,* 49). Pierre meets the challenge by pledging his undying allegiance to Isabel and to the dark revelations she presents. He is fully pre-pared to acknowledge the summons to his moral being; he will atone for his father, will act out the demands on "Conscience" and of "Pity" and "Love," and will do so because Isabel's gloomy disclosures, and the mystery which attaches to them, ring with the "Truth." All of this represents Pierre's "practical resolve" (*P,* 141) toward Isabel's person, and, as for Isabel as symbol, "Pierre renounced all thought of ever having Isabel's dark-lantern illuminated to him," and he "determined to pry not at all into this sacred problem" (*P,* 141).

This is the point at which Pierre begins to run something like the course of Ahab's peril, for, if like Ahab he acknowledges the reality of the wonder-world, he responds to it in kind. When he is "unmanned" by Isabel's dark revelations, as when Ahab had been maimed by the white whale, Pierre assumes that he has received a final revelation, thinks that he has seen through to its absolute and universal meaning, and elevates that singular meaning to the level of "one sensational truth." Isabel becomes for Pierre, as Moby Dick became for Ahab, the "apex of all wonders" (*P,* 49) and for Pierre, as for Ahab, the apex abolishes the efficacy of all other elements, aspects, and forms of the wonder-world and becomes the object of an intensely monistic vision which issues in an undeviatingly practical resolve. When confronted with Isabel's dimly imaged midnight knowledge, Pierre concludes that all his previous experience has been fraudulent, that it has led him "through gay gardens to a gulf," and that he must discard his bright life and assume this dark angel Isabel. He convinces himself that the ultimate wisdom lies in the woe surrounding Isabel and that he has achieved such wisdom in his "unfallible presentiment . . . that not always doth life's beginning gloom conclude in gladness."

Despite Pierre's dismissing his early experience so utterly that he now dates his "life's beginning" with the gloom he has found in Isabel and despite his frenzied assertions of the infallibility of his vision, the narrator, now pulled completely away from Pierre's point of view, knows full well that the youth's early world was not false and that it was only Pierre's one-sided perception of it that was false, a fallacy he will now enact again by making Isabel's truth absolute. The narrator, sharing the retrospective Ishmael's sense of the nature of the world, recognizes that the green and golden world is intermingled with the "deep stunted pine forest," that portents of one are not exclusive, do not abolish portents of the other, and that the disclosures of both only relativize the disclosures of each. Further, the narrator realizes that Pierre is imperiled not only by his elevation of one portentous disclosure but also by his insistence that he has gained the final meaning of life in that disclosure. Knowing with Ishmael that in the symbol there is silence and concealment as well as revelation, the narrator possesses, and the reader gains, the insight Pierre will never achieve. Just as Ahab swears by his woe, Pierre confines himself with Isabel, and, just as Ahab must refuse the validity of the sunset that would soothe his tormented spirit, Pierre will refuse Lucy, whose "more recent life" (*P*, 327) has given her a portentousness of light fully equal to Isabel's darkness: "That unsullied complexion of bloom was now entirely gone, without being any way replaced by sallowness, as is usual in similar instances. And as if her body indeed were the temple of God, and Marble indeed were the only fit material for so holy a shrine, a brilliant, supernatural whiteness now gleamed in her cheek. Her head sat on her shoulders as a chiseled statue's head; and the soft, firm light in her eye seemed as much a prodigy, as though a chiseled statue should give token of vision and intelligence" (*P*, 328). Isabel and Pierre are "most strangely moved by this sweet unearthliness in the aspect of Lucy" (*P*, 328), but Pierre is by now completely confirmed in his woe and will not admit the validity of the happier, consoling allusiveness of the wonder-world portended by Lucy's symbolic presence. Later, "before the eyes of seated Lucy, Pierre and Isabel stood locked; Pierre's lips upon her cheek" (*P*, 334). He embraces his darkness in the midst of the light.[8]

Like Ahab, Pierre forms a practical resolution on the basis of, and with the hope of surmounting, the vision of woe which hems him in, and, as with Ahab, the failure of the resolution leads Pierre to the exclusive concentration on his own limitations. Ahab would strike through "the paste-board masks" figured for him by Moby Dick and would thus locate the inscrutable thing which maddens him. Pierre would atone for the sins of his father and would thus master the ambiguities which haunt him. Just as Ahab finds his own image reflected to him in the doubloon which is the white whale's talisman, however, Pierre finds that he contains in himself ambiguities exceeding any others. From his first presentiment of Isabel, Pierre had sought the reason of the subtler secret within himself:

Wonder interlocks with wonder; and then the confounding feeling comes. No cause have we to fancy, that a horse, a dog, a fowl, ever stand transfixed beneath yon skyey load of majesty. But our soul's arches underfit into its; and so, prevent the upper arch from falling on us with unsustainable inscrutableness. "Explain ye my deeper mystery," said the shepherd Chaldean king, smiting his breast, lying on his back upon the plain; "and then, I will bestow all my wonderings upon ye, ye stately stars!" So, in some sort with Pierre. Explain thou this strange integral feeling in me myself, he thought—turning upon the fancied face—and I will renounce all other wonders, to gaze wonderingly at thee. (P, 51)

The "confounding feeling" remains with Pierre to the last just because he renounces "all other wonders to gaze wonderingly" at the ambiguities with which Isabel's dark presence leaves him. At the last, just as the white whale eludes Ahab's ability to know him and returns the captain to his own woe, Pierre suffers the same epistemological despair because he cannot plumb the depths of his own interiority.

If Ishmael has touched upon an ultimate being, has recognized his limits, and has returned to a world in which wonder is manifest everywhere, Pierre, like Ahab, has seen the disclosive presence of the transcendent in his experience, has refused to accept his inability to penetrate to its ultimately hidden character, and has been returned to a world which taunts him with its inscrutability. As the narrator observes in an aside to the reader, Pierre "had not as yet procured for himself that enchanter's wand of the soul, which but touching the humblest experiences in one's life, straightaway it starts up all eyes, in every one of which are endless significancies" (P, 284). The Ahab who would pierce the white whale's hidden life must finally "burst his hot heart's shell" against the impenetrable externality of the whale. The Pierre who would resolve the ambiguities must finally drown in the immense amplitude of his own ambiguous interiority. Neither has seized the meaning of the transcendent; both can only rail at the skies to disclose all. And neither has gained the full significance of the wonder-world they inhabit, for both refuse aspects of that world's portentousness which would support their passage.

When the opportunity arises for Pierre to accept the squeeze of the hand held out to him in Lucy's tenderness and sympathy,

he has by now become so thoroughly afloat in the seas of his own
interior woe that he can no more receive this offering than Ahab
could seize the similar occasion presented him by Pip. Pierre has
learned that, because God permits him to suffer his anguish, he
must look at life with eyes prepared for ill, and, because he looks
with eyes clouded by woe, he can only suspect that what Lucy
now brings to him is only another element to contribute to the
ambiguity of his situation. Moreover, Pierre, again like Ahab,
will not put down his iron crown of woe because he has turned
the concentrated cannon of his self-centeredness to a prideful
sense of the nobility of the task in which consists his practical
resolve. By atoning for the sins of his father, he will, he continues to believe, clear away the ambiguities, and thus he will
accept, with a strong sense of his martyr's cause, all the self-
abuse which he assures himself goes into the atonement. Even
the punishment of himself itself finally becomes ambiguous: his
virtue remains unrewarded except in his own egotistical self-
congratulation.

In passing through these stages, Pierre embodies the dilemma
posed in Plinlimmon's pamphlet: "'What man who carries a
heavenly soul in him, has not groaned to perceive, that unless he
committed a sort of suicide as to the practical things of this
world, he can never hope to regulate his earthly conduct by that
same heavenly soul?'" (*P*, 213). Now, although the narrator
recognizes that this statement by Plinlimmon is more "the ex-
cellently illustrated re-statement of a problem, than the solution
of the problem itself" (*P*, 210), Pierre, consciously or not, adopts
it as a method: by cloistering himself from the world, he "committed a sort of suicide" in order to pursue his sense of virtuous-
ly regulated "earthly conduct." When this mode of response fails
him and leaves him with a conduct of life which only issues in
more suffering and more ambiguity, his pride will not permit him
to relent, to receive the partial return of his "worldly felicity"
(*P*, 209). His narrowly concentrated and self-returning vision
prevents his seizing and possessing the meaning of the portents
which appear to him. Because he cannot "solve" the earth, cannot surmount the ambiguities with his suffering atonement,
Pierre is at last "struck with the sort of infidel idea [articulated

in the pamphlet], that whatever other worlds God may be Lord of, he is not the Lord of this; for else this world would seem to give the lie to Him; so utterly repugnant seem its ways to the instinctively known ways of Heaven" (*P,* 213). Pierre wants a God and a world which answer to his human sense of virtue and justice, and, when the world will not so answer, he repudiates it outright, rejects Lucy *and* Isabel and the element of the wondrous which belongs to each. He cannot return like Ishmael to a world touched with wonder because his unilateral interpretation of experience precludes his taking the span of portents. The narrator has known all along that Pierre's attempts to live as if he had gained the ultimate knowledge of the transcendent were bound to be doomed, for the source of the wonder-world, the hidden God, remains finally hidden to human knowing: "That profound Silence, that only Voice of our God, which I before spoke of; from that divine thing without a name, those imposter philosophers pretend somehow to have got an answer; which is as absurd, as though they should say they had got water out of stone; for how can a man get a Voice out of Silence?" (*P,* 208). Because he has lived exclusively on the answer he thinks disclosed absolutely in Isabel, because he refuses the full range of the wonder-world, Pierre never gains any sense of the significance of his own suffering, fails to realize that the portents can "betray to Pain" and that woe can "come in the path to God" (*P,* 159–60), and, withal, he fails finally to transcend "the fine hammered steel" of his own anguish. If the earth will not satisfy his infallible sense of the known ways of Heaven—the ways of virtue rewarded and justice made clear—that earth cannot be redeemed in his eyes; he cannot at last be returned to it by the reasons of the heart, cannot accept its ambiguity which, in its full range, might have supported him. The would-be master of the ambiguities becomes the slave of his own limitations; if he had wanted to resolve the ambiguities by atoning for his father, he is finally his mother's child—the son of the Mrs. Glendinning who declares "'I hate a mystery'" (*P,* 47). Against the world of mystery, then, Pierre turns a "wolfish heart," and against the mystery of his own interiority, he turns a suicidal hand.

Now, this parade of failures, this procession of characters

from Queequeg to Pierre whose responses imperil them in the wonder-world, does not mean that Melville felt the necessity to reject the vision Ishmael had so laboriously gained. He was not prepared, after surveying the successive demises of Ahab and Pierre, to conclude that the wonder-world was false, regardless of how intractable and frustrating that world became for these epistemological heroes. Despite his obvious, if not unmixed, admiration for the assaults on the heavens by Ahab and Pierre— his sense, articulated by the narrator of *Pierre,* that "whoso storms the sky gives best proof he came from thither!" (*P,* 347) —Melville retained the view that neither Ahab nor Pierre was betrayed by the world but was, rather, betrayed by his own flawed responses to it. The fact that the narrator of *Pierre* has now become a third-person omniscient narrator is significant because the transition indicates that the vision achieved by Ishmael's first-person struggle is now the organizing vision of Melville's fiction, a vision to which, in *Pierre,* the author himself recommits himself. In his rehearsal of Pierre's failure, and the failure of Ahab from which it in part stems, he was apparently seeking to expose those failures of response for the same reason that he presented the "perilous" responses of other, less grand, characters. The successive appearances of all the faulty and perilous modes of responding to experience signal Melville's realism about the public world in which he knew his fictive vision would have to be ratified. Convinced of the reality of the wonder-world, and the correlative necessity to take the span of portents, Melville felt that he was submitting his model of self-transcendence, and the view of the world in which it could be achieved, to an audience whose eyesight was seriously impaired. Having used his fiction in *Moby-Dick* and *Pierre* to assay the perils of human vision, he might well have despaired about the odds against his own vision of human possibility. But the most severe test of his own sense of life's conciliatory dimension was yet to come. In *Billy Budd,* Melville's last major fiction, the possibilities for man in a world to which the transcendent is present collide with the realities of life perceived after the more habitual human responses to a man-of-war world.

CHAPTER EIGHT

IN PARTIBUS INFIDELIUM
Billy Budd *and the Part of Wonder in a Man-of-war World*

In *Billy Budd,* the last of his major fictions, Herman Melville returned to the metaphor for the fallen world—the pent-up wickedness of five hundred men aboard a man-of-war—which he had developed in his first book, *Typee.* All his realism about life had convinced him that there was that in man, as he had hypothesized in "The House-Tops" (1863), which "corroborated Calvin's creed." If his fictions had been pressed into the service of seeking out and articulating a ground and a mode of transcending the condition of that fallen life, he had, after *Typee,* assumed that fallen condition was not only a trope but a reality. Indeed, the reconciliation of man with the ground of his experience—with the model figured in Ishmael which delineated the form and the possibility of that self-transcending activity—was only necessary because of what he took to be the signs of man's fallen life. Those signs are everywhere evident and acknowledged in Melville's fictions: they come in the forms of some nameless woe which haunts the protagonists in their early careers because they cannot find in their experience that which buoys them up, supporting their lives with meaning and richness; they come in the forms of several species of flawed perception about experience which preclude characters' recognition of and proper response to the context of ultimacy present to them. Indications are also to the fore in Melville's work that the world of experience itself in its variety had within it that which could incline human perception toward perilous response: there is a demonic element apparently built into the structures of the created order; there is the presence of the snake which, if exclusively accredited, could ravish human perception and instill in it its own demonic principles. Melville had seen "The Maldive Shark"—that "pale ravener of horrible meat"—and he knew that this incipient cannibalism in the created order was duplicated in human life, violently feeding on its own frail humanity and thus enacting the basest impulses of its fallen nature. Nowhere were these signs of the Fall more profoundly apparent to Melville than in the microcosmic world of the man-of-war. There, he found all the truncated sense of ultimacy which goes with nationalistic fervor, the deeply flawed perception about the nature and possibility of human experience, the inclination of man to bare the "serrated teeth" of his shark-like nature in order to feed on his kind. There Melville found imaged in the total architectonics of the ship—its theory, design, purpose, and use—the acknowledgment by man about man that he is fundamentally and inherently a man "of war." To this world of the man-of-war Melville's unfaltering realism returns him in *Billy Budd*.

To suggest that Melville is brought back by his realism to a world which corroborates Calvin's creed, however, is not at all to conclude that he had finally resigned himself to such a world and had surrendered his vision of the wonder-world. The fact that he returns to the world perceived in microcosm as a man-of-war indicates only that Melville retained a strong sense of the historical contexts in which his fictive vision would have to find its proper life. He knew that vision had no possibility of transfiguring the vision of the culture unless it could be shown to be a realistic possibility, recognizable by the culture in its own prevailing terms. This is the challenge always faced by imaginative efforts which seek to transform the attitudes and perceptions they address. As Ray L. Hart has written: "Imagination is therefore ineluctably bound up with the historical possibilities of human being. With that imagination is not a license to invent *ex nihilo;* it cannot, in an undemented self, intend a world that is not bound to the historical past it renews; indeed, renewal means the disclosure of ontological possibility funded in the ontic,

temporal past, that now must be brought forward historically." [1]
In the amplitude of sea-room afforded by the "four several cruising-grounds" of *Moby-Dick,* Ishmael locates and enacts the integral response to a world exhilarated with the wondrous—a
world the vision of which Melville could affirm to the extent that
its demands become, in *Moby-Dick* and *Pierre,* the test of human response. It was just this vision that Melville was seeking
to give to his age, for he was convinced that this world, instinct
with significances, was a world enabled by the deepest ontological possibilities. Convinced as he was of the reality of the wonder-world gained by Ishmael's strenuous questing, however,
Melville knew realistically that Ishmael was outcast and that his
vision was a decidedly alien one in the age. With Ishmael, he
had bottomed upon the truth, but Melville realized that this
truth would appear ridiculous to contemporaries whose versions
of reality were framed after a different fashion. Still, like the
reformer, Melville felt that he had, as Father Mapple had extra-
polated in the case of Jonah, "to preach the Truth to the face of
Falsehood" and to hope, with that literary preaching, to transform the imagination of his age.

The significance of Melville's returning to the fictive world
represented by the man-of-war is that it signals the author's seriousness about the question of the potential of a literary vision to
give to the regnant historical perception a new, transfiguring idea
of the experience which is its essential condition. It was fundamentally a question of the capacity of Ishmael's responses to
find ratification in the face of, and therefore to supersede, more
characteristic responses to experience which belonged to the
times. The degree of Melville's seriousness becomes apparent in
the selections he made for his final fiction, for in *Billy Budd* he
pits the validity of Ishmael's location of a redemptive possibility
for man against the conception of man dramatized in his most
fallen aspect by confronting the potentiality of the wonder-world
with the historical reality of the man-of-war world; in short, he
forces Ishmael's affirmations into a context which, by its very
nature, calls those affirmations most radically into question. In
Billy Budd, the truth Ishmael has located in a vast sea-room
must now reach adjudication on the narrow decks of a line-of-

battle ship. If the wonder-world had tested characters' perceptions in *Moby-Dick* and *Pierre*, if the demands of that world had exposed peril in man, the issue in *Billy Budd* becomes the efficacy of the appeal of the reign of wonder to a man, Captain Vere, whose entire view is committed to his sense of the reality of a man-of-war world.

The dimension of the wondrous occurs to Vere within the martial setting of the narrative in two signal portents—Billy Budd and John Claggart—which start everything up to themselves in a strange, unfettered, and exhilarated atmosphere. With all their symbolic resonances, these two characters, in themselves and in their clashing, present a portentous time of some extended periodicity, a time entered, if unknowingly at first, by Captain Vere. Brought by the situation into the encounter with the symbolic forms, Vere recognizes the wondrous dimension disclosed to him, but he cannot shake off the habits of a lifetime which preclude his taking the span of portents. The form of perilous response he enacts is the most destructive one possible, flowing as it does out of the very nature of the man-of-war vision of life, and the response itself adumbrates the significance of Melville's having brought the vision of the wonder-world into the presence of a man for whom the promises of wonder remain *in partibus infidelium.*

I

Like the narrator of *Pierre,* the narrator of *Billy Budd* shares all the senses of the nature and requirements of the wonder-world that belong to Ishmael's retrospective account in *Moby-Dick.* From the outset, the narrator of *Billy Budd* brings to his auditors' attention the fact that the tale he tells occurs in the midst of charged times. The opening remarks of his prefatory passage establish the mise-en-scène: "The year 1797, the year of this narrative, belongs to a period which, as every thinker now feels, involved a crisis for Christendom not exceeded in its undetermined momentousness at the time by any other era whereof there is record. The opening proposition made by the Spirit of the Age involved rectification of the Old World's hereditary wrongs" (*B,* "Preface").[2] Under Melville's firm control, then, the narrator returns his attention to an historical moment in which the old forms of life were being called into question by new energies. It was a moment, he as much as tells us, the presaging quality of which is indisputable, and Melville makes his narrator insistent about this fact because he wanted to provide a realistic context, historically recognizable, which itself partook even in its martial aspect of the unfettered and exhilarated moment. The "historical" description in the "Preface" constructs just such a huge, electric, critical time: "Straightway the Revolution itself became a wrong-doer, one more oppressive than the kings. Under Napoleon it enthroned upstart kings, and initiated that prolonged agony of continual war whose final throe was Waterloo. During those years not the wisest could have foreseen that the outcome of all would be what to some thinkers apparently it has since turned out to be—a political advance along nearly the whole line for Europeans" (*B,* "Preface"). Even in its demonic forms, the moment brimmed with the currents of its own periodicity; all of the energies of it—some promising, some menacing—made it a profoundly contingent time, abundant with power and obscure meaning, containing crises for history itself and putting man in anxiety about the terms of his living. Life is suddenly charged and instinct with significance at every turn, with each moment calling the preceding one into question. In short, the epoch borrows for description from the vocabulary attaching to the wonder-world.

Having established this intensified epoch as a historical stage on which the drama of life grows larger, the narrator narrows the epoch to maritime life in order to depict, again from historical record, that drama in smaller form:

Now, as elsewhere hinted, it was something caught from the Revolutionary Spirit that at Spithead emboldened the man-of-war's men to rise against real abuses, long-standing ones, and afterwards at the Nore to make inordinate demands—successful resistance to which was confirmed only when the ringleaders were hung for an admonitory spectacle to the anchored fleet. Yet in a way analogous to the operation of the Revolution at large—the Great Mutiny, though by Englishmen naturally deemed monstrous at the time, doubtless gave the first latent prompting to most important reforms in the British navy. (*B*, "Preface")

But the narrative interest is more specific still. If the tale will have as its largest backdrop the critical times of the revolutionary aftermath and if, within that momentous time for Christendom, the circumambience of the tale will be defined by the radically contingent and anxious awareness of time which surrounds the Great Mutiny, the narrator's concern is with a presaging moment which plays itself out in yet a smaller theatre: "Passion, and passion in its profoundest, is not a thing demanding a palatial stage whereon to play its part. Down among the groundlings, among the beggars and rakers of garbage, profound passion is enacted. And the circumstances that provoke it, however trivial or mean, are no measure of its power. In the present instance the stage is a scrubbed gun deck, and one of the external provocations a man-of-war's-man's spilled soup" (*B*, 78–79). The narrator lures the reader into a wonder-world *within* the context of those historical times which the reader cannot doubt were instances brimming over with crisis, moment, and passion. The effect, and no doubt the purpose, of this telescopic narrative technique—this ranging across Europe, narrowing to Spithead and the Nore, and focusing at last on the gundecks of the *Bellipotent*—is to lend credence to the validity of the fiction because the implication left with the reader is that the wonder-world he has entered possesses all the momentousness, energy, and significance of the encompassing, historically verifiable time. With introduction onto this less than palatial stage of John Claggart and Billy Budd, whose undeniably portentous characters bode a dimension which transcends the "scrubbed gun-decks" whereon they walk, the establishment of the possibility of wonderment even in a man-of-war world is complete.

In the figurement of Claggart, the master-at-arms, there is clearly the kind of allusiveness and yet secrecy, disclosure and yet concealment, command and yet mystery, which make him stand as a symbol after the fashion of the symbols in Ishmael's wonder-world. His face is a "notable one . . . [with] features all except the chin cleanly cut as those on a Greek medallion," and this chin "had something of a strange protuberant heaviness in its make" (B, 64). Claggart's visage "seemed to hint of something defective or abnormal in the constitution and the blood," but his aspect is nonetheless commanding because the mark of "his eye could cast a tutoring glance" which tyrannized those around him. His singularity marks him off from the ordinary because "his general aspect and manner were . . . suggestive of an education and career incongruous with his naval function" (B, 64). For the time, however, everything about Claggart comes in hints, suggestiveness, indirection—through allusion to Greek medallions, Tecumseh, Titus Oates—and the narrator must own that Claggart's "portrait I essay, but shall never hit it" (B, 64). At this early point in the narrative, then, Claggart "conceals" as symbol. If his appearance and presence are allusive, he remains in an "official seclusion from the sunlight" in which the other seamen know each other; he is a man "who for reasons of his own was keeping incog" (B, 64). As symbol, then, his depth is unsounded: "nothing was known of his former life," and "the dearth of exact knowledge as to his true antecedents [the thing apparently defective or abnormal signalled by his pallor] opened to the invidious a vague field for unfavorable surmise" (B, 64–65).

Fully as singular as Claggart in his aspect is Billy Budd, who is portrayed by the narrator in the early pages as possessing the same symbolic allusiveness and furtiveness which yet portends different substance. In the genre of the "Handsome Sailor" to which he belongs, Billy moves among other seamen "like Aldebaran among the lesser lights of his constellation" and is most notable for his "off-hand unaffectedness of natural regality" (B, 43). When removed from his merchant's ship to board the *Bellipotent,* Billy's aspect, the commanding officer exclaims, makes him "'Apollo with his portmanteau!'" (B, 48)—an allusion suggested by Billy's "youth, and free heart" (B, 49). According to the narrator, moreover, Billy "showed in face that humane look of reposeful good nature which the Greek sculptor in some instances gave to his heroic strongman, Hercules" (B, 51). Like Claggart, then, Billy arrives and is presented in suggestiveness and allusion; he can only be described, it seems, with reference to Aldebaran, Apollo, Hercules, Adam before the Fall: "The ear, small and shapely, the arch of the foot, the curve in mouth and nostril, even the indurated hand dyed to the orange-tawny of the toucan's bill, a hand telling alike of the halyards and the tar-bucket; but, above all, something in the mobile expression, and every chance attitude and movement, something suggestive of a mother eminently favored by Love and the Graces" (*B*, 51). Further like Claggart, Billy's countenance stands "in direct con-tradiction to his lot" aboard ship, for "noble descent was as evident in him as a blood horse" (*B*, 52). Just as Claggart's allu-siveness makes him seem to refer to the savage and insidious and dark, all of Billy's resonance refers to models of peace and inno-cence and light. If Claggart's dark eye can quail, Billy comes "welkin-eyed" (*B*, 44); if Claggart secludes himself, Billy is wide open; if Claggart becomes the subject for invective, Billy, at least aboard the *Rights of Man,* stands as "cynosure" (*B*, 50), a "sig-nal object," evoking "the spontaneous homage of his shipmates" (*B*, 43). But, like Claggart, Billy unavoidably conceals more than he discloses at this early point in the narrative. When he is asked "'Who was your father?'" Billy can reply that only "'God knows, Sir'" (*B*, 51).

As symbols, then, Claggart and Billy are characterized by nothing so much as their disclosive and yet finally hidden na-tures, which demarcate both from the round of the ordinary. They present to the world of the *Bellipotent* what Carlyle refers to as "the wondrous agency of Symbols," for both contain in themselves that which enlarges the moment: both refer, in their resonances, to another, spiritual world, and yet both conceal any ultimate knowledge of that transcendent factor which lies at their source. Like the symbolic objects which had evoked Ish-mael's wonderment in *Moby-Dick,* Claggart and Billy throw up barriers to any epistemological inquiries which would seek to plumb their uttermost depths. As a part of his presentation of them, the narrator of *Billy Budd* assures the reader that these two signally portentous characters can, finally, only be won-dered at because each contains a depth-dimension, an arcane center at their hearts, to which human knowing cannot com-pletely penetrate. At one time, the narrator reports, he had thought any man—"however singular a study"—can be known by what he refers to as "'knowledge of the world'" (B, 74). In "turning on the hidden nature of the master-at-arms" (B, 76–77), however, the narrator recognizes the validity of lessons taught him "long ago . . . [by] an honest scholar" (B, 74) about the difficulty earthly knowledge has in its attempts to "define and denominate certain phenomenal men" (B, 75).[3] The scholar had lectured him about the gains of earthly knowledge:

"[It gives," he says,] . . . "but a superficial knowledge of it, serving ordinary purposes. But for anything deeper, I am not certain whether to know the world and to know human nature be not two distinct branches of knowledge, which while they may coexist in the same heart, yet either may exist with little or nothing of the other. Nay, in an average man of the world, his constant rubbing with it blunts that fine spiritual insight indispensable to the understanding of the essential in certain exceptional characters, whether evil ones or good. In a matter of some importance I have seen a girl wind an old lawyer about her little finger. Nor was it the dotage of senile love. Nothing of the sort. But he knew law better than he knew the girl's heart. Coke and Blackstone hardly shed so much light into obscure spiritual places as the Hebrew prophets. And who were they? Mostly recluses." (B, 75)

In short, then, the narrator realizes that at the heart of the symbol that is Claggart there resides one of those "obscure spiritual places" which men, with their "constant rubbing" against the man-of-war world, will not have the "spiritual insight" to enter.

These lessons of the scholar about the incapacity of earthbound men to sound the innermost hearts of certain supraordinary characters apply equally to the symbolic aspect of Billy Budd. The ultimately clouded center of Billy's nature and the inability of mere worldly wisdom to grasp it arise in the attempt of the narrator to define Billy's motives for submitting to the secret meeting with the afterguardsman who suggests mutiny and for remaining silent about it:

But shrewd ones may opine that it was hardly possible for Billy to refrain [later] from going up to the afterguardsman and bluntly demanding to know his purpose in the initial interview, so abruptly closed in the forechains. Shrewd ones may also think it but natural in Billy to set about sounding some of the other impressed men of the ship in order to discover what basis, if any, there was for the emissary's obscure suggestions as to plotting disaffection aboard. Yes, the shrewd may so think. But something more, or rather something else than mere shrewdness is perhaps needful for the due understanding of such a character as Billy Budd's. (*B*, 89–90)

Like Claggart, in this sense, Billy presents himself as a figurement of something which can only be wondered at and which cannot finally be solved. Both have in them that which refers to an ultimately hidden world of spirit, and both, even with this revelatory aspect, conceal in their opaqueness that which lies within and beyond themselves. In the very portentousness which marks them off, which connotes their association with the wonder-world, resides their mysteriousness—the spiritual quality which increases when they clash as symbols to form, in their conflict, the signal portentous episode of the narrative.

However much of concealment belongs to Claggart and Billy as symbols, they are, in their disclosive aspect, unmistakably clear as the narrator presents them to the eyes of the reader. Everything about Claggart, including his mystery, refers to his association with the element of evil organic in the fallen creation. After a digression into Plato, the narrator is forced to conclude that Claggart, in his revelatory aspect as symbol, borrows of "natural depravity": in him "was the mania of an evil nature, not engendered by vicious training or corrupting books or licentious living, but born with him and innate, in short 'a depravity according to nature'" (*B*, 76). The master-at-arms has about him that inexplicable "mania of an evil nature" which places him in direct lineage with the "'mystery of iniquity'" (*B*, 76) which can, in civilization, be cloaked in "the mantle of respectability" (*B*, 75). His depravity, with an outward countenance "dominated by intellectuality," has the look of reason about it, according to the narrator:

But the thing which in eminent instances signalizes so exceptional a nature is this: Though the man's even temper and discreet bearing would seem to intimate a mind peculiarly subject to the law of reason, not the less in his heart he would seem to riot in complete exemption from that law, having apparently little to do with reason further than to employ it as an ambidexter implement for effecting the irrational. That is to say: Toward the accomplishment of an aim which in wantonness of malignity would seem to partake of the insane, he will direct a cool judgment sagacious and sound. (*B*, 76)

In Claggart, such a nature is concentrated, "surcharged with energy," and with no recourse "left to it but to recoil upon itself and, like the scorpion for which the Creator alone is responsible, act out to the end the part allotted it" (*B*, 78). Each disclosure of him, however hidden its source and center, tends him toward the malignant.

   In Billy the revelatory aspect is equally clear. Everything about him, including his centric mystery, refers to an element of purity and innocence which belongs to transcendent goodness. If Claggart is the incarnation of natural depravity, Billy is the embodiment of all that is conceivable of natural goodness in a fallen world. He has the stutter that signals the interference of "the envious marplot of Eden" (*B*, 53), but, for all of that, Billy arrives as "little more than a sort of upright barbarian, much such perhaps as Adam presumably might have been ere the urbane Serpent wriggled himself into his company" (*B*, 52). If Claggart possesses a rabid heart and the sort of diabolical brain which can hide beneath civilized appearances of reason, Billy has nothing if not a pure heart and a mind utterly free of guile:

Billy, though happily endowed with the gaiety of high health, youth, and a free heart, was yet by no means of a satirical turn. The will to it and the sinister dexterity were alike wanting. To deal in double meanings and insinuations of any sort was quite foreign to his nature.
   As to his enforced enlistment, that he seemed to take pretty much as he was wont to take any vicissitude of weather. Like the animals, though no philosopher, he was, without knowing it, practically a fatalist. (*B*, 49)

In Billy, then, there is concentrated the nature of the "peacemaker," as he had been identified by his previous captain, for his passivity flows from pure acquiescence. Each disclosure of his nature, however unaccountable might be its sources, resounds with "virtues pristine and unadulterate" (*B*, 53).

II

Exhilaratedly symbolic as Claggart and Billy are, their clashing —in the world in which both appear—leaves no doubt that Billy is the major object of wonder in the narrative. However surcharged with energy Claggart might be as a symbolic character, his disclosiveness is of an order which the vision of a man-of-war world does not find astonishing when it is present. The narrator, early on in his general, historical description, had taken pains to point out that in such a world—no matter how presaging and significant and, indeed, wondrous are the times—"insolvent debtors," criminals, "lame ducks of morality," and the like find "in the navy a convenient and secure refuge" because "aboard a King's ship, they were as much in sanctuary as the transgressor of the Middle Ages harboring himself under the shadow of the altar" (*B*, 66–67). The theory and effect of the man-of-war—founded on the firm and continuously corroborated knowledge of human evil and corruption and violence—institutionalizes the very cannibal behavior against which it is designed to protect. John Claggart is no surprise to such knowledge; his rabid heart is simply one more symptom of the status quo which makes the man-of-war both possible and necessary. Perhaps because of his sheer "wantonness of malignity," covered by a dissembling nature, Claggart not only finds security and refuge on the floating envoy of civilization but is placed, as master-at-arms, at the very center of the vortices of power which make up such a world: "Of this maritime Chief of Police the ship's corporals, so called, were the immediate subordinates, and compliant ones; and this, as is to be noted in some business departments ashore, almost to a degree inconsistent with entire moral volition. His place put various converging wires of underground influence under the chief's control, capable when astutely worked through his understrappers of operating to the mysterious discomfort, if nothing worse, of any of the sea-commonalty" (*B*, 67). Far from being surprising to this world, Claggart's portentousness of evil is part and parcel of the basic perception of this world. His boding malignancy poses no apparent threat, for his pale cast of eye, which can give a "tutoring glance," makes him fully acceptable and useful in such a world. Further, Claggart has the mark of intellectuality, literacy, civilized life about him which, as the narrator has observed, allows the man-of-war world to enfold his evil in the mantle of respectability.

It is Billy Budd, rather, whose presence is to be marvelled at in such a world as that in which Claggart has his sphere of influence; it is Billy whose nature is strange and incongruous in this martial world, for he is, as his former captain had identified him, a "'jewel'" (*B,* 47) which glitters up even in the midst of the foulness around him. In his figurement is portended the possibility of human innocence and openness even in a strife-torn and anxious time, and thus all his disclosiveness as symbol poses a threat, however mildly embodied, to the vision and action of the man-of-war world in which those disclosures occur. Billy appears as cynosure of pacific humanity, and his very presence, hardly imaginable in the world in which it must make its appeal, calls into profound question the status quo which permits a Claggart security and influence. Claggart recognizes both the promise and the threat in Billy's spiritual resonances:

If askance he eyed the good looks, cheery health and frank enjoyment of young life in Billy Budd, it was because these went along with a nature that, as Claggart magnetically felt, had in its simplicity never willed malice or experienced the reactionary bite of that serpent. To him, the spirit lodged within Billy, and looking out from his welkin eyes as from windows, that ineffability it was which made the dimple in his dyed cheek, supplied his joints, and dancing in his yellow curls made him preeminently the Handsome Sailor. One person excepted the master-at-arms was perhaps the only man in the ship intellectually capable of adequately appreciating the moral phenomenon presented in Billy Budd. And the insight but intensified his passion, which assuming various secret forms within him, at times assumed that of cynic disdain, disdain of innocence—To be nothing more than innocent! Yet in an aesthetic way he saw the charm of it, the courageous free-and-easy temper of it, and fain would have shared it, but he despaired of it. (*B,* 78)

Billy's promise of peace is the portent whose span must be taken, for its presentation makes it the paramount object of wonder in the narrative; it is that which challenges astonishment and calls for a profound transformation of the regnant vision of the day. In Billy's form, there is disclosed that ineffable thing which withholds the promise of a new life and which demands, in its mild and graceful presence, to be acknowledged.

Thus, the question central to the drama of the entire narrative is brought into focus by the nagging doubts implicit in the narrator's description of Billy's transfer to the *Bellipotent*—the question of what will become of "such a novice in the complexities of factitious life, [in] the abrupt transition from his former and simpler sphere to the ampler and more knowing world of a great warship" (*B*, 50). Claggart, the representative par excellence of the world of the warship, and "with no power to annul the elemental evil in him" (*B*, 78), will bend all his energy to the effort of annihilating Billy's promise and, so, of ending Billy's threat. But Claggart, as symbol, only acts out "the part allotted" him: he is capable of "apprehending the good, but powerless to be it" (*B*, 78). If Claggart must attempt to destroy Billy, there is, the narrator hints, another "in the ship intellectually capable of adequately appreciating the moral phenomenon presented in Billy Budd." Starry Vere, like Claggart, is a resident of the prevailing man-of-war civilization, but the narrator's implication is that Vere, who "had a marked leaning toward everything intellectual" (*B*, 62), is capable of "apprehending the good." In any event, it is Captain Vere who must decide Billy's case: it is Vere who must adjudge this moral phenomenon, Vere who must answer the question of Billy, whose presence arrives "as if indeed exceptionally transmitted from a period prior to Cain's city" (*B*, 53), Vere who must ask Billy the question, addressed to Fabian, "'What hath thee . . . to the the city brought?'" (*B*, 53). It is Vere, at last, who is asked to take the span of portentousness of Billy Budd.

Until the time of the secret interview at which Vere asks Billy to answer to his accuser, the captain is not fully aware either of the extent of Claggart's civilized malignity or of the deep mystery of Billy's pristine innocence. In Claggart, Vere had located that which gives rise to "a vaguely repellent distaste" (*B*, 91), but Claggart had "hitherto...shown considerable tact in his function" (*B*, 93), had not at all startled Vere, accustomed to the man-of-war, with his malign presence aboard ship. Billy, on the other hand, had presented to Vere's observation a much stranger aspect—he "who in the nude might have posed [Vere thinks] for a statue of young Adam before the Fall" (*B*, 94)—altogether alien to, and wondrous in, the world of the *Bellipotent*. Vere has the capacity for wonder at this "signal figure," for it is "with unfeigned astonishment" (*B*, 94) that he hears Claggart name Billy as a mutineer. Faced with the necessity of encountering a portentous clash of symbols, Vere begins at this moment to enact the perilous form of vision which will render the possibilities of the reign of wonder *in partibus infidelium*. Although he will come to recognize the full portentousness of the moment which extends before him, although he will see the promise of Billy's revelations, he will respond to the portent out of the habits accrued for a lifetime, without acknowledging its efficacy, and will not take its span.

In the cabin, as Billy meets his accuser, Vere stands "prepared to scrutinize the mutually confronting visages" (*B*, 98), and he begins to seize the full depth of the portentousness of the moment, for Claggart and Billy, as always, are unmistakable in their disclosures. After Claggart reiterates the accusation and faces Billy, his countenance presents his unquestionable connection with the "mystery of iniquity":

Not at first did Billy take it in. When he did, the rose-tan of his cheek looked struck as by white leprosy. He stood like one impaled and gagged. Meanwhile the accuser's eyes, removing not as yet from the blue dilated ones, underwent a phenomenal change, their wonted rich violet color blurring into a muddy purple. Those lights of human intelligence, losing human expression, were gelidly protruding like the alien eyes of certain uncatalogued creatures of the deep. The first mesmeric glance was one of serpent fascination; the last was as the paralyzing lurch of the torpedo fish. (*B*, 98)

If Billy did not at first understand Claggart's menace, Vere has not missed its revelation. Still, Vere turns to the transfixed Billy and is "struck by his aspect even more than by Claggart's" (*B*, 98). Vere recognizes Billy's vocal impediment immediately, and everything he reads in Billy's face suggests to Captain Vere the sacrificial innocent brought to slaughter, the pure in heart, the peacemaker, brought down by violence. He sees in Billy's face an expression "like that of a condemned vestal priestess in the moment of being buried alive," for Vere locates there that "which was as a crucifixion to behold" (*B*, 99). There can be no doubt that Vere has seized upon the substance of these disclosures to him, and there can be no doubt that he recognizes in them the presence of some transcending goodness. When the surgeon arrives to examine the dead Claggart, Vere exclaims to him that "'it is the divine judgment on Ananias,'" that Claggart has been "'struck dead by an angel of God'" (*B*, 100–101).

Now, despite Vere's recognition of the transcendent presence that looms through Billy and the promise there of that which would redeem the man-of-war world, the captain will not meet the demands of the portent he encounters, for he cannot accredit its efficacy and cannot possess its significance for his life. Even before his exclamations to the surgeon, indeed even before he and Billy have picked up the prone Claggart, which was "like handling a dead snake" (*B*, 99), Captain Vere has adjudged the case. Almost instantaneously with Billy's striking Claggart, Vere has whispered that Billy is a "'fated boy'" (*B*, 99). He decides the case at the very moment that it occurs before him, for he "knows" what is required of him.[4] After his "passionate interjections" to the surgeon, then, Vere reverts to "something of his wonted manner" and calls together a "drumhead court" (*B*, 101) to try Billy's case.

As baffled with wonderment as he is in the face of Billy's resonance with divinity, as certain as he is of Billy's symbolic disclosures of peace and innocence, Vere refuses the rule of wonder and resumes the "spirit of common sense" with which he has been characterized from the outset and which he validates by his reading of "books treating of actual men and events" (*B*, 62):

In this line of reading he found confirmation of his own more reserved thoughts—confirmation which he had vainly sought in social converse, so that as touching most fundamental topics, there had got to be established in him some positive convictions which he forefelt would abide in him essentially unmodified so long as his intelligent part remained unimpaired. In view of the troubled period in which his lot was cast, this was well for him. His settled convictions were as a dyke against those invading waters of novel opinion social, political, and otherwise, which carried away as in a torrent no few minds in those days, minds by nature not inferior to his own. While other members of that aristocracy to which by birth he belonged were incensed at the innovators mainly because their theories were inimical to the privileged classes, Captain Vere disinterestedly opposed them not alone because they seemed to him insusceptible of embodiment in lasting institutions, but at war with the peace of the world and the true welfare of mankind. (B, 62–63)

On the basis of these considerations pertaining to Starry Vere, his instantaneous judgment on Billy and his summoning of the drumhead court should come as no surprise, for he responds to Billy's "wondrous" aspect in the same way that he responds to anything novel—by casting up the "dyke" of his "settled convictions" against the "invading waters." But much else about Vere is revealed here which explains why he will not be able to ratify and receive Billy's promise. Vere is a man who approaches his experience without the capacity to be altered by what it contains; he "forefeels" life and thus will remain "essentially unmodified" by it. All of his forefelt convictions make him scrutinize Billy Budd not in an effort to seize the disclosiveness there but, rather, in an attempt to assess the practical course of action with which Billy's act leaves him. Vere is a man ruled over by facticity, by his sense of the actual, and "his intelligent part" is thus persuaded immediately that the possibilities presented by Billy are incapable of "embodiment in lasting institutions." It is just this consideration which is finally decisive in Vere's judgment that Billy must be punished, for all of the captain's loyalties are to the forms of civilization which secure the order and, in his sense of things, "the peace of the world." Starry Vere has located such peace in the forms of order of the man-of-war world; as the poem from which he receives his nickname puts it, he has been "'in a domestic heaven nursed'" (B, 61). Vere's peace lies in the rules of order of the King's navy; aboard the *Bellipotent* he finds his "domestic heaven"; Billy must die, he is wont to say, because "'forms, measured forms are everything; and that is the import couched in the story of Orpheus with his lyre spellbinding the wild denizens of the wood'" (B, 128).

At Billy's trial, the sources and nature of the measured forms Vere swears by are betrayed fully out of the captain's own mouth. The drumhead court itself is summoned for a pro forma function—simply to ratify the decision Vere made instantaneously about Billy—but Vere is grateful for it because "it would not be a variance with usage" to share "the perils of moral responsibility" (*B,* 104). While on the face of it, Vere's arguments at the hearing seem to stem only from a sense of authoritative discipline for authority's sake, discipline because discipline is the rule, the roots of his defense of measured forms are actually in his settled convictions about the nature of man. Following the suggestion that Billy's punishment be mitigated, Vere launches the "argument of consequences" which clearly indicates his view that man corroborates Calvin's creed: "You know what sailors are. Will they not revert to the recent outbreak at the Nore? Ay. They know the well-founded alarm—the panic is struck throughout England. Your clement sentence they would account pusillanimous. They would think that we flinch, that we are afraid of them—afraid of practising a lawful rigor singularly demanded at this juncture lest, it should provoke new troubles. What shame to us such a conjecture on their part" (*B,* 112–13). Vere's argument reveals in a dramatic way both how little he has been grasped by Billy's portentousness and how thoroughly his common sense commits him to the "factitious life . . . of a great warship" (*B,* 50). Having encountered Billy, whose promise—if received—would go to contravene Calvin's creed, Vere's convictions about man remain "essentially unmodified," and the reasons for this are revealed during an earlier stage of his argument for the drumhead court. Sensing that the jurors are prey to the disclosures of transcendent innocence obvious in Billy's countenance, Vere, although he acknowledges that "the case is an exceptional one," reminds them that they are not "casuists or moralists" and that the case falls "under martial law practically to be dealt with" (*B,* 110): "But the exceptional in the matter moves the hearts within you. Even so too is mine moved. But let not warm hearts betray heads that should be cool. Ashore in a criminal case, will an upright judge allow himself off the bench to be waylaid by some tender kinswoman of the accused seeking

to touch him with her tearful plea? Well, the heart here, sometimes the feminine in man, is as that piteous woman, and hard
though it be, she must here be ruled out" (*B*, 111). Vere can
never take the span of Billy, can never be reigned over by wonder, because he rules out of consideration the reasons of the
heart. If he has seen Billy's promise of peace, if he is aware of
the transcendent dimension which lies within and beyond it, if
indeed he is convinced about Billy's innocence that "at the Last
Assizes it shall acquit" (*B*, 111), he brackets off the aspect of
wonder, refuses the demand of the transcendent, and thus narrows the context of ultimacy, and the context of his loyalties, to
the Articles of War.

Having touched on the level of the transcendent, in short,
Captain Vere insists that the deliberations "recur to the facts"
(*B*, 111), and the "facts," of course, substantiate the necessity of
the measured forms of the man-of-war. Having touched on the
possibilities of wonder and spurning the reasons of the heart,
Vere cannot return to a world whose cannibal aspect has been
ameliorated by the possibilities that portents like Billy present to
it; Vere's intelligent part, rather, inclines him away from the
vision of the possible toward the confirmation of what his common sense assures him are the practical necessities. In view of the
actualities of the outrages at the Nore, which corroborate Calvin's creed, Vere agonizingly casts the decisive vote for maintain-
ing the status quo of the man-of-war world—the world which,
in order to combat evil, gives evil refuge and security and influence at its own center. For Starry Vere, the reign of wonder remains *in partibus infidelium,* lost to the view of man and the
facts which are capable of embodiment in lasting institutions like
the man-of-war and which are indomitable.

III

In the dramatization of Vere's decision, a decision which to all
accounts appears inevitable because of his deep-seated and abid-
ing convictions about the nature of man and the consequent
necessity of the man-of-war, Melville acknowledges the remoteness of the possibility that the vision of a wonder-world could

be brought to birth in such a factitious world. Vere is the paradigmatic case, in a sense, because, among all the others aboard
the ship, he alone seems fully capable of seeing and seizing Billy's
disclosures in their significance for human life. When he refuses
this possibility, his action, controlled by Melville's historical realism, suggests that if Billy's revelations will be dismissed by
Vere as irrelevant in the situation then the possibility of reifying
the integral response to Billy has no chance at all. Vere represents
a kind of last resort; despite the drumhead court which seems to
share the responsibility for judging Billy's case, Vere recognizes
that he alone "is the one on whom the ultimate accountability
would rest" (*B,* 104). And thus the decision against Billy is
handed down from the very seat of authority of the man-of-war
world on behalf of what that authority takes to be the actualities
and necessities of that world. At the moment of Billy's hanging—
at the moment, that is, during which he is most completely repudiated by the world—Billy's character is disclosed most fully. He
confers a benediction on Vere, the sources of which are unmistakably transcendent, which comes with "a phenomenal effect,
not unenhanced by the rare personal beauty of the young sailor,
spiritualized now through late experiences so poignantly profound" (*B,* 123). But Vere is locked to the last into his martial
context: hearing Billy's words, the captain "stood erectly rigid as
a musket" (*B,* 124). With Vere's decision before him, Melville
had to own that Billy's promise of peace would not redeem the
man-of-war world because the vision necessary to take the full
span of portents, to seize the significance of the wonder-world
for human life, could not be reified aboard the *Bellipotent.*

To say that Melville's sense of realistic consistency could not
avoid or avert the failure of imagination implicit in Vere's trun-
cation of his context of ultimacy is not, however, to say that
Melville himself revoked either his sense of the reality of the
wonder-world or the mode of response he felt best answered to
the presence of the wondrous in human experience. Indeed, after
Vere's initial decision to disregard that which is exceptional in
the matter, Billy's portentousness is put on the increase. Attempting to minister to the manacled Billy, the chaplain finds
that the measured forms of his Christianity "had no consolation

to proffer which could result in a peace transcending that which he beheld" (*B*, 120) in Billy's countenance: "Without movement, he lay as in a trance, that adolescent expression previously noted as his taking on something akin to the look of a slumbering child in the cradle when the warm hearth-glow of the still chamber at night plays on the dimples that at whiles mysteriously form in the cheek, silently coming and going there. For now and then in the gyved one's trance a serene happy light born of some wandering reminiscence or dream would diffuse itself over his face, and then wane away only anew to return" (*B*, 119–20).[5] Billy's portentous revelation of innocence and peace does not occur simply to the eyes of the chaplain, for his benediction on Vere runs through "the ship's populace" like "some vocal current electric" (*B*, 123). For all eyes, the hanging of Billy becomes a moment filled with a significance: "The hull, deliberately recovering from the periodic roll to leeward, was just regaining an even keel when the last signal, a preconcerted dumb one, was given. At the same moment it chanced that the vapory fleece hanging low in the East was shot through with a soft glory as of the fleece of the Lamb of God seen in mystical vision, and simultaneously therewith, watched by the wedged mass of upturned faces, Billy ascended; and, ascending, took the full rose of the dawn" (*B*, 124). With this, Billy's connection with "another world" is culminated for all who watch.[6] In him, it must be acknowledged at last, there is "beheld the prodigy of repose" in the midst of the martial atmosphere. If the possibilities Billy brings into the world are acknowledged, however, the chaplain, the sailors, and all who behold, are as powerless as Vere to seize those possibilities, to convert life, to accept the promise. The chaplain "reluctantly withdrew," for, although he "is the minister of the Prince of Peace" (*B*, 122), he receives "his stipend from Mars" (*B*, 120), the god of war. The sailors are called back to arms by a "strategic command" (*B*, 126), for, although they have been dumbstruck by wonder at the ascension of Billy, they can only think that "the penalty was somehow unavoidably inflicted from the naval point of view" (*B*, 131).

Despite Melville's having to portray realistically the fact that all returned to the "naval point of view," he could affirm the reality of the portentous as well; despite the narrator's having to conclude after Vere's decision that this is a "conviction, without appeal" (*B,* 114), Melville could maintain the conviction, with Billy's surpassing transcendent disclosures, that, as William Ellery Sedgwick has observed, there is a "radiant visage of life, whose shining secret is, it has its salvation in its own keeping." [7] Finally, the lessons of *Billy Budd* are clear: a promise of redemption appears in the world of human experience but is repudiated by the regnant, martial perception of experience; but the very presence of the "radiant visage," having been refused, itself grows in moment and power to the extent that it casts into radical doubt the validity of the man-of-war world which spurns its promise. If Vere's decision is a conviction without appeal, Billy's increasing radiance makes its own appeal to the reader in unmistakable terms. The absolute clarity with which the lessons are taught and the unmistakable aspect with which Billy's appeal is made contain their own complexities, however, for they point in a subtle way to a shift in Melville's sense of his vocation, its function, and its possibilities.

CHAPTER NINE

DELPHIC DELIVERANCES
Narrative Didacticism and
the Tragedy of Herman Melville

Billy Budd, Herman Melville's last major effort in fiction, has frequently been understood as culminating Melville's literary career—at least in the sense that, because it was his last work and was completed shortly before he died, it seems to stand as something like a denouement in relation to the issues which, however interpreted, run throughout Melville's work. For some critics, the radiant visage that is undeniable in Billy Budd's life and character has signalled Melville's affirmation of life—or at least his resigned acceptance of the existence of good and evil—after what they understand as Melville's pessimistic or nihilistic rejection of life in works like *Moby-Dick, Pierre,* and *The Confidence-Man.*[1] For others, who have seen the slaughter of the innocent Billy as the key to the work, *Billy Budd* has been interpreted to suggest that Melville had dipped his pen in the fire for a last time to resist, by way of his fiction, the evil he saw built into the very structure of human existence as its definitive characteristic.[2] Still others regard this final work as a mixed resolution, as Melville's ironic demonstration that pure acquiescence will not suffice—however radiant its aspect—in a world plagued by evil.[3]

As argued in the preceding chapter, *Billy Budd* does seem to present, in its narrative lessons, a significant addition, if not a decisive conclusion, to Melville's continuing vision of life in his fiction. The early works—and especially *Typee, Redburn,* and *White-Jacket*—had the effect, if not the intention, of ferreting through, and exposing the inadequacy of, some characteristic modes of perception in Melville's time, and these beginning labors in fiction served as well to adumbrate, at least slowly in their cumulative development, what Melville thought was a more integral response to the terms of experience. In *Moby-Dick,* now more fully in control of his craft, Melville had utilized the gains of the early works in order to articulate, in the structures of Ishmael's retrospective narration, a mode of vision which would enable man to recover a sense of the presence of the transcendent in the precincts of human experience and to present, in the career of Ishmael's responses to the possibilities and demands of such a vision, a model of full experiencing which would issue in man's transcending the bankruptcy of his fallen life. This was the truth upon which Melville sensed he had "bottomed," and, with this vision of the wonder-world, he wanted, like the reformer, to transfigure the perception of his fellows. And thus, in *Moby-Dick* and *Pierre,* among other works, he in effect ratified the validity of the vision by demonstrating that it remained intact despite the variety of perilous responses which prevented some men's ever seizing its promises.

With *Billy Budd,* the terms of the engagement shifted slightly, for with this final work Melville sought to bring his vision to birth for his times by forcing it to gain certification in the most trying possible situation, among men who swear by, and are confined by, the doctrines of their own fallen natures. The vision of the wonder-world fails to enter history, however, for Melville's historical sense admitted in the dramatic action of the narrative that the claims of the man-of-war world were too much with his age. Nonetheless, the character of Billy's promise—the possibility of such a wonder-world as Billy's portentousness adumbrates —was retained, and the peril of life after its man-of-war fashion was exposed. On the face of the matter, then, *Billy Budd* seems to provide a denouement—to wit, Melville's affirmation that experience itself contains its own redemptive principle, an opportunity for fallen man to reconcile himself with the ground of his being, even if such a principle, the occasion for the opportunity, is refused. Understood in a slightly different way, therefore, Lewis Mumford's "summary" of *Billy Budd* is to the point:

Good and evil exist in the nature of things, each forever itself, each doomed to war with the other. In the working out of human institutions, evil has a place as well as good: Vere is contemptuous of Claggart, but cannot do without him: he loves Budd as a son and must condemn him to the noose: justice dictates an act abhorrent to his nature, and only his inner magnanimity keeps it from being revolting. These are the fundamental ambiguities of life: so long as evil exists, the agents that intercept it will also be evil, whilst we accept the world's conditions: the universal articles of war on which our civilizations rest.[4]

The lessons of *Billy Budd*, then, are painfully clear. As Mumford writes: "the meaning is so obvious that one shrinks from underlining it."[5] As curious a statement as this seems about a work which has been the subject of so much, and so diverse, critical interpretation, there is justice in it, for regardless of the subtle nuances of peripheral matters in the story, which critical inquiries continue to bring to light, the central substance of the narrative, with only slight variations of reading, cannot be debated: Claggart is evil; Billy is good; their conflict is inevitable and Vere must judge it; Vere—a man of unquestionable responsibility—judges in favor of the necessity of order; Billy transcends the world which tries his case.

The question about *Billy Budd*, then, is not about its meaning in broad outline but, rather, about its significance—the most decisive clue to which is just that obviousness of the central action of the narrative. *Billy Budd* reveals by way of its own clarity Melville's final, desperate sense of the diminishing possibilities of his vocation. Clarify itself is not a vice in fiction, of course, but the peculiar terms of the perspicacity of *Billy Budd* leave the reader with a Melville to whom he is not accustomed. The dramatic shift in narrative technique from *Moby-Dick* to *Billy Budd* —both works which seek to present essentially the same kind of vision—suggests the image of a Melville beleaguered by the facts that he had no audience, that his vision was ignored or misunderstood, that his final work would have to be committed to a last-ditch effort to rechart the course of his age away from the man-of-war direction in which it continued to drift. This image is not at all uncomplicated, however, for if he had worked in *Moby-Dick* with the conviction that fiction was the place wherein one could undertake "the great art of telling the truth," he was now filled with uncertainty about the capacity of fiction to alter life in any measurable way or even to address life in any convincing way. This uncertainty comes profoundly to the fore in Melville's narrative insistence on making matters unmistakably clear in *Billy Budd*. With that insistence, the implication is that the author, now, will leave no doubt whatever about the necessity of his culture to assume to its heart a transfigured conception of itself and to "revision" its environing world. In that insistence, however, Melville endangers the vision of the wonder-world by clarifying what at its center should remain unclarified. With this the narrator of *Billy Budd* is caught, like Melville, in the desperate and finally untenable position of having either to fail to bring the vision to birth or, by explaining it thoroughly enough to do so, to rob it of its definitive dimension, wonderment. At last, then, the image has its tragic aspect—the Melville who wanted to act on behalf of his fellows, who wanted to chart for his age a renewed idea of its deepest possibilities of being, but who finally thinks that he must fail as reformer of life and find himself left only to record its dangerous trend or else to cry in the wilderness, like the prophet, with the frail hope that someone would hear.[6]

The extraordinary didacticism which characterizes the narrative technique of the tale invites an assessment of what this technique signals about Melville's ending sense of himself and of what his final resolution portends for the reader of his work. The narrator of *Billy Budd*—surely one of the most obtrusively self-conscious of Melville's narrators about the manner in which he tells his tale—is set so strenuously on convincing the reader of the truth and reality of the wonder-world that he presents the portents—their promise, demand, meaning, and significance—in a way previously unwonted by Melville's fiction. In doing so, he strips the portentous world of the very opacity and abundance, richness of meaning and mystery, which had been, in Ishmael's view, its definitive characteristic. This narrator, then, compromises the vision in his efforts to plead its case in unmistakable terms, and he grows all-the-more anxious, and all-the-more reductionist with the terms of the vision, as he becomes progressively aware that, despite the clarity of his meaning, it will not be accepted by the public world he addresses. And Melville so shared the anxiety of his narrator that he could not, apparently, control the narrator's increasing betrayal of the vision —a betrayal marked by all the dubiety that went into the last-ditch effort.

I

Ishmael, following the labyrinthine course of scrutiny required by the diverse symbolism of the whale, assures his auditors that, "in a matter like this, subtlety appeals to subtlety, and without imagination no man can follow another into these halls," but the narrator of *Billy Budd* wants nothing of this subtlety or imagination from his readers, even if his purpose, like Ishmael's, is to bring before the reader the nature and possibility of the world for eyes capable of wonder. If Ishmael's narrative is designed to repossess the sense of the transcendent and to record the drama of his own encounter with moments brimming over with the holy, and if his technique is experientially constructed to evoke the capacity for wonder in the reader, the narrator of *Billy Budd* designs his narrative less for dramatic purposes than for homiletic ones and wants less to evoke wonder than to convince his readers intellectually. If Ishmael deals in prolepsis—beginning with the intractable materialities and discovering what is funded there—the narrator of *Billy Budd* works in abstractions to teach his readers what they ought to see. As Lewis Mumford has observed:

Billy Budd . . . is not a full-bodied story: there is statement, commentary, illustration, just statement, wise commentary, apt illustration: what is lacking is an independent and living creation. The epithets themselves lack body and colour: Billy Budd has nothing to compare with the description of boiling whale oil in Moby Dick—"a wild Hindoo odour, like the left wing of the Day of Judgement."

Billy Budd . . . lacks the fecundity and energy of White Jacket: the story itself takes place on the sea, but the sea itself is missing, and even the principal characters are not primarily men: they are actors and symbols.[7]

In these ways, the story is, as Mumford notes, "stripped for action" with characters who possess "a Platonic clarity of form."[8] The action, however, is finally heuristic; *Billy Budd* is stripped for clarity of form in order to pursue didactic purposes.

The "wild Hindoo odour" of *Moby-Dick* is discarded in *Billy Budd* just because of the narrator's ostensible feeling, indicated by his narrational habits, that such odorous realities can be misconstrued by readers whose interpretive abilities are to be distrusted. The characters are not even symbols—in any sense that Ishmael would warrant—for, at last, their meanings are in the singular, without the ambiguous and opaque quality which would give them the necessary resonances of the hidden transcendent. They are, rather, allegorical, presented in the unmistakable terms of their static and abstract equivalencies. No hieroglyphic Queequeg appears in *Billy Budd* to pose the riddle of the earth in the inscriptions of his sinewy body, for the narrator cannot afford a conundrum which would lead to bafflement in his readers, and he suspects that even a full-bodied character might contain complexities which would subvert the abstract lessons he seeks to teach. Ultimately even the central portents— Claggart and Billy themselves—are stripped of their attributes of mystery, apparently because the narrator will not risk misunderstanding. Ishmael presents in *Moby-Dick* the experience of wonder, and even his commentary stems from ruminations on the objects of wonder, but the narrator of *Billy Budd* wants to teach the necessity of the vision of the wonder-world as doctrine, and his entire rhetorical control of the narrative will leave nothing to wonderment. All of his technical strategy—his elaborate staging of the situation, his homiletical asides to the reader, his glossing vocabulary on the scenes he presents, and his "functional" digressions—all, indeed, of his narrational virtuosity, is marshalled to the cause of making the lessons of the wonder-world absolutely clear.

DELPHIC DELIVERANCES

At an early point in the story, the narrator suggests to the reader that the narrative will be "restricted . . . to the inner life of one ship and the career of an individual sailor" (*B,* 54), but throughout, he will seek to stage the situation aboard the decks of the *Bellipotent* against the backdrop of the revolutionary zeitgeist of western Europe and the rebellions at Spithead and the Nore and has already associated Billy with Aldebaran, "young Alexander," Apollo, Hercules, and Adam. His avowed "restricted" concern, with all its unrestricted background and allusiveness of character, immediately reveals the tension in the narrator's sense of how he must tell his tale. He needs to prove to his readers, he suggests in an aside, that "profound passion" does not demand "a palatial stage whereon to play its part" (*B,* 78), and yet, at the same time, he needs to associate the present stage—the gundeck of the man-of-war—to the momentousness of the era in order to convince his readers that the importance of his tale is not confined to those narrow decks. With the portraiture of Billy, the narrator labors under a similar tension: he must assure the reader that Billy is a recognizable possibility, that he is real, that "he is not presented as a conventional hero . . . [and] that the story in which he is the main figure is no romance" (*B,* 53); and yet, because Billy is the locus of wonder, the narrator must increase his portentousness beyond "the career of an individual sailor" by attaching to Billy the names of mighty figures in order to make clear that the proper vision of Billy's possibility is paramount. The point is that the narrator, from the outset, suffers the problem of having to persuade his readers that the wonder-world is credible and significant without, at the same time, having to try too severely the imaginations of those same readers. He must convince them of the reality and promise of portentous mystery in experience without simultaneously leaving them bewildered.

This tension in the double necessities of the narrator's mode is also apparent in the heuristic and homiletic asides to the reader with which he frequently interrupts the narrative. His dealing with the "certain phenomenal men" in the story is one case in point. With the case of Claggart, he literally begs his assertions that the master-at-arms, as an object of wonder, is "as much

228

charged with that prime element of Radcliffian romance, *the mysterious,* as any that the ingenuity of the author of the *Mysteries of Udolpho* could devise" (*B,* 74). At practically the same moment that he insists on Claggart's connection with mystery, however, the narrator, apparently fearful that his readers will be baffled, steps forward to clarify the matter by stating unequivocally that Claggart is "the direct reverse of a saint" (*B,* 74). His purpose is obvious: he will explain "whatever of enigma may appear to lurk in the case" (*B,* 74) by launching into his thorough explication of Claggart's "depravity according to nature" (*B,* 75). In his portrayal of Billy, the narrator similarly reveals his double motive, for he is as declamatory about Billy's signal mystery as about Claggart's and as quick to reduce Billy's mystery as he had been with that of his counterpart. Only "God knows" Billy's paternity, the narrator wants Billy to point out, and thus Billy's purity of form and innocence of bearing have their obvious associations with an uncanny dimension. But what Billy presents cannot be mistaken because the narrator exerts all of his energies to the effort of leaving no doubt in the reader's mind that Billy touches the orbit of transcendental goodness. Finally, then, the narrator's asides serve didactic purposes—to clarify beyond any uncertainty the meaning of his phenomenal and prodigious characters. As such heuristic elements, the asides function to tear away the complex concretions which might have accrued to Claggart and Billy as genuine symbols, to rob them of what Ishmael would have recognized as the necessary opaqueness which belongs to the mysterious agency of symbols, and to convert them, instead, into the less-textured, but clearer, stuff of allegory. In his strenuous efforts to clarify the reality of the wonder-world in human experience, then, the narrator drives his objects of wonder away from experience into the realm of abstractions about experience.

Even after his elaborate staging and after his establishing in a crystalline way the allegorical antipathy of Claggart and Billy, the narrator cannot rest from his anxiety to steer the reader to the proper understanding; he feels obliged to provide a gloss on every instance and scene in the narrative which he suspects might perplex his auditors. One of the functions of Billy's meetings with the old Dansker is, strategically, toward the end of specifying further still that something signal in importance is occurring and that a conflict will ensue. However obscure the Dansker's "Delphic deliverances" (B, 86) seem to Billy, the reader knows enough by this point to understand the sage old man perfectly. Although the inevitability of an encounter between the abstractions of Claggart and Billy is perfectly clear by virtue of the ways the narrator has presented them, and has reiterated their conflicting character in the oracular hints of the Dansker, the narrator cannot, even so, resist his compulsive need to point out, as if the reader could not be expected to know it, that "something decisive must come of it" (B, 90). This is the narrator's habitual technique throughout the narrative: he simply cannot rest until he has satisfied himself that there is no mistaking his message.

More of what Mumford refers to as "wise commentary" appears with obvious intentionality on the narrator's part in his gloss on the chaplain's interview with Billy. The narrator virtually leaps at the opportunity to hammer his point home:

Marvel not that having been made acquainted with the young sailor's essential innocence the worthy man lifted not a finger to avert the doom of such a martyr to martial discipline. So to do would not only have been as idle as invoking the desert, but would also have been an audacious transgression of the bounds of his function, one as exactly prescribed to him by military law as that of the boatswain or any other naval officer. Bluntly put, a chaplain is the minister of the Prince of Peace in the host of the God of War—Mars. As such, he is as incongruous as a musket would be on the altar at Christmas. Why then is he there? Because he indirectly subserves the purpose attested by the cannon; because too he lends the sanction of the religion of the meek to that which practically is the abrogation of everything but brute Force. (B, 121–22)

The function of this passage in the narrative is betrayed by its own rhetorical makeup. Sensing that his readers might miss the point of the paradox localized in the presence of the chaplain aboard the man-of-war, the narrator seizes the occasion to explain, for he finds in this scene the didactic moral of his story— the "abrogation" of Billy's promise in favor of loyalty to the "law" of "brute Force," Vere's response encapsulated in the response of the chaplain, Vere's refusal of Billy in a sense ameliorated because even the chaplain can do no other when the context of ultimacy is abridged to the gundecks of a line-of-battle ship. Even the parenthetical aside within the larger aside pleads with the reader *not* to "suppress" the "heretic thought" of Billy's transcendent innocence—a notion heretical only in relation to the military context which presumes his guilt. "Marvel not" about any incongruity, the narrator instructs, for, he could well go on to say, "I shall explain all." He anticipates the reader's perplexity by posing his own rhetorical question about the chaplain—"why then is he there?"—and, of course, as is his wont, the narrator supplies the answer immediately. Insistent as he had earlier been about the reality of wonder, the narrator has here reached the point at which he even admonishes the reader to "marvel not." Earlier, with the most significant portent in the narrative, Billy himself, the narrator had issued similar instructions when he sensed that Billy's behavior might baffle the reader: "This is to be wondered at," the narrator insists, begging for a proper imagination of wonder on the reader's part, but then, having declared the necessity of wonder, he distrusts the reader's response to it and must add hastily "yet not so much to be wondered at" (*B*, 86). Again, then, as with virtually every mysterious facet of his tale, he proceeds to explicate the complexities of the case in point to the extent that no room is left for wonder, subverting his hard-taught lessons by his own "hard-teaching" of them.[9]

This narrative didacticism also characterizes the narrator's self-conscious digressions and, again, ends with similar results. Whatever other purposes the narrator's extended consideration of the case of Lord Nelson might have, it clearly serves to present this "'greatest sailor since our world began'" (*B*, 58) as a counterpoint to Starry Vere. Nelson's "impassioning" nature "vitalizes into acts" heroic "exaltations of sentiment" (*B*, 58), and it is "by force of his mere presence" (*B*, 59), responding reflexively to the experience he encounters, that Nelson overcomes the anxieties of captaincy in revolutionary times. The narrator suggests that he will "err into such a by-path" as the digression on

Nelson simply because "some by-paths have an enticement not readily to be withstood," but the strategy, again, is heuristic and glossarial as he asks "if the reader will keep me company" (*B*, 56). Obtruding on his story as he does, he is able to suggest with respect to Nelson's brilliance that "personal prudence even when dictated by quite other than selfish considerations surely is no special virtue in a military man" (*B*, 58), and this observation seems crafted especially with a view toward Captain Vere who is shortly to be introduced to the reader as a man "who whatever his sturdy qualities was without any brilliant ones" (*B*, 61), as a man who is marked distinctively by "personal prudence," as a man whose "honest sense of duty" is not, like Nelson's, impassioned to respond reflexively to life. The function of the digression, once more, is to allow the narrator to clarify the case of Vere for the reader's enlightenment—specifically, here, to point out the personal prudence, regardless of its motive, which Vere will interpose between himself and his experience of Billy Budd and, therefore, to explain Vere's failure.

II

If the digression on Nelson is designed, at least in part, to expose the terms of Vere's failure, the end digressions which close the narrative teach in a painstaking way both what Vere and his man-of-war world have lost and what the consequences of such a loss are. The allegorical action has run its course: the abstract equivalencies of Claggart and Billy have been reversed—in an altogether obvious way—by the judicial proceedings of the man-of-war trial, and the lesson or moral of the tale seems, in a word, indisputable. But the narrator, seeing that the man-of-war world either ignores or misunderstands Billy's spiritual promise, continues to be driven by the suspicion that his readers will similarly disdain or misapprehend the necessity of the proper vision of Billy which is the whole plan of the narrative. On the basis of this anxious suspicion, the narrator places, as addenda to the story proper, the five digressions which serve even further to clarify and to enforce the idea of what Billy is, how he has been spurned or misperceived, and what results from the failure of the world to seize hold on his significance.

In the first two digressions, the narrator provides exposition of the wonderment evoked by Billy's hanging—exposition designed, it seems, to demonstrate both that Billy's resonances of the transcendent are actual and that they have been turned down. As the purser and the surgeon debate the issues raised by Billy's lack of muscle spasm after the hanging, it is quite clear that Billy shares in the transcendent but, as well, that he cannot be grasped by either man. The purser ascribes the "phenomenal incident" to "'the force lodged in will-power'" (*B*, 124), but the surgeon, although agreeing that "'it was phenomenal,'" wants to bracket off the question of sources: "'an appearance,'" he argues, "'the cause of which is not immediately to be assigned'" (*B*, 125).[10] In the second digression, the wonderment among the sailors is examined by the narrator for the same purpose of pointing out as clearly as possible that Billy's portentousness refers to the transcendent and, at once, that the sailors misunderstand its demands. The "emphasized silence" at the moment of execution is an awed and reverential quietude among the seamen, and it is followed by a hushed and "muffled murmur" of "seeming remoteness" in a "sound not easily to be verbally rendered" (*B*, 126). As struck with wonderment as they are, however, the men fail to recognize and respond to the implicit demands of the wondrous moment they have encountered; they foreswear any allegiance to the moment because they are brought back all too easily by the "strategic command" (*B*, 126) of the man-of-war. The narrator realizes the inevitability of their failure, and makes it clear to the reader, when he suggests aside that "true martial discipline long continued superinduces in average man a sort of impulse whose operation at the official sound of command much resembles in its promptitude the effect of an instinct" (*B*, 127). This also is the point of the last digression—the "impulse of docility" to the man-of-war world—for here the narrator wants to reiterate the misperception on the sailors' part that Billy's "penalty was somehow unavoidably inflicted from the naval point of view" (*B*, 131).

Apart from the end digressions, there are also misapprehensions of Billy revealed in the poem "Billy in the Darbies," written, according to the narrative, by one of the sailors. The sailor-poet ascribes to Billy some all-too-human attributes which are belied by Billy's symbolic figurement. For instance, Billy's association with "Bristol Molly" seems an addition made by the poet, for the Billy the reader has come to know, through the narrator's portraiture, belongs to a completely asexual world in which the female of the poem seems an interloper. Further, the poet's rendition of Billy's utterances does not seem commensurate with the image of the "upright barbarian." When he has Billy ask "aren't it all sham?" the poet contradicts the narrator's earlier observations that Billy was "by no means of a satirical turn" and that "to deal in double meanings and insinuations of any sort was quite foreign to his nature" (B, 49). In short, the sailor-poet attributes to Billy the very sense of irony which the narrator claims Billy lacks. Or, again, when the poet wants to suggest Billy's fear by having him ask "Sentry, are you there?" the question seems one alien to the Billy Budd who, the narrator has informed the reader, "was wholly without irrational fear" (B, 120) of death. The point seems to be that the sailor's poem is designed to commemorate Billy as sailor and thus to give to him those human characteristics which seem necessary. Nowhere in the poem, however, is there evidence that Billy has been understood symbolically by the sailor bard, and, of course, without that understanding, he too misses the message of the narrator.

The penultimate digression—the newspaper report—is presented by the narrator, with the apparent purpose of objectivity, in a way which exposes the broader, public allegiance to the man-of-war understanding of life, for given the immobility of the status quo, the report simply assumes on the face of the evidence that Billy was guilty and that Claggart was beyond reproach; Billy, the report concludes, bears out Dr. Johnson's sententia that "patriotism is the last refuge of a scoundrel" (B, 130), but the narrator knows, and has exposed to the reader, the fact that the man-of-war gave, and gives, at its very center, refuge to the likes of Claggart. The imputations of guilt and innocence made by the newspaper account are not altogether different in purpose than the ascriptions to Billy made by the anonymous sailor-author of "Billy in the Darbies" in the sense that, like the sailor, the newspaper writer supplies an interpretation of Billy which satisfies his own sense of things; the sailor wants Billy to be a sailor, and the newspaper writer wants Billy to be vindictive and depraved both because naval justice is vindicated and the sense of the status quo is not complicated. The juxtaposition by the newspaper comes pat to the narrator's purposes, yet once more, of pointing out the misperceptions and refusals of what Billy brought into the world.

The consequences of such repudiation are dramatized distinctly, heuristically, and, at last, unmistakably in the narrator's digression on the death of Vere. He launches this digression because, he says, the "truth" demands it: "The symmetry of form attainable in pure fiction can not so readily be achieved in a narration essentially having less to do with fable than with fact. Truth uncompromisingly told will always have its ragged edges; hence the conclusion of such a narration is apt to be less finished than an architectural finial" (*B*, 128). Despite the disclaimers of the smooth edges of fable, however, the narrator's presentation of Vere's death at the hands of the *Athée*—perhaps the least subtle deus ex machina in American literature—is a decided "finial" for the didactic pursuits of the narrator. If he seeks to tell the "truth uncompromisingly," the narrator can nonetheless find in the incident of Vere's death the culminating and enforcing element of his point disclosed in allegorical terms. Vere dies, almost literally, but in any case obviously, for his lack of faith: disdaining the promise of the transcendent and swearing loyalty, however tacitly, to the man-of-war, his case—as he had suggested Billy's would be—is judged by "the last Assizes." The point, again, is all too clear. If a man lives by the atheist impulses of a man-of-war world, he will die by them. If "Billy Budd" is the last thing on Vere's lips, it does not seem to gainsay the fact that he had foresworn Billy's promise. The retributive justice of Vere's death—poetic or theological—signals the consequences of such foreswearing. Although the narration has ragged edges and requires digressions for the purposes of the truth, then, that didactically presented truth has a perfect symmetry of form which does not so much indicate any idea, on Melville's part, of a punitive God as it suggests the inevitable results of failures of human imagination. Vere is singled out for punishment—only allegorically—because his refusals are "representative" ones; his fatality belongs to the fatal end, it seems, toward which the world, on its man-of-war course, is tending.

Withal, the end digressions of the narrative acknowledge the narrator's awareness and admission that the reign of wonder must, by the nature of the case, remain *in partibus infidelium* in a world which swears by the man-of-war sense of its condition. But what is also betrayed by the mode of the narrator's admission is Melville's suspicion that this fatal response must be put before the eyes of his readers in no uncertain terms. If, earlier in the narrative, the author's purpose and mode had been to use his narrator to clarify, and to plead the case for, the necessity for the proper vision of wonder, Melville seems to have sensed by the end of his narrative that that necessity, however clearly presented, would not be recognized and accepted. With this developing sense, the narrator converts his reformative thrust to the new purpose of a didactic chronicle which, as Mumford has noted, is full of "wise commentary" about events, trends, and attitudes which he now admits, in the very mode of the final digressions, he cannot change with his art. He has moved from a sense of himself as reformer to a sense of himself as seer, from the commitment to change life to the less-empowered, and more oracular, intention to record life's course and necessity, and this altered sense of the function and possibility of fiction indicates that Melville's poetic faith—his loyalty to the idea that literature could reform life, could bottom human history on a new idea of the truth—has been tried, has been found wanting, and has been abandoned. The painstakingly self-conscious and shifting didacticism of the narrator of *Billy Budd*—first, in arguing for the necessity of the vision of the wonder-world and finally, in teaching the lessons of the refusal of such a vision—leaves the reader with a Melville apparently full of dubiety from the outset of *Billy Budd* about the capacity of fiction to transform life, a Melville so anxious about the efficacy of fiction that his narrator strips and reduces the very vision of life he wished to accredit for his readers.

To the last, then, Melville clings to the vision of experience worked out by Ishmael in *Moby-Dick,* but, at the last, he despaired, as his final fiction betrays, of actualizing that vision for his age. The sententious thrust in the all-too-obvious closure of *Billy Budd* suggests that by the end of the narrative Melville had advanced, or retreated, to the archetypal vision of the old Dansker, he who has seen it all, who recognizes "Baby" Budd and *Jemmy Legs* for what they are, who knows that Billy's promise will be spurned, but who is powerless to be more than "the salt seer," the "old sea-Chiron" (*B,* 71) who "seemed to divine more than he was told" and, yet, whose "bitter prudence . . . never interferes in aught" (*B,* 86).[11] The closure of *Billy Budd* suggests Melville's realization that the vision will not transform life, for it stands as something like the "Delphic deliverances" (*B,* 86) of the Dansker—seeing, foretelling of, warning about what lies ahead but unempowered to alter the direction in which life runs. In this shifted sense of the possibilities of his vocation lies the hint of the tragedy of Herman Melville. He had put his fiction in the service of exploring and articulating the deepest senses of the condition and possibility of his age, and he had, in plummeting to the bottom of human experience, tapped what was withheld there to present to his age a new idea of what was significant in reality. He had acted on behalf of life to bring to life a richer conception of its context of ultimacy and sources of meaning, and he had wrestled with "the angel, Art," even in his last fiction to release the potencies and energies of this fictive vision for quickening the religious and historical imaginations of his time. But the testimony of that last fiction contains in its own narrative structures the suggestion of Melville's tragic sense of his failure to renew the terms and possibilities of the imagination of his age. No one can deny the sheer literary power of *Billy Budd;* as Newton Arvin has observed, it leaves "a permanent stamp on the imagination."[12] After all is said, however, that power emerges from what is a tour de force, the very virtuosity of which reveals the author's increasingly anxious sense that he is failing, his fear

237

that for all its literary power it could not break its way into history. The final testimony, then, presents the tragic aspect of a Melville reduced in his own sense of himself to the desperate situation of watching life drift on its destructive man-of-war way while he holds futilely out to it the possibility of a different course.

Perhaps it is too late in the seventh decade of the twentieth century to provide an *aggiornamento* for Melville's full vision. The vicissitudes of experience have profoundly altered what might now comprise an integral imagination of wonder and an adequate recovery of the sense of the transcendent, even if his fictions might well contain elements which would aid in such an imaginative recovery. Indeed, the full substance of his vision is probably lost to the twentieth century as much as Melville feared it to be lost to his own age. But what is not lost, however ignored or spurned it might have been then and might be now, is the mode of his engagement with life, the capacity of the deep-diving literary imagination to plunge to the bottom of human experience and to find there what is funded as ontological possibility. Melville's work fully embodies this capacity and stands as example, and thus, if his final sense of himself partook of the tragic, it issued, as tragedy does frequently, in its own justification—by adding to life images of being which would not otherwise have been gained. When we look back to his age, that age in direct lineage with which we stand, we find an age immeasurably richer for Melville's having imagined the terms of its experience. And, as we look back, as men must, in an attempt to grasp the kind of history which is recoverable there, we meet the example of Melville, challenging the contemporary imagination to enter its own experience at an analogous depth. Only that image-making capacity, searching life for its deepest resources, can bring into full view the conditions of present experience which make a repossession of the past meaningful. Imagination, the challenge tells us, is the idiom of our possibilities even as we fear that the once-green world "is getting grey and grizzled now."

NOTES

NOTES

Chapter One

1. R.W.B. Lewis, *The American Adam* (Chicago: University of Chicago Press, 1955), passim.

2. F. O. Matthiessen, *American Renaissance* (New York: Oxford University Press, 1941), p. 221n.

3. For samples of reviewers' responses to *Typee*, see Hershel Parker, ed., *The Recognition of Herman Melville* (Ann Arbor: University of Michigan Press, 1967); and Hugh W. Hetherington, *Melville's Reviewers, British and American, 1846–1891* (Chapel Hill: University of North Carolina Press, 1961).

4. Arthur O. Lovejoy, *Essays in the History of Ideas* (Baltimore: Johns Hopkins University Press, 1948), pp. 228–53.

5. Perry Miller, "Melville and Transcendentalism," in *Nature's Nation* (Cambridge, Mass.: Belknap Press of Harvard University, 1967), p. 196.

6. Ibid., p. 185.

7. As John Seelye has pointed out, Tommo, at this earliest stage of the book, presents himself as a kind of sailor-historian who bases his romantic conception of the interior part of the island not on his own certain knowledge but on his reading of "a guidebook and tall-tale miscellany of attractions and frights" (*Melville: The Ironic Diagram* [Evanston: Northwestern University Press, 1970], p. 14).

8. Seelye thinks this voice of "the hero-narrator" is an "insufficient instrument" in *Typee* to carry the "romantic ironies" Melville sought (ibid., p. 23). My own view is that the voice succeeds just because the irony of the book is internal to Tommo's retrospective voice—a voice which stems from the self-recognition implicit in Tommo's final "change" of mind.

9. Richard Chase, *The American Novel and Its Tradition* (Garden City, N.Y.: Doubleday, 1957), p. 209.

10. As quoted by Perry Miller, *The Raven and the Whale* (New York: Harcourt, Brace and World, 1956), p. 153.

11. For accounts of Melville's attitude toward, and problems with, the missionaries, see Daniel Aaron, "Melville and the Missionaries,"

New England Quarterly 8 (September 1935): 404–8; and Charles Roberts Anderson, *Melville in the South Seas* (New York: Columbia University Press, 1939), chap. 6.

12. For an opinion of *Typee* which is somewhat similar to this conclusion, see Richard Ruland, "Melville and the Fortunate Fall: Typee as Eden," *Nineteenth Century Fiction* 23 (December 1968): 312–23. Unlike Ruland, however, I see no evidence in *Typee* to suggest that the Fall is a fortunate one. The fallen condition of modern man which Melville discerns in his first book must await later books, as the succeeding chapters will argue, in which Melville adumbrates a principle of reconciliation to answer to the deepest needs of that condition.

Chapter Two

1. Hershel Parker, ed., *The Recognition of Herman Melville* (Ann Arbor: University of Michigan Press, 1967), p. 7.

2. For the authoritative account of the biographical sources of *Redburn,* see William H. Gilman, *Melville's Early Life and "Redburn"* (New York: New York University Press, 1959).

3. *Journal of a Visit to London and the Continent,* ed. Eleanor Metcalf Melville (Cambridge, Mass.: Harvard University Press, 1948), p. 23.

4. For another interpretation of the ways that *Redburn* can be viewed in the context of this current situation, see Sacvan Bercovitch, "Melville's Search for National Identity: Son and Father in *Redburn, Pierre,* and *Billy Budd,*" *CLA Journal* 10 (March 1967): 217–28.

5. Many of the primary documents in this debate are reproduced in Robert E. Spiller, ed., *The American Literary Revolution, 1783–1837* (Garden City, N.Y.: Doubleday, 1967); and, for the terms in which Melville probably became aware of the debate, see Perry Miller, *The Raven and the Whale* (New York: Harcourt, Brace and World, 1956), especially book two, "Young America."

6. For a succinct account of the modes and motives of the "party of memory," see R.W.B. Lewis, *The American Adam* (Chicago: University of Chicago Press, 1955), especially the prologue.

7. This phrase, of course, occurs in Henry James, *Hawthorne* (1879), a volume prepared for the English Men of Letters series.

8. This shifting "center of consciousness" detected by F. O. Matthiessen has been the source of some debate (*American Rennaissance* [New York: Oxford University Press, 1941], p. 397). For further dis-

cussion of this problem, see William Dillingham, *An Artist in the Rigging* (Athens, Ga.: University of Georgia Press, 1972), pp. 32–34; Hershel Parker, "Historical Note," *Redburn* (Northwestern-Newberry edition), pp. 348–49; and Merlin Bowen, "*Redburn* and the Angle of Vision," *Modern Philology* 52 (November 1954): 100–109.

9. As reproduced in Jay Leyda, ed., *The Melville Log*, 2 vols. (New York: Gordian Press, 1969), 2:576.

10. The phrase comes from Melville's poem "The House-Top: A Night Piece" (1863) in which the persona of the poem reflects on the atrocities of the draft riots in New York during the summer of that year, atrocities which seem to ratify the idea of man's inherent depravity.

11. Gilman notes that "here and elsewhere in *Redburn*, his [Melville's] technique of symbolism is proleptic, in that he elaborates his higher meaning from the foundation of real things" (*Melville's Early Life and "Redburn,"* p. 226). While Gilman is no doubt correct in adducing that Melville commits Redburn to work from "real things," my own view is that there is finally no genuine symbolism in the book, at least as readers of *Moby-Dick* will see it, much less any authorial "technique of symbolism." What technique there is in the narrative belongs to Redburn, and he elaborates on objects, events, and persons *as* objects, events, and persons, and *not* as symbols.

12. Cf. Merlin Bowen, *The Long Encounter: Self and Experience in the Writings of Herman Melville* (Chicago: University of Chicago Press, 1960), p. 131.

13. At least one recent interpretation of the book argues that Redburn's lack of perception with respect to Harry Bolton "earns him the reader's contempt." See Terrence G. Lish, "Melville's *Redburn:* A Study in Dualism," *English Language Notes* 5 (December 1967): 113–20. While I agree that young Redburn's misapprehension of his experience with Harry cannot simply be dismissed, I find this failure a more venial one, particularly in the context of Melville's total body of work before *Moby-Dick*. A conclusion akin to my own, although stemming from a much different argument, is John J. Gross, "The Rehearsal of Ishmael: Melville's *Redburn*," *Virginia Quarterly Review* 27 (Autumn 1951): 581–600.

Chapter Three

1. This dichotomy is suggested in the juxtaposition of the title with the subtitle of the work. "White-Jacket" refers to the private man; his jacket, indeed, is the only thing which keeps him from being anonymous

for much of the narrative, and his namelessness points immediately to his lack of identity. The subtitle, "The World in a Man-of-War," refers, on the other hand, to the public realm of the institution and the society.

2. Howard Vincent suggests that "*White-Jacket* also celebrates heroism—how man in a society corrupt by nature and by structure, finds some way to assert and to fulfill his essential manhood, whether he be Jack Chase or magnificent old Ushant" (*The Tailoring of Melville's White-Jacket* [Evanston: Northwestern University Press, 1970], pp. 4–5). Vincent's book is a most studious and careful compilation of the reading and experience on Melville's part which went into the making of *White-Jacket*, but I think the question of the nature and sources of "essential manhood" precede in importance in the narrative any celebration of achieving that manhood.

3. Indeed, the earlier White-Jacket is frequently recalled in ways which suggest that the retrospective narrator hardly recognizes him. During a moment early in the book, for instance, the narrator clearly thinks of that White-Jacket as a "third person": "White-Jacket . . . was a long time rapt in calculations, concerning the various 'numbers' allotted him by the *First Luff,* otherwise known as the First Lieutenant. In the first place, White-Jacket was given the *number of his mess;* then, his *ship's number,* or the number to which he must answer when the watch-roll is called; then, the number of his hammock; then, the number of the gun to which he was assigned; besides a variety of other numbers" (*W,* 11). This passage serves a double function in the narrative: first, it indicates immediately the attempt of the institution to reduce the man to a numerical cipher, and second, it implies the discrepancy in the places where the early White-Jacket and the retrospective White-Jacket stand since the latter hardly seems to think the former an earlier version of himself.

4. The quest for human community occurs frequently in Melville's fictions, and it is true that with the fellows of "the top" White-Jacket secures himself into a group of men with whom he has some rapport. But this temporary location of *communitas* is not the most important aspect of his climbing to the top of the masts, for there he is in effect alone with himself. It is this significance which the narrator himself ultimately discerns.

5. Ishmael will later express his sense of the dangers implicit in such a blending of the self with the "All" when he imagines slipping off of the masthead. But White-Jacket learns these dangers as well, for as his self-consciousness "glides" away, he nearly slips himself, and, at all events, is mistaken for a ghost, with the whiteness of his jacket, on the

yard-arm. Still, in this moment he senses his relation to a context which quite overarches any that he has located until now.

6. While White-Jacket does not have to put into action this newly discovered sense of himself because others intercede on his behalf, he nonetheless seizes within himself in this moment a resource which has its origins quite apart from the contexts within which he had hitherto sought his manhood.

7. Here, then, is the first hint of that "infinite obscure" which Melville admired in Hawthorne's characteristic mise-en-scène, which he would mention in a later review of Hawthorne's work, and which finally would become the wonder-world of *Moby-Dick*.

8. *The Letters of Herman Melville,* ed. Merrell R. Davis and William H. Gilman (New Haven: Yale University Press, 1960), pp. 91–92.

Chapter Four

1. Perry Miller, "Benjamin Franklin—Jonathan Edwards," in *Major Writers of America,* ed. Miller, 2 vols. (New York: Harcourt, Brace and World, 1962), 1:84.

2. More accurately, *Moby-Dick* does not so much alter the vision of the early works as it deepens and extends the understanding of Tommo, Redburn, and White-Jacket to the extent that those understandings, as Melville appropriated them, become the resources for Melville—in mode and goal—in his presentation of Ishmael's vision of experience.

3. Vincent Buckley, *Poetry and the Sacred* (London: Chatto and Windus, 1968), p. 146.

4. In short, then, this chapter will not seek to provide a reading of *Moby-Dick* or, indeed, to attend to the interpretive problems posed by the text in any way beyond this issue of the generic intentionality of the work. The inquiry here, rather, is meant to stand in relation to the text only as a prolegomenon which seeks to clarify something of the authorial situation from which the shape of the text emerged.

5. *Harper's New Monthly Magazine* 4 (December 1851): 137.

6. *The Letters of Herman Melville,* ed. Merrell R. Davis and William H. Gilman (New Haven: Yale University Press, 1960), p. 142.

7. Henry A. Murray, "'In Nomine Diaboli,'" in *Melville: A Collection of Critical Essays,* ed. Richard Chase (Englewood Cliffs, N.J.: Prentice-Hall, 1962), p. 66. This article originally appeared in *New England Quarterly* 24 (December 1951): 435–52.

8. Ibid., p. 70. "God is incarnate in the whale," Murray claims, if for no other reason than the "fact" that Moby Dick has received "the

projection of Captain Ahab's Presbyterian conscience, and so may be said to embody the Old Testament Calvinist conception of an affrighting Deity" (pp. 68, 69). The psycho-literary aggression which, Murray thinks, Ahab acts out on Melville's behalf results from the deep "frustration of Eros" (p. 71). Melville, imprisoned by "an incompatible marriage," temporarily succumbs to the "insurgent Id" (Ahab), and attacks the "oppressive cultural Superego" (Moby Dick), the conception of God, and its derivative ethic, which prevented a divorce (p. 70).

9. Lawrance Thompson, *Melville's Quarrel with God* (Princeton: Princeton University Press, 1952), p. 149.

10. Ibid., p. 148.

11. Ibid., p. 150. Naturally, Melville wanted the book to sell, Thompson remarks, and consequently he could not openly admire Ahab's epic *taille* or condone his satanic defiance in the face of a pious public. Nonetheless, Thompson contends, it is Ahab who must be seen as the "brave and heroic pursuer [of the white whale, the Christian conception of God]," (p. 151). In this view, Ishmael's narration represents "allegorical triple-talk" (p. 182) which is ironically designed to commend Ahab's actions during the very moments Ishmael, on the surface, seems most appalled by those actions. Any critic who disagrees with this interpretation of the anti-Christian thrust of *Moby-Dick,* Thompson repeatedly emphasizes, has been taken in by Melville's duplicity: even as early as the first chapter, "enough anti-Christian insinuations have been brought together to serve as fair warning to the reader" (p. 159). Finally, Thompson concludes that, "badly stated . . . Melville's underlying theme in *Moby-Dick* correlates the notions that the world was put together wrong and that God is to blame; that God in his infinite malice asserts a sovereign tyranny over man and that most men are seduced into the mistaken view that this divine tyranny is benevolent and therefore acceptable" (p. 242).

12. William Braswell, *Melville's Religious Thought* (Durham: Duke University Press, 1943), pp. 72–73.

13. Ibid., p. 60. In Braswell's understanding of the book, the captain of the *Pequod* reasons that, "if God is omnipotent, evil must be attributed to him" (p. 58), "expresses the suspicion that there is no first cause" (p. 62), and "conceives that God . . . [is] without love for mankind" (p. 64). Having declared his own sovereign nature, then, Ahab directs his fury toward Moby Dick, "an imposing symbol of divine power" (p. 59). And Melville, with his reading in tow, with his personal experience of disillusionment on hand, and with Ahab's suffering and

doom before him, relented wholly, in Braswell's opinion, to profound pessimism.

14. Joseph Haroutunian, *Piety versus Moralism: The Passing of the New England Theology* (New York: Harper and Row, 1970), p. 171.

15. Ibid., p. 176.

16. For a discussion of the unreasoning responses with regard to evil and suffering made by this strident Calvinism to interrogation from "enlightened" views of the day, see Haroutunian, *Piety versus Moralism*, pp. 177–219.

17. To conclude from this as Lawrance Thompson does (see note 11 above) that Herman Melville was anti-Christian, however, is to traffic in critical innuendo. While Melville has some obvious sympathies for Ahab's dilemma, especially the epistemological issue, it is also evident that Melville recognized Ahab's reasoning about his experience to be too narrow and Ahab's furious theological constructions to cohere only in monomania. The God Ahab conceives is not Melville's God so much as the God of the punitive Calvinism Melville rejected.

18. Haroutunian, *Piety versus Moralism*, p. 180.

19. Perry Miller, *Nature's Nation* (Cambridge, Mass.: Belknap Press of Harvard University, 1967), pp. 90–120, presents a discussion of the ways in which the sense of covenant with God in American Protestantism was enacted in the period of the American Revolution and the ways in which, after the victorious emergence of the new nation from the war, the covenant seemed to have been fulfilled and the divine destiny of the American people to have been insured. For a somewhat different account of the ways in which religion and politics converged in Melville's period, see Michael T. Gilmore, *The Middle Way: Puritanism and Ideology in American Romantic Fiction* (New Brunswick, N.J.: Rutgers University Press, 1977).

20. Haroutunian suggests the distance the New England theology had come when he observes that now "men could be Calvinists on Sunday and eighteenth-century rationalists on week-days" (*Piety versus Moralism*, p. 180); this "enlightened" attitude, of course, carried the faithful easily into the nineteenth century: "the transition from Calvinism was thus smooth and quiet" (ibid.) for this orthodoxy. In a sense, one might add, this remnant of Calvinism did not so much surrender to the modern as it simply gave way to some of its own earlier impulses. For instance, the construction of a covenant of grace by the Federal Theology served severely to diminish the absolute sovereignty of Calvin's God and optimistically to inflate the ability of man to "keep cove-

nant." For a fuller discussion of this idea of covenant and shifts from the spirit of Calvin, see Perry Miller, *Errand into the Wilderness* (New York: Harper and Row, 1964), the chapter entitled "The Marrow of Puritan Divinity."

21. For accounts of this dream of destiny at the heart of American Protestantism during the first half of the nineteenth century, see Martin E. Marty, *Righteous Empire: The Protestant Experience in America* (New York: Dial Press, 1970), especially part 1; and Sidney E. Mead, *The Lively Experiment: The Shaping of Christianity in America* (New York: Harper and Row, 1963), chapters 5 and 6, both of which discuss the appearance and nature of this civic morality.

22. Without rehearsing the rise of "civil religion," the pervasiveness of this view among Americans can be demonstrated in a surprising way by recourse to one of the most visible books of the day, Richard Henry Dana, Jr.'s *Two Years before the Mast* (1840; New York: Doubleday and Co., n.d.), a book which is ordinarily understood as having raised religious and humanitarian objections to the practise of flogging aboard vessels of the United States. In his "Concluding Chapter," as Dana ponders "what may be done for seamen" (p. 376), he does not, however, condemn flogging at all. Although he sees it as an evil, Dana believes it is a necessary evil to be retained. He insists that, given the general character of sailors, flogging serves logically as a deterrent: "I should not wish to take command of a ship tomorrow," Dana declares, knowing "that I could not, under any circumstances, inflict even moderate [corporal] punishment" (pp. 382–83). Religious activism or civil legislation against flogging will not solve the problem, he argues. What is necessary, rather, is the slower work of instructing seamen about the life of religion because "a sailor never becomes interested in religion, without immediately learning to read" (p. 390). The hours spent in reading and study, Dana reasons, will "raise the character of sailors" (p. 393) and will reclaim them "from indolence and vice, which [naturally] follow in the wake of the converted man" (p. 390). Further, religious reading will in turn lead the sailor to read materials about national issues and world affairs, and this will make him a more responsible citizen. Then he will not commit the errors which require his being flogged, and the practise of flogging will slowly die from disuse.

23. Herman Melville, "Hawthorne and His Mosses," in Miller, ed., *Major Writers of America*, 1:893. This review originally appeared in *The Literary World* (August 1850).

24. For accounts of Melville's relationships and problems with the missionaries, see, for example, Daniel Aaron, "Melville and the Mis-

sionaries," *New England Quarterly* 8 (September 1935): 404–8; and
Charles Roberts Anderson, *Melville and the South Seas* (New York:
Columbia University Press, 1939), the chapter entitled "Missionaries
and Cannibals."

25. Nathan A. Scott, Jr., "Eliot and the Orphic Way," *Journal of
the American Academy of Religion* 42 (June 1974): 227.

26. Further, as Randall Stewart has pointed out, the passage un-
doubtedly reveals as much about Hawthorne himself as about Melville:
"Hawthorne himself had reasoned much concerning Providence and
futurity and the things that lie beyond human ken, and although . . .
he seems to imply the futility and unwisdom of such an occupation, he
continued to be deeply concerned with these matters until the end of his
days. . . . It was Hawthorne's dilemma as well as Melville's—and indeed the dilemma of many other serious minds—to find it difficult
either to believe or to be comfortable in unbelief" ("Melville and Hawthorne," in *Moby-Dick Centennial Essays,* ed. Tyrus Hillway and
Luther S. Mansfield [Dallas: Southern Methodist University Press,
1953], pp. 156–57).

27. In William Braswell's interpretation of *Moby-Dick* (see note 13
above), it was Melville's inability to accept the easy epistemology of
the natural theology of his day which forced him into skepticism and
finally into pessimism. Although Braswell provides an adequate account
of the epistemological dilemma Melville faced, there are problems with
the way Braswell advances his argument on the basis of Melville's reading. His argument presents a theory of a chronological development of
pessimism in Melville's work up to and through *Moby-Dick,* but Braswell informs the reader in his opening chapter that, in citing influences
on Melville's religious reflections, he will proceed "with little regard for
chronology" (p. 10). Thus, one is informed early in the book of "the
kinship of Melville to [Schopenhauer]" (p. 15), for instance. Although
Braswell observes that Melville purchased his personal copies of Schopenhauer's works late in his life, the implication is that he must have
read much earlier in the writings of the great German pessimist. There
is nothing, however, to indicate that Melville read Schopenhauer before
1891, the year Melville died and forty years after the publication of
Moby-Dick (See Jay Leyda, ed., *The Melville Log,* 2 vols. [New York:
Gordian Press, 1969], 2:832–33; and Merton M. Sealts, Jr., *Melville's
Reading: A Checklist of Books Owned and Borrowed* [Madison: University of Wisconsin Press, 1966], p. 91). And there are other, similar
problems of discrepancy between implied influences and the known
chronology in Braswell's argument about Melville's early turn to pes-

simism. But the point here is not to invalidate the conclusions of that argument, for pessimism was in the air Melville breathed; the point, rather, is to suggest that there are enough problems with such an argument, very influential in recent years, to warrant one's not regarding such conclusions about Melville's early pessimism as a settled matter.

28. The Edwards I have in mind here is the writer of the "Dissertation Concerning the End for Which God Created the World," who sees spirit in the world as "an emanation of . . . [God's] own infinite fulness" (*The Works of President Edwards*, 10 vols. [1817; reprint ed., New York: Burt Franklin, 1968], 1:460). Hereafter, all quotations, unless otherwise indicated, will be from this edition of this "Dissertation." For Edwards, of course, these "emanations" also make possible the validity of the typological imagination of his *Images or Shadows of Divine Things* (ed. Perry Miller [New Haven: Yale University Press, 1968]), in which moments, objects, and activities in the world are seen as inspirited by the surplusage of divine fulness. The rainbow figurement in the whale's spouting, which gives Ishmael "intuitions of some things heavenly," proves to Edwards, as an instance, that "the works of nature are intended and contrived of God to signify and indicate spiritual things [for this] is particularly evident concerning the rainbow" (Image 55; p. 60). For a discussion of the Puritan conception and uses of typology and the relations of this aspect of Puritanism to Melville, see Ursula Brumm, *American Thought and Religious Typology*, trans. John Hoaglund (New Brunswick, N.J.: Rutgers University Press, 1970).

29. Rudolph Otto, *The Idea of the Holy*, trans. John W. Harvey (New York: Oxford University Press, 1958), pp. 12–13. The catalyst for these feelings, Otto argues, is the *mysterium tremendum* character of the *numen* which discloses itself in one of its awe-ful and majestic forms and whose mystery, far more than being merely furtive, is most aptly and strikingly expressed in the term *wholly other*—"that which is quite beyond the sphere of the usual, the intelligible, and the familiar, which therefore falls quite outside the limits of the 'canny,' and is contrasted with it, filling the mind with blank wonder and astonishment" (p. 26).

30. In the interpretation of *Moby-Dick* provided by T. Walter Herbert, Jr., in his *Moby-Dick and Calvinism* (New Brunswick, N.J.: Rutgers University Press, 1977), Melville's inability to square with his personal experience the conceptions of God in the Dutch Reformed tradition and the Unitarian tradition, (at least as these conceptions reached him as a young man) led him to a profoundly defiant skepticism

which, in turn, channeled his energies in *Moby-Dick* to the effort to "dismantle" the theocentric conception of life of both traditions. Although Herbert provides a sensitive and well-documented account of the ways these orthodoxies might have influentially entered the fabric of Melville's familial experience, however, he fails to see that Melville's rejections of the contemporary religious alternatives, as much as creating skepticism in him, pulled him more deeply into the epistemological issues and, finally, brought him to a more theologically thoughtful position. What troubled Melville the most about the conservative and the liberal religious practises of his time, and what no doubt drove him after knowledge of "Providence and futurity," was his sense of the inadequacies of their species of "God-talk." Melville simply could not share their confidence about "naming the Whirlwind," to borrow a phrase from Langdon Gilkey (*Naming the Whirlwind: The Renewal of God-Language* [Indianapolis: Bobbs-Merrill, 1969]). Instead, his efforts to locate a radical view of human experience had taught him to think that that experience stood in a theologically more profound situation when it touched on its limits, when it acknowledged that the whirlwind could not be named. In this respect at least, Melville belongs to a vital tradition in Christian thought which reaches, in its well-known instances, from Augustine to the great Protestant reformers and, as I am arguing here, to Jonathan Edwards. Like many of the exemplars of this tradition—which frequently runs deeper than any orthodox or institutional expression of it—Melville thought that although the reality of God is disclosed in revelations which issue from an overflowing of divine abundance and power, the final character of this reality is veiled and hidden within and beyond any particular revelation of itself. For a discussion of this doctrine of God at the heart of Protestant Christianity, see B. A. Gerrish, "'To the Unknown God': Luther and Calvin on the Hiddenness of God," *Journal of Religion* 53 (July 1973): 263–92. And for a succinct but thoughtful exploration of the ways in which Melville entered the epistemological questions which confront such a tradition, see Thomas Werge, "*Moby-Dick* and the Calvinist Tradition," *Studies in the Novel* 1 (Winter 1969): 484–506. The point here is that the encounter with the hidden God does not automatically lead to skepticism or pessimism. Another more deeply committed alternative—the course followed by an Edwards, for instance—was to explore the dimensions of the presence of this hidden God in order to calculate its significance for an understanding of human experience. For an account of the ways in which this doctrine of God provides a rich resource, as well as an epistemologically chastening experience, for the Protestant imagination, see Carl Michalson, "The Real Presence of the Hidden God," in *Faith and Ethics*, ed. Paul Ramsey (New York: Harper and Row, 1957), pp. 245–67. And it is this alternative, I want to demonstrate, that Melville, after some preliminary recoil, determined to follow.

31. Michalson, "The Real Presence," p. 249.

32. This is Michalson's phrase, of course, to indicate both the reality and the presence of God. But it is likely that Melville touched on this reality neither "as a fact at the end of a line of reasoning" nor as "a hope at the end of the rope of despair" (though Ishmael seems to do the latter). Melville came to it, rather, as a condition of experience realized in the process of his "radical interrogation of the meaning of man." In this he seems to have followed a course similar to that of Augustine who, as Hannah Arendt has noted, distinguishes between the questions "who am I?" (which man poses to himself) and "what am I?" (which man poses to God). Both questions—the *Tu, quis es?* and the *Quid ergo sum, Deus meus?*—begin in the anthropological problem as Augustine understood it, *quaestio mihi factus sum*, which, as Arendt writes, "is a question raised in the presence of God, 'in whose eyes I have become a question for myself' ([*Confessions,*] x.33). In brief, the answer to the question 'Who am I?' is simply: 'You are a man—whatever that may be'; and the answer to the question 'What am I?' can be given only by God who made man. The question about the nature of man is no less a theological question than the question about the nature of God; both can be settled only within the framework of a divinely revealed answer" (*The Human Condition* [Doubleday and Co., 1959], p. 302n).

33. For a somewhat different discussion of the ways in which Melville appropriated some contours of Calvinism, see William B. Dillingham, *An Artist in the Rigging* (Athens: University of Georgia Press, 1972), pp. 138–43; and for a comparison of Melville's thought with an element in Martin Luther's theology, see Thomas Werge, "Luther and Melville on the Masks of God," *Melville Society Extracts* 22:6–7.

34. *The Letters of Herman Melville*, ed. Merrell R. Davis and William H. Gilman (New Haven: Yale University Press, 1960) p. 125. A sizeable number of critics have concluded that this remark to Hawthorne constitutes Melville's saying "no" to life itself. In the context of the letter, however, it seems obvious that it is the "*yes*-gentry . . . [who] travel with heaps of baggage" for their own human comfort in their conceptions of God against whom Melville rails. Those who, like

Hawthorne, bring only the naked human heart to that encounter, says Melville, "why, they are in the happy condition of judicious, unincumbered travellers in Europe; they cross the frontiers into Eternity with nothing but a carpet-bag,—that is to say, the Ego."

35. Ibid., pp. 153–61. All quotations in this paragraph are from this famous letter.

36. How little Melville felt one could completely "live in the all" is revealed when he responds to this recommendation by Goethe by remarking to Hawthorne that "as with all great genius, there is an immense deal of flummery in Goethe" (Ibid., p. 131). And although Melville is willing to accredit momentary feelings of the "all," his sense of their hidden sources is expressed in a *nota bene* to Hawthorne which is tucked snugly into the postscripts of the same letter: "This 'all' feeling, though, there is some truth in. You must often have felt it, lying on the grass on a warm summer's day. Your legs seem to send out shoots into the earth. Your hair feels like leaves upon your head. This is the *all* feeling. But what plays mischief with the truth is that men will insist upon the universal application of a temporary feeling or opinion."

37. Of course, the essay in which Emerson elaborates his notion of the poet as visionary is "The Poet," in *Essays: Second Series* (1884). Although it might seem somewhat incongruous to discuss Melville's thought first in terms of Jonathan Edwards's doctrine of the world and then in terms of Emerson's notion of "how to see," Perry Miller has prepared a nuanced account of the transitions between the thought of the two men in *Errand into the Wilderness,* the chapter entitled "From Edwards to Emerson."

38. Melville, "Hawthorne and His Mosses," p. 893. All quotations in this paragraph are from this review. If Perry Miller began to trace out the continuities between Edwards and Emerson, it was F. O. Matthiessen, of course, who first suggested the ways in which Emerson, Hawthorne, and Melville, among others, could be understood together because of their shared conception of the nature of symbolism. See *American Renaissance.* Giles Gunn calls special attention to, and explores the implications of, this perception on Matthiessen's part in his *F. O. Matthiessen: The Critical Achievement* (Seattle: University of Washington Press, 1975), pp. 68–104. What I am arguing here, in part, is that the three shared some epistemological concerns as well, even if Hawthorne and Melville located "restraints" on their knowing which were influential in their theories of fiction.

39. Ordinarily, this "power of blackness" phrase has been under-

stood to be the key to any connections between Edwards and Melville (and, by association, Hawthorne) in its apparent allusion to a cruel and sinister universe ruled over by a dark and wrathful God. It is in this respect that Henry Bamford Parkes, for instance, observes that "if Edwards is judged as an American poet, then only Melville can be said t [sic] have surpassed him in depth and intensity of spiritual experience" (*The American Experience* [New York: Random House, 1947], pp. 86–87). But Parkes has in mind in this statement the Edwards of the famous Enfield sermon, "Sinners in the Hands of an Angry God" (1741), and a Melville characterized with a decidedly Ahabian cast of mind, and it seems just as appropriate in the context of the review to regard "the blackness of darkness beyond" the "upper skies" as an epistemological acknowledgement of the hidden transcendent whose power must also be acknowledged because it is against "the infinite obscure of . . . [this] background" that human experience is to be understood in its most radical terms. Edwards would no doubt have concurred with both acknowledgements.

40. "Preface to *The House of Seven Gables*," as reprinted in Perry Miller, ed., *Major Writers of America*, 1:790.

41. Melville, "Hawthorne and His Mosses," p. 895.

42. There is something like a consensus that chapters 14, 33, and 44 of *The Confidence-Man*, as brief as they are, and the review "Hawthorne and His Mosses" constitute the fullest available statements by Melville of his theory of fiction. See, for instance, Willard Thorp, "Herman Melville," in *Literary History of the United States*, 3d ed., rev., ed. Robert Spiller et al. (London: Macmillan Co., 1963), pp. 459–60; and Allen Hayman, "The Real and the Original: Herman Melville's Theory of Prose Fiction," *Modern Fiction Studies* 8 (Autumn 1962): 211–32.

43. Melville, "Hawthorne and His Mosses," p. 895.

44. Ibid.

Chapter Five

1. *The Letters of Herman Melville*, ed. Merrell R. Davis and William H. Gilman (New Haven: Yale University Press, 1960), p. 127. All quotations in this and the next paragraph are from this letter.

2. *White-Jacket* also contains such moments, of course, but, as I have suggested in the preceding chapter, the retrospective narrator seems much better equipped to handle them than either Tommo or Red-

burn because he can possess such moments for his life. His organicism suffers nothing of the attenuations which characterize Redburn's efforts, and his burgeoning symbolic imagination makes him, in that respect at least, more nearly like Ishmael. In this chapter, I discuss only *Typee* and *Redburn* among the early works because the failures of their narrator-protagonists in the encounter with these resounding moments provide a distinct counterpoint to Ishmael's attempts to take possession of such moments.

3. In this chapter I am concentrating exclusively on the *retrospective* Ishmael and how his representation of the world of *Moby-Dick* bespeaks his sense of the nature of that world. *How* he has come—that is, his record of his *progress* to "the flood-gates of the wonder-world"—will be the subject of the next chapter.

4. When I use the term *metaphysics* here, I do not mean to point to any fully elaborated system of thought but, rather, to indicate an orientation toward experience and a mode of searching experience, as bearing evidence of a controlling reality which overarches experience. Still, the term metaphysics has a special denotation in the American context—Emerson's wanting to know the "ultimate reason" of the "meal in the firkin" and the "milk in the pan," for instance—in which the goal of speculation and the object of scrutiny seem to coincide. It is in this context, I think, that Melville's metaphysics must be understood.

5. James Richmond, *Theology and Metaphysics* (New York: Schocken Books, 1971), p. 96.

6. The phrase, of course, is from Thomas Carlyle's *Sartor Resartus,* but it has been appropriated by Tony Tanner who sees just such a "reign" at the heart of the American literary tradition. See Tanner, *The Reign of Wonder: Naivety and Reality in American Literature* (Cambridge: Cambridge University Press, 1965). Although Tanner does not discuss Melville at any length, I want to argue that Ishmael, in retrospection at least, is a subject of the "reign of wonder" but that he is not overtaken by the "sleep of reason" or the "predilection for the strategy of the naive vision" which ordinarily characterize the American tradition.

7. This phrase has been borrowed from Giles Gunn, who uses it in a different context in his "F. Scott Fitzgerald's *Gatsby* and the Imagination of Wonder," *Journal of the American Academy of Religion* 41 (June 1973): 171–83.

8. "The Problem for Metaphysics," in *The Future of Metaphysics,* ed. Robert E. Wood (Chicago: Quadrangle Books, 1970), p. 13.

9. London *Spectator* 24 (25 October 1851): 1026.

10. Hershel Parker, ed., *The Recognition of Herman Melville* (Ann Arbor: University of Michigan Press, 1967), p. 36. This review originally appeared in New York *Daily Tribune*, 22 November 1851.

11. Charles Feidelson, in his *Symbolism and American Literature* (Chicago: University of Chicago Press, 1953), argues most persuasively for the view that Melville does not, in his fiction, impute value and significance to elements in experience but, rather, discerns significance inherent in those elements. Melville, Feidelson writes, "treats the meaning as substantive, not adjectival" (p. 178). This argument is all the more convincing in the light of Melville's own statement that the most commanding and significant elements in experience cannot be devised but only discovered. He writes: "There would seem but one point in common between this sort of phenomenon in fiction and all other sorts: It cannot be born in the author's imagination—it being as true in literature as in zoology, that all life is from the egg" (*C*, 261).

12. Paul Tillich, *The Protestant Era* (Chicago: University of Chicago Press, 1957), p. xv.

13. Ibid., p. 43. Now, Tillich is here discussing *kairos* in terms of the interpretation of history as epoch, as a stage of history with extended periodicity. He is fully aware, however, that the *chronos-kairos* understanding of time can be localized, as it were, into personal time: the appearance of a *kairos,* he writes, "may happen in a derived form again and again, creating centers of less importance on which the periodization of history [including personal history] is dependent" (p. xv). What I am suggesting, then, is that Ishmael's perception that chronological time is periodically displaced by singularly presaging and abundant moments is only a personal version of the interpretation of history that Tillich describes.

14. Ibid., p. 47.

15. Ibid., p. 42.

16. Henry James, *The Altar of the Dead* (New York: Charles Scribner, 1909), p. xix.

17. Walter E. Bezanson provides a discerning account of the types of symbolic forms in *Moby-Dick* and of the ways in which the symbols transcend the rhetoric of Ishmael's narration. See his *"Moby-Dick:* Work of Art," in *Moby-Dick Centennial Essays,* ed. Tyrus Hillway and Luther S. Mansfield (Dallas: Southern Methodist University Press, 1953). While Bezanson thinks that Ishmael *creates* symbols by means of his rhetoric (p. 47), however, Feidelson seems more accurate in ob-

serving (cf. note 11 above) that Ishmael *discovers* symbolic forms in the structure of the "unfettered" world he inhabits and that his rhetoric is the mode of his exploration of their mysterious contours.

18. Thomas Carlyle, *Sartor Resartus* (London: J. M. Dent and Sons, 1908), p. 165. That Melville was aware of *Sartor Resartus,* there can be little doubt, for the "clothes-philosophy" seems obviously to have made its way into *White-Jacket.* Indeed, we know that Melville borrowed the book—in the Munro edition of 1840 or the Wiley and Putnam edition of 1846—from Evert Duyckinck during the summer of 1850. See Merton M. Sealts, Jr., *Melville's Reading: A Check-List of Books Owned and Borrowed* (Madison: University of Wisconsin Press, 1966), p. 48 (item 123).

19. Carlyle, *Sartor Resartus,* p. 164.

20. Dorothy Emmet, *The Nature of Metaphysical Thinking* (London: Macmillan and Co., 1961), p. 104.

21. Ibid., p. 105.

22. *The Letters of Herman Melville,* p. 131.

23. Carlyle, *Sartor Resartus,* p. 165.

24. Ibid., p. 167.

25. For a persuasive exposition of the relationship between metaphysics and faith, see Emmet, *Nature of Metaphysical Thinking,* especially the chapter entitled "Revelation and Faith," pp. 115–45.

26. Tillich, *Protestant Era,* p. 47.

Chapter Six

1. Of course, the tone of the poem is sardonic, for the "portent" the persona faces is the beckoning of a prostitute. Rather than fronting this portent, he flies from it—amusing himself with the notion that he, like the "divine Ulysses," does not think it a "shame to run" from one of the "Sirens, waylayers in the sea." By refusing to face the portent, he convinces himself, he has been "brave" and "wise" to avoid a "peril in man."

2. Paul Brodtkorb's phenomenology of Ishmael's narration leads him to think that "Ishmael's book is founded in his own boredom, dread, and despair" and that "Ishmael goes to sea in endless repetition to create meaning out of emptiness" (*Ishmael's White World* [New Haven: Yale University Press, 1965], p. 148). As far as Brodtkorb is concerned, then, Ishmael never gets past this narcissistic stage but always projects meaning where none can be found. I want to argue here

that Ishmael does not *devise* meaning but *discerns* it as substantively inherent in the stuff of his experience, as I have suggested in the preceding chapter. In this chapter I will define the ways in which Ishmael learns to see the "other" in his experience and not merely to locate there projections or reflections of himself.

3. *Walden and Civil Disobedience,* ed. Sherman Paul (Cambridge, Mass.: Riverside Press, 1957), pp. 62–63.

4. Giles Gunn, "F. Scott Fitzgerald's *Gatsby* and the Imagination of Wonder," *Journal of the American Academy of Religion* 41 (June 1973): 182.

5. Rudolph Otto, *The Idea of the Holy,* trans. John W. Harvey (New York: Oxford University Press, 1958), p. 17. For a discussion of the relationship between "the holy" and "the demonic" see Paul Tillich, *Systematic Theology,* 3 vols. (Chicago: University of Chicago Press, 1951–63), 1:215–18.

6. Paul Ricoeur, *The Symbolism of Evil,* trans. Emerson Buchanan (New York: Harper and Row, 1967), p. 356.

7. *Ibid.*

8. *The Letters of Herman Melville,* ed. Merrell R. Davis and William H. Gilman (New Haven: Yale University Press, 1960), p. 132 (letter 85).

9. Thomas Carlyle, *Sartor Resartus* (London: Chapman and Hall, 1870), p. 40.

Chapter Seven

1. Walter E. Bezanson, "*Moby-Dick:* Work of Art," *Moby-Dick Centennial Essays,* ed. Tyrus Hillway and Luther S. Mansfield (Dallas: Southern Methodist University Press, 1953), p. 41.

2. The fact that I am arguing here with a concern to demonstrate how these characters fall under the judgment of the wonder-world does not mean that I think this is the only rubric under which they can be discussed. Queequeg himself, for instance, can be understood as something of a norm for making judgments—as Ishmael recognizes—at least in the measure that his instinctive humanity pales habitually poor moral responses by his civilized, Christian "superiors." Starbuck could well be discussed in terms of his "mercantile" theory, for his readiness to do the bidding of the owners of the ship, a readiness which stems from his pious sense of his duties, makes him a pawn of the "Captains of Industry" as well as of Captain Ahab. Still, even these aspects of their

characters fall within the terms of the discourse established by Ishmael's imagination of wonder.

3. Of course, Ahab himself discerns in Starbuck and Pip some of his own longing and something of his "peril." His continual taunting of Starbuck about the mate's "sunlight" vision betrays how much the comfort of such a point of view might have appealed to Ahab in different circumstances, and, indeed, the captain finds in Starbuck's reminders of Nantucket that which stirs his admittedly splintered heart. In Pip, after his being "cast away," Ahab senses their bond; both have chanced to see, he says, "'the omniscient gods oblivious of suffering man'" (*M*, 125).

4. Passages like this one raise to a pitch the question of fate in the book. But Ishmael has worked his way out of woe, has changed, and thus provides an answer—at least in his case—to such a question. It is not at all surprising, I think, that when the question of fate arises with respect to Ahab's situation, it is Ahab who raises it and who does so out of his own self-concentration. Ishmael senses that if there is fate in the case at all it is not merely a matter of something external to Ahab which forces him along his "iron rails" but, rather, that some element of Ahab's interiority coalesces with his external situation and impels him forward.

5. If Ishmael has surpassed the narcissistic temptation, however, it is true that he resubmits himself for a time to his other initial peril—the reliance on secondary authority. He accepts Ahab's version of Moby Dick and says, "I gave myself up to the abandonment of the time and the place; but while yet all a-rush to encounter the whale, could see naught in that brute but the deadliest ill" (*M*, 41). It is significant to note, however, that Ishmael accepts the authority of Ahab's view of Moby Dick and of all whales *before* "the first lowering"—before, that is, Ishmael encounters the whale directly. Just as significant is the fact that his submission to Ahab's interpretation is followed immediately by his musing on "the whiteness of the whale," for in that brooding on matters he begins to pull away from Ahab's view because he recognizes that it cannot do justice, after its monistic fashion, to the immensity and fecundity of the whale.

6. *The Letters of Herman Melville*, ed. Merrell R. Davis and William H. Gilman (New Haven: Yale University Press, 1960), p. 146.

7. For the idea in this paragraph, I am indebted to Professor Merlin Bowen of the University of Chicago, who, in conversation, provided a clue for me, although I have perhaps used it in a different fashion.

8. As with the case of Ahab in *Moby-Dick,* the question of fate is posed in *Pierre* with respect to the protagonist's inability to free himself from Isabel, within whose gloom he is exclusively arboured. But, as the retrospective Ishmael recognized about Ahab, the narrator in *Pierre* thinks that what there is of fate belongs to character, that one's actions are not simply determined by some external element. In an aside to the reader, he examines Pierre's sense of himself as "fated" by Isabel: Pierre's "profound curiosity and interest in the matter—strange as it may seem—did not so much appear to be embodied in the mournful person of the olive girl, as by some radiations from her, embodied in the vague conceits which agitated his own soul" (*P,* 51).

Chapter Eight

1. Ray L. Hart, *Unfinished Man and the Imagination* (New York: Herder and Herder, 1968), p. 225.

2. This and the following two extended quotations cite material which frequently has been used to precede the text of *Billy Budd,* as in William Stafford's edition of the work (Belmont, Cal.: Wadsworth Publishing Co., 1961), from which I quote p. 3. The Hayford-Sealts edition, which is generally accepted as authoritative and which will hereafter be used, omits this "preface," regarding it as a spurious inclusion by Melville's wife who did not realize that it was superseded by materials in the text proper. Without entering fully into the debate about the validity of this prefatory material, I want only to suggest that, if included, it serves a telescoping function which reveals the narrator's insistence about seeing the story aboard the *Bellipotent* against the milieu of revolutionary Europe, a backdrop frequently evoked in the work.

3. The term *phenomenal* recurs frequently in the narrative, and in each case the context in which it appears suggests that Melville wanted it to be understood as connoting that which is prodigious and not to be read, in its more acceptable philosophic sense, as alluding to that which is accessible to the human senses. In this it seems that Melville was taking advantage of a current unconventional usage of the term. According to the *Oxford English Dictionary on Historical Principles,* 7:772, the primary use of the term is the Kantian sense of it, that "cognizable by the senses," but a second, less admirable usage refers to that which is "very notable or remarkable, extraordinary, exceptional; 'prodigious.'" The currency of this "perversion" of the term was obvi-

ously useful to Melville in just the senses that Eric Partridge's *Dictionary of Slang and Unconventional English*, 7th ed., rev. (New York: Macmillan Co., 1970), renders it: a *phenomenon* is "a prodigy; a remarkable person, occ., animal, or thing" (p. 662). Indeed, in the debate between the purser and the surgeon about whether Billy's not having an erection at his hanging was "phenomenal," the purser—"more accurate as an accountant than profound as a philosopher" (*B,* 124)—wants to use the term in its unconventional sense while the surgeon, by implication the more philosophically adept of the two, wants to question this use of the term by the purser. Even the surgeon must finally admit, however, that "'the absence of spasmodic movement ... was phenomenal, Mr. Purser, in the sense that it was an appearance the cause of which is not immediately to be assigned'" (*B,* 125). In short, the one challenge in the narrative to the unconventional usage of *phenomenal* must own that there looms through Billy that which is not "cognizable by the senses." Still, the surgeon disdains the purser's insistence that Billy bodes something "prodigious."

4. One of the functions of the narrator's digression on Lord Nelson seems to be to suggest that in Nelson there is figured an alternative to Vere's rigid adherence to rules. Nelson, the narrator explains or "shows," responds to his experience reflexively and not, as is the case with Captain Vere, by "fore-feeling" what is necessary.

5. The vocabulary here even borrows of Ishmael's diction of wonder, for under the transparent pool at the center of "The Grand Armada" Ishmael has seen the gaze of the newborn whales which "while yet drawing mortal nourishment, be still feasting upon some unearthly reminiscence." Billy's face expresses a similarly "wandering reminiscence," and the narrator assures the reader that "Baby" Budd, like the suckling whales, stands near to "unadulterate Nature" (*B,* 120–21).

6. Billy's "ascension" suggests to some readers an "apotheosis." See, for instance, R.W.B. Lewis, *The American Adam* (Chicago: University of Chicago Press, 1955), pp. 149–55; and Ray B. Browne, *Melville's Drive to Humanism* (Lafayette, Ind.: Purdue University Press, 1971), pp. 393–94. For Lewis, Billy represents "the apotheosis of Adam"; for Browne, Billy stands finally as Melville's "apotheosis of humanity." Both views misunderstand, I think, the fact that it is the transcendent presence in Billy, looming through his concrete form, which partakes of divinity and not Billy himself who is, after all, mortal and finite and conditioned; he is the vessel of the unconditional but he is not himself unconditioned.

7. William Ellery Sedgwick, *Herman Melville: The Tragedy of Mind* (1944; reprint ed., New York: Russell and Russell, 1962), p. 249.

Chapter Nine

1. Representative of this view are E. L. Grant Watson, "Melville's Testament of Acceptance," *New England Quarterly* 6 (June 1933): 319–37; William Ellery Sedgwick, *Herman Melville: The Tragedy of Mind* (1944; reprint ed., New York: Russell and Russell, 1962) pp. 231–49; F. O. Matthiessen, *American Rennaissance* (New York: Oxford University Press, 1941), pp. 500–514; and Jean Jacques Mayoux, *Melville*, trans. John Ashberry (New York: Grove Press, 1960) pp. 125–28. Of course, there is some very real disagreement among these critics about whether *Billy Budd* affirms life or merely accepts its conditions.

2. In varying ways, and with varying degrees of sophistication, this argument has been waged by Harry Levin, *The Power of Blackness* (New York: Alfred A. Knopf, 1958), pp. 194–97; James E. Miller, Jr., "*Billy Budd:* The Catastrophe of Innocence," *Modern Language Notes* 73 (March 1958): 168–76; and his "Melville's Search for Form," *Bucknell Review* 8 (December 1959): 275–76; and Lawrance Thompson, *Melville's Quarrel with God* (Princeton: Princeton University Press, 1952), pp. 331–32, 335–414.

3. Arguing that the resolution to be discerned in *Billy Budd* is "mixed" and perhaps ironic are Phil Withim, "*Billy Budd:* Testament of Resistance," *Modern Language Quarterly* 20 (June 1959): 115–27; Joseph Schiffman, "Melville's Final Stage, Irony: A Re-Examination of 'Billy Budd' Criticism," *American Literature* 22 (May 1950): 128–36; Geoffrey Stone, *Melville* (New York: Sheed and Ward, 1949), pp. 206–19.

4. Lewis Mumford, *Herman Melville: A Study of His Life and Vision* (New York: Harcourt, Brace and World, 1929), p. 356.

5. Ibid.

6. I am not arguing here that *Billy Budd* itself qualifies as tragedy, although Richard Harter Fogle, among others, is persuaded to this end. See his "*Billy Budd*—Acceptance or Irony," *Tulane Studies in English* 8 (1958): 107–13, and his "*Billy Budd:* The Order of the Fall," *Nineteenth Century Fiction* 15 (December 1960): 189–205. Murray Krieger calls the view of *Billy Budd* as tragedy into question in his *The Tragic Vision* (New York: Holt, Rinehart, and Winston, 1960), pp. 256, 260,

263–64. But I am less interested here in the generic question than in the question of significance. Nor am I arguing however, that Melville's career can be understood as a *tragedy* in any classical sense of that term. I mean only to suggest that *Billy Budd* reveals, by virtue of its mode, something in Melville's late-life sense of himself in his vocation which has a tragic dimension—to the extent at least that his version of the "truth" left him in an ineluctably "fated" situation with respect to the moral community in relation to which he felt he had to act.

7. Lewis Mumford, *Herman Melville: A Study of His Life and Vision* (New York: Harcourt, Brace and World, 1929), p. 353.

8. Ibid., p. 354. But Mumford believes that "the story gains something by this concentration" (ibid.), while I am convinced that the "stripping" reduces the vision Melville wanted to promote and that the "concentration" betrays what is a shrill insistence on the author's part.

9. In short, the narrator's habits are to "tell" the reader what he, and apparently Melville, think the reader should know instead of allowing that knowledge to come out slowly by way of the dramatic activity of the story. Now, of course, Wayne Booth, in *The Rhetoric of Fiction* (Chicago: University of Chicago Press, 1961), is no doubt correct in his argument that "telling" is not inferior to "showing" in fiction; it is simply a different rhetorical strategy which does not automatically indicate a failure of imagination or of technique by the author. But in the case of *Billy Budd* the habit of "telling" does suggest, as I am arguing, Melville's anxious sense that he must not fail to get his message across.

10. Cf. note 2 of chapter 8.

11. I am indebted here to James Baird's interpretation of the Dansker as "the archetype of the wise man" (*Ishmael* [Baltimore: Johns Hopkins University Press, 1956]). Baird writes: "The Dansker is wise with the weary wisdom of the Furies and the Norns, heavy with the knowledge of human error and distorted purpose" (p. 250). Although my conclusions are somewhat different, I think the wisdom of the Dansker, his possession of the knowledge Baird mentions, is essentially correct, and I want only to suggest here that Melville, in his last fiction, was himself approaching, or indeed gaining, such "weary wisdom . . . of human error and distorted purpose," and that he sensed himself, like the Dansker, powerless to correct it with his art.

12. Newton Arvin, *Herman Melville* (1950; reprint ed., New York: Viking Press, 1966), p. 294. But Arvin thinks that this stamp of power "triumphs even over the stiff-jointed prose, the torpidity of the movement, the excess of commentary, and Melville's failure to quicken any

of the scenes with a full dramatic life" (ibid.). My own view, as I have argued it above, is that these matters—what Arvin refers to as "blemishes of form and manner"—are perhaps more telling in themselves than the "power" of *Billy Budd,* that they reduce the wonder-world even as they establish an undeniably powerful allegory, an abstraction of that world.

INDEX

INDEX

Characters in Melville's fiction are identified with a parenthetical reference to the book in which each appears. The abbreviations used are listed on p. xi.

267

Index

Index

About the Author

Rowland A. Sherrill is assistant professor of religious studies and English at Indiana University–Purdue University, Indianapolis, Indiana.